IMAGES
of America

McCurtain County

ON THE COVER: A camp of horse traders is pictured in the vicinity of the present Idabel Warriors Football Stadium. (Courtesy of the McCurtain County Historical Society.)

IMAGES
of America

McCURTAIN COUNTY

Kenneth and Kayla Sivard

ARCADIA
PUBLISHING

ISBN 978-0-7385-8269-6

Published by Arcadia Publishing
Charleston, South Carolina

Printed in the United States of America

Library of Congress Control Number: 2011927449

For all general information, please contact Arcadia Publishing:
Telephone 843-853-2070
Fax 843-853-0044
E-mail sales@arcadiapublishing.com
For customer service and orders:
Toll-Free 1-888-313-2665

Visit us on the Internet at www.arcadiapublishing.com

We dedicate this book to the "Two Lewises," Dr. Lewis Stiles of Broken Bow and Louis Coleman of Idabel. Both of these men have worked countless hours to preserve and educate others about the great history of McCurtain County. Both are former presidents of both the McCurtain County Historical Society and the Oklahoma Historical Society. Both have also been inducted into the Oklahoma Historians Hall of Fame. They have served as inspiration to many, including the authors of this book.

Contents

ACKNOWLEDGMENTS

We would like to extend our thanks and gratitude to the following people, businesses, and organizations who helped us greatly in making this book a reality: the McCurtain County Historical Society, Bunch–Singleton Funeral Home, Idabel Weyerhaeuser, Jimm and Jackie Jacobs, Wanda and Robert Brisbois, Ted Gerstle, Winnie Rodgers, and Joe Walker.

Thank you all for the great help you lent us in producing this book.

INTRODUCTION

McCurtain County's rich heritage stretches back thousands of years when the county's first inhabitants, the Woodland Culture of Indians, which later became tribes such as the Caddo Indians, made their homes and ancestral hunting grounds within its borders. Later, in the early 1700s, French explorer Bernard De La Harpe became the first documented white explorer to come into the county, creating several camps including one near present-day Idabel.

In 1803, President Jefferson made the famous Louisiana Purchase from France, which included what is now the state of Oklahoma. The land that makes up McCurtain County was charted as part of Miller County, Arkansas, on April 1, 1820, being the first county created in the Arkansas Territory and named for the territory's first governor, James Miller. Miller County's seat was situated in a small community seven miles southeast of present-day Idabel, known as Shawneetown.

After the formation of Miller County, white settlers began to come into the area. Caddo Indians petitioned to the US government that white settlements had infringed on and, in some cases, destroyed ancestral hunting grounds. Their plight was ignored, however, and white advancement continued until 1824 with the signing of the Treaty of Doaks Stand.

The Treaty of Doaks Stand ceded the land that made up much of Miller County, Arkansas, including what is now McCurtain County, to the Choctaw Nation. In return, white settlers were ordered out of the territory. Many were so disgusted that they moved south across the Red River to Texas, which was Mexico at that time. Residents burned down their houses and even their county courthouse rather than let the new inhabitants make use of them.

In 1830, the Treaty of Dancing Rabbit Creek was signed, and Choctaws were told that they could stay in Mississippi, receive 40 acres of land, and become citizens of the state of Mississippi without the right to vote; their tribal government would have to cease to operate. Rather than do this and lose their cultural identity, many chose to come to the tribe's land west of the Mississippi River, in what is now the southern half of the state of Oklahoma.

In 1831, the first wave of Choctaw immigrants into the county came into Eagletown on the Trail of Tears. The Choctaws began the long, difficult task of digging into their new lands and learning the plants, layout, soil, and terrain. Many died of disease and malnutrition in the first years of inhabitation.

Once settled onto their new lands, the Choctaws created the first constitution west of the Mississippi River and implemented a tribal government, which ruled its territory for 76 years. In 1855, the Choctaws revised their government and established county courts in the three districts that made up the nation. Eagle, Bok Tuklo, Bok Homma, Nashoba, and Towson Counties all had land and county seats within the borders of what is now McCurtain County. All of what is now McCurtain County rested in the Apukshunnubbee District, the capital of which was at Alikchi, near Ringold, in McCurtain County.

Many missionaries came with the Choctaws to their new territories. These missionaries included men such as Cyrus Byington, Alfred Wright, Lorring S. Williams, and Cyrus Kingsbury, all of who settled in what is now McCurtain County. They moved themselves, and most of the time their entire families, to the untamed Western Frontier to minister to the Choctaws and help their people and society grow. Cyrus Byington developed the Choctaw written language and penned many hymns and books of the Bible in the Choctaw language. Alfred Wright, along with Williams, Kingsbury, and Byington, established day and boarding schools. These schools later set the stage for the Choctaw Nation's national education program.

In 1898, the Atoka Agreement was signed, and the Choctaw Tribe started the long road to relinquishing its government's hold on the territory. The land that made up the Choctaw Nation was surveyed, and the Dawes Commission came in with the agenda of creating a Native American census in order to allot lands to individuals, whereas in the tribal government there was collective ownership of land. This set the stage for the fall of the Choctaw Nation, and it was led from one of the tribe's very own, Chief Green McCurtain.

McCurtain also allowed railroads to be built through the Choctaw Nation and, as a result, the Frisco Railroad built a line through the southern portion of the county. Many towns were established as a direct result of the railroad construction, such as Bok Homma, Haworth, Idabel, and Garvin.

With the 20th century came the idea of Oklahoma statehood. At first, the state of Sequoyah was suggested being made of the Indian Territories. An election was held in the county to see which town would hold the county seat; Lukfata, Haworth, Garvin, and Idabel were all in the running. Garvin received only one vote, Lukfata received two, and Idabel received the rest. However, the state of Sequoyah never developed, and when the plans for Oklahoma statehood were drawn, Idabel was again selected as the county's seat.

On November 16, 1907, Oklahoma became the 46th state admitted into the United States. Federal judge Spaulding swore in the official first family of McCurtain County. There was no courthouse immediately following statehood—nor would there be for almost a year. The county's first judge, T.J. Barnes, held court wherever he could find an open room and carried court documents around in his pockets.

McCurtain County would first inhabit a courthouse on the corners of Madison and Central Streets in Idabel. When the government outgrew the two-story frame building, it moved into a two-story brick building on East Main Street, which was owned and rented out by Judge Barnes.

In the 1920s, the county passed a bond to build the first county-owned courthouse. Unfortunately, shortly after being constructed, it burned down. Though the exterior of the massive brick and marble building was salvaged, the interior had to be completely rebuilt. In the rebuilding of the courthouse, cheaper labor and materials were used, and the basement flooded so heavily that a maintenance man recorded getting in a small boat to change a lightbulb. The last straw came when one of the large columns in the building's lobby fell completely through the floor and into the basement. The building was deemed unsafe. It was replaced with the county's current structure in 1964.

Within the years immediately following statehood, many business prospects arose in the county. The Choctaw Lumber and Coal Company bought many timber assets in McCurtain County and established a railroad through the midsection of the county to transport raw materials to the business's two company-owned towns, Broken Bow and Bismark (later Wright City). Lumber companies contributed greatly to the early success of many of the McCurtain County's towns, such as Garvin, Millerton, and America.

Farming and ranching have also long been key players in McCurtain County's economy. After the Choctaws arrived, some established plantation-style farms using slave labor to farm and ranch thousands of acres in the county. In the early 20th century, many poor whites sharecropped, as did the many African American citizens, especially in the southern portion of the county known as the Red River Bottoms. Communities such as Harris, Forest Grove, Farmers Hill, Mt. Zion, Clear Lake, Tom and Chili Flatts, and even towns such as Idabel, Valliant, and Haworth relied heavily on the cotton and corn market to maintain the economy.

The Great Depression affected McCurtain County citizens the same way it did most in the state. Many were without jobs or were happy to find work for $1 a day. A great number of the county's men eked out a living hacking railroad ties out of raw timber on government lands in the northern and southern portions of the county. Some even squat farmed on US government land.

McCurtain County was affected greatly by Pres. Franklin D. Roosevelt's New Deal. Many of the county's men received jobs with the Works Progress Administration (WPA) and the Civilian Conservation Corps (CCC), which had several camps within the county. A large number of the county's young girls found work with the National Youth Administration (NYA). As a result of all of this activity, the county has more than eight buildings constructed by the WPA still in existence.

After World War II, the county changed tremendously. Choctaw Electrical Co-op grew rapidly in the years following the war and brought electricity to many of the county's rural homes. Farming and timber industries changed with the use of new machinery. People began to buy homes in town, moving away from the country, and towns such as Idabel, Valliant, and Broken Bow began to prosper.

In 1969, Dierks Lumber, owners of the Choctaw Lumber and Coal Company, sold all timber interests in McCurtain County to the Weyerhaeuser Company of Tacoma, Washington, including lumber mills in Wright City and Broken Bow. The Broken Bow Mill, in operation since 1910, was closed, but the Wright City Mill would run until 2009, when it was closed after 99 years of sawing the timber of McCurtain County. During the 1970s, the Weyerhaeuser Company built a paper mill in Valliant that was, at the time, the largest one in the world. It was sold only a few years ago to the International Paper Company. In December 2007, the Weyerhaeuser Company announced that it was purchasing the Bibler Brothers Sawmill in Idabel from its owner, Terry Freeman. It is a mill that it still owns and operates today.

In 1959, the Flood Control Act of 1958 authorized a dam to be built on the Mountain Fork River near Hochatown. Construction began in October 1961, and the project was finished in 1968. The result was the formation of Broken Bow Lake. With this accomplishment, McCurtain County entered into a new aspect of its economy—tourism. Today, the tourism industry has brought millions of dollars into the county and employees many of its people.

Another large employer of people in the county is the Choctaw Nation, which operates two casinos, two health clinics, three travel plazas, and many tribal offices within the county, employing many from their tribe.

With this book being a brief overview of the diverseness of McCurtain County, it is hoped that one will catch a glimpse of the broad history that created the legacy of the county as well as what carries it on today.

One

People

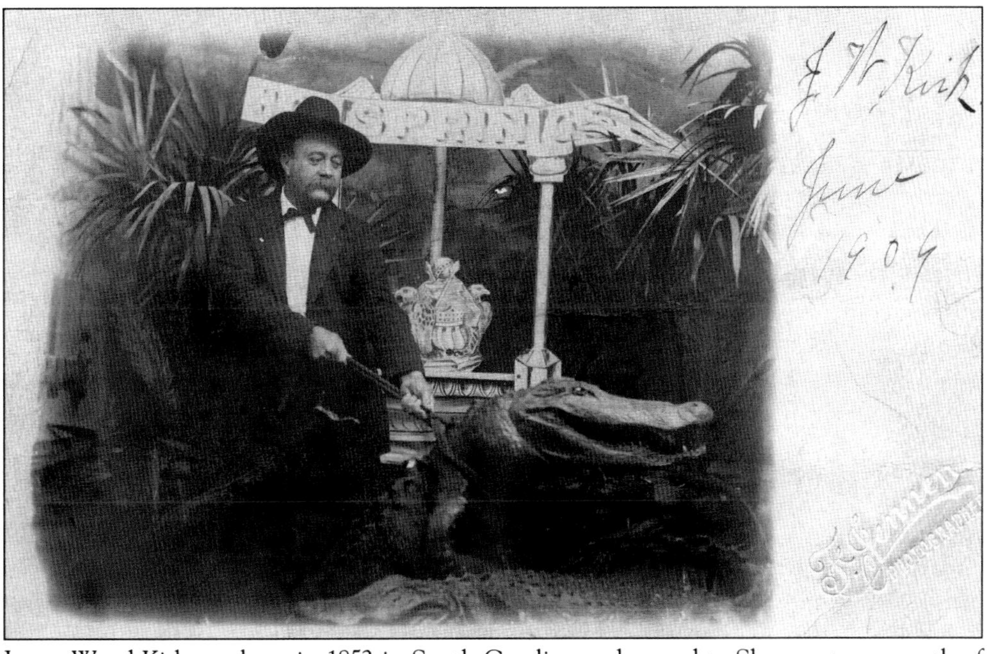

James Wood Kirk was born in 1852 in South Carolina and moved to Shawneetown, south of present-day Idabel, to help his cousin run a store there. He later settled in the Forest Hill vicinity and became a personal advisor to Choctaw chief Isaac Levi Garvin and later married Garvin's daughter. Kirk established a trading post and post office in 1894 and named it Garvin, in honor of his late father-in-law. He died in 1916 and is buried in the Water Hole Cemetery in the Iron Stobb community. (Kenneth Sivard Jr. collection.)

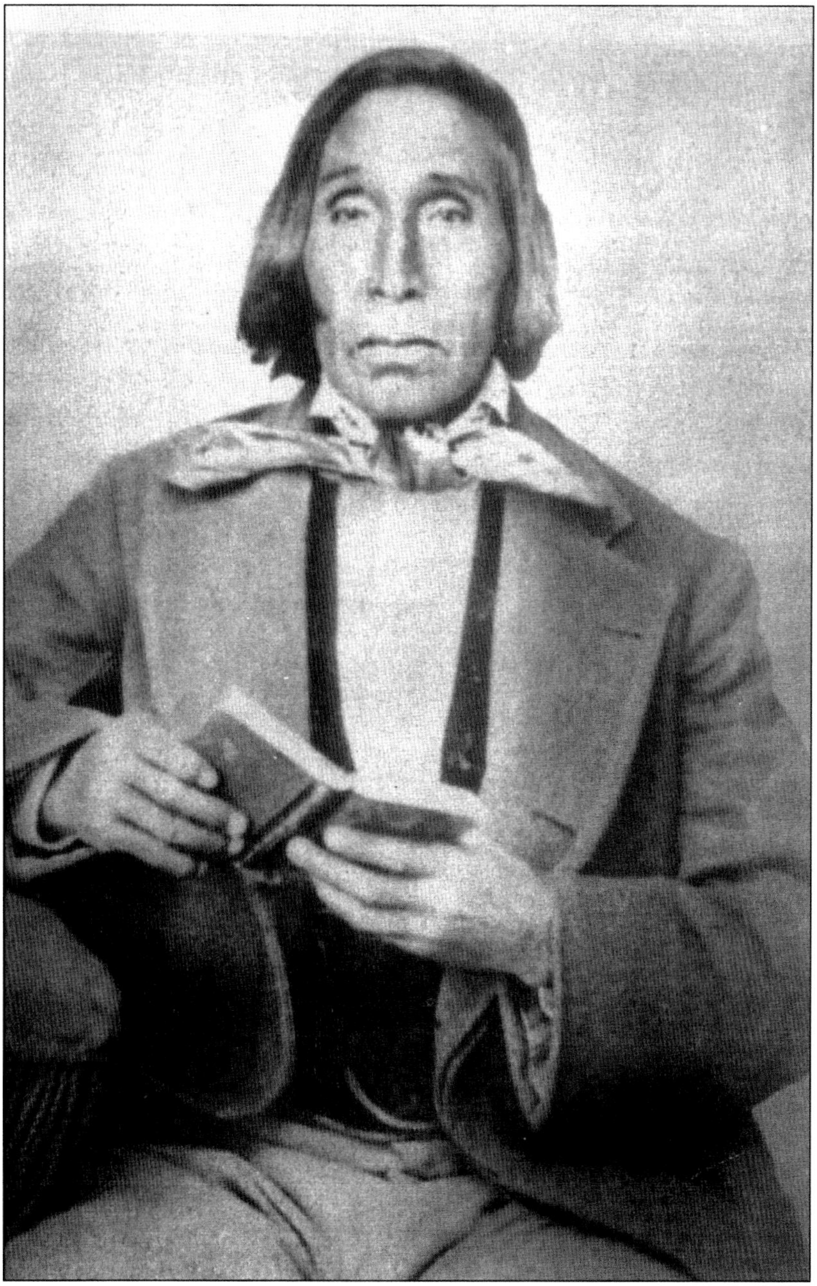

Choctaw chief George Hudson settled in Eagletown after arriving while on the Trail of Tears. He was only half Choctaw; his father was white. His mother died on the journey to Indian Territory from Mississippi. He practiced law in Eagle County and the Apukshunnubbee District and later served as a representative to the Choctaw Council and presided over the Constitutional Convention of 1860, which appointed him the first principle chief of the Choctaws. He guided the Choctaw Nation into joining the Confederacy during the Civil War against the advice of his advisor and friend, Peter Pitchlynn. Hudson's tenure as chief ended in 1862, and he lived out the rest of his life in his Eagletown home where he was buried in an unmarked grave. (Courtesy of the McCurtain County Historical Society.)

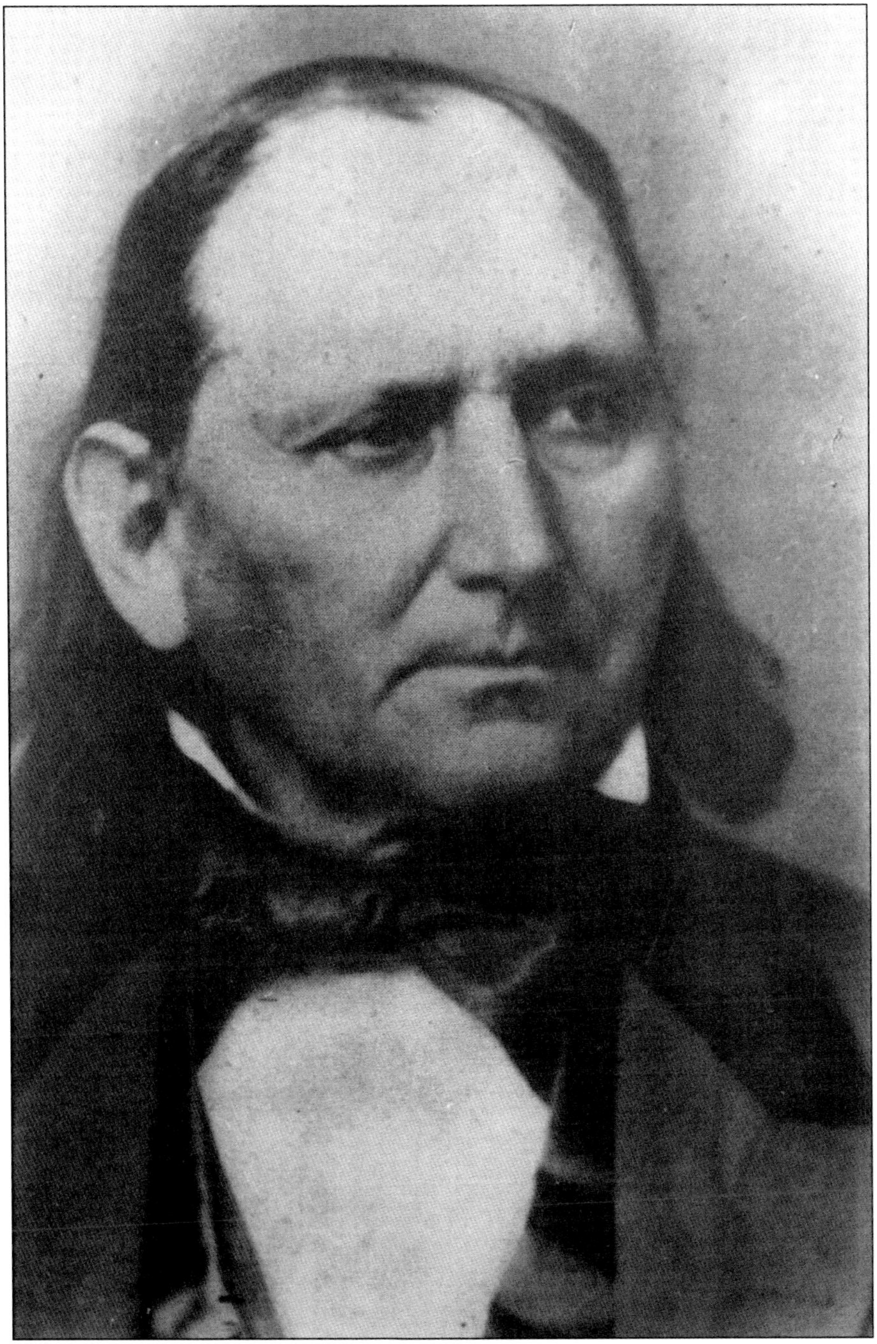

Choctaw chief Peter Perkins Pitchlynn made his home east of Eagletown in 1834 and farmed more than 1,000 acres of land with slave labor. Pitchlynn became chief after the term of his brother-in-law Samuel Garland and was responsible for surrendering Choctaw Confederate forces to the 111th Volunteer Infantry of Illinois in 1864. Pitchlynn worked for the Choctaw Nation after his term as chief representing them in Washington, DC, where he lived for more than 20 years. He is buried in the Congressional Cemetery in Washington, DC. (Courtesy of the McCurtain County Historical Society.)

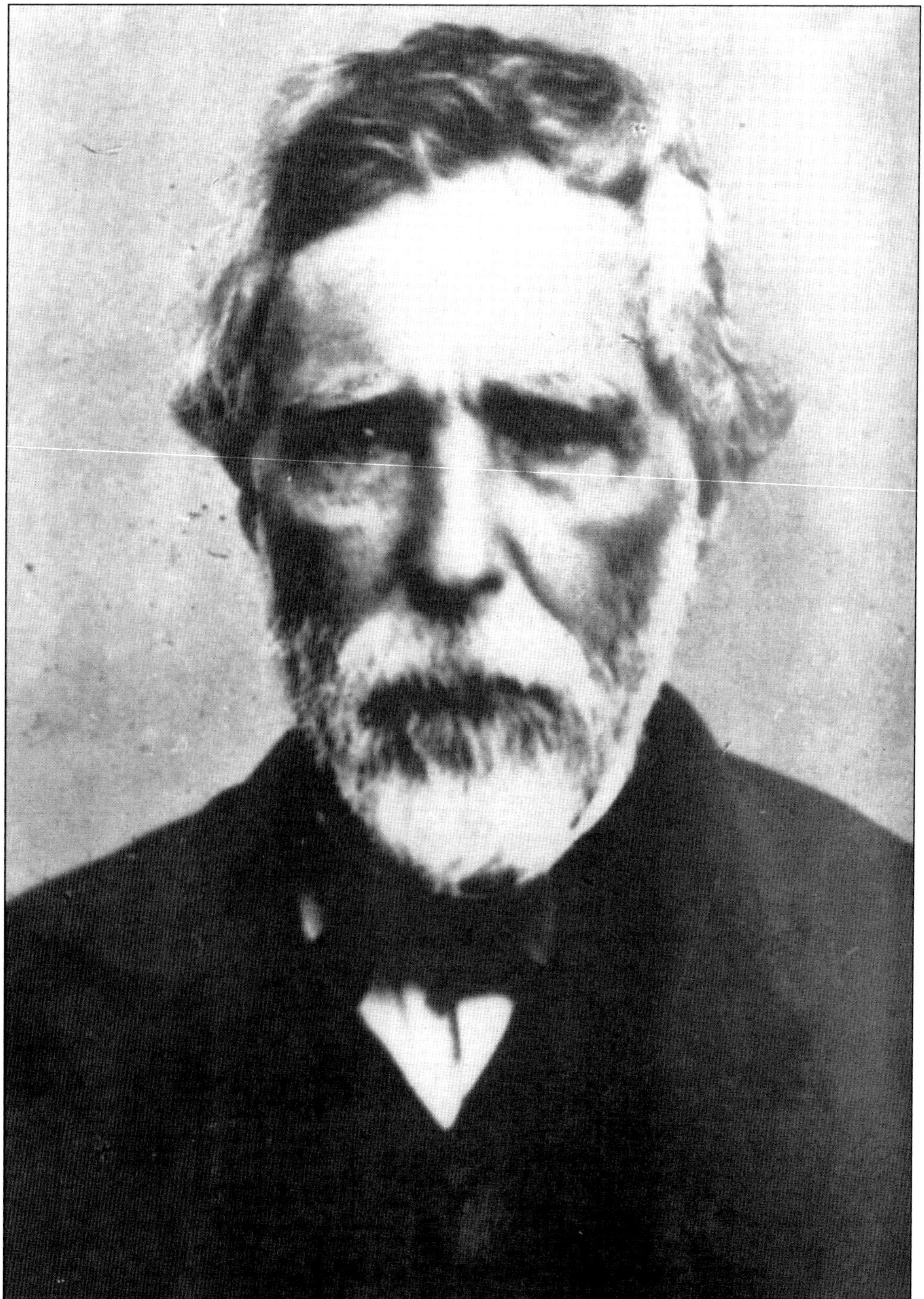

Samuel Garland was Choctaw chief from 1862 to 1864. He was married to a sister of Peter Pitchlynn and made his home in the Janis community near present-day Tom. There, Garland farmed 600 acres with the labor of slaves. After his service as Choctaw chief, he served as the Supreme Court justice of the Choctaw Nation. (Courtesy of the McCurtain County Historical Society.)

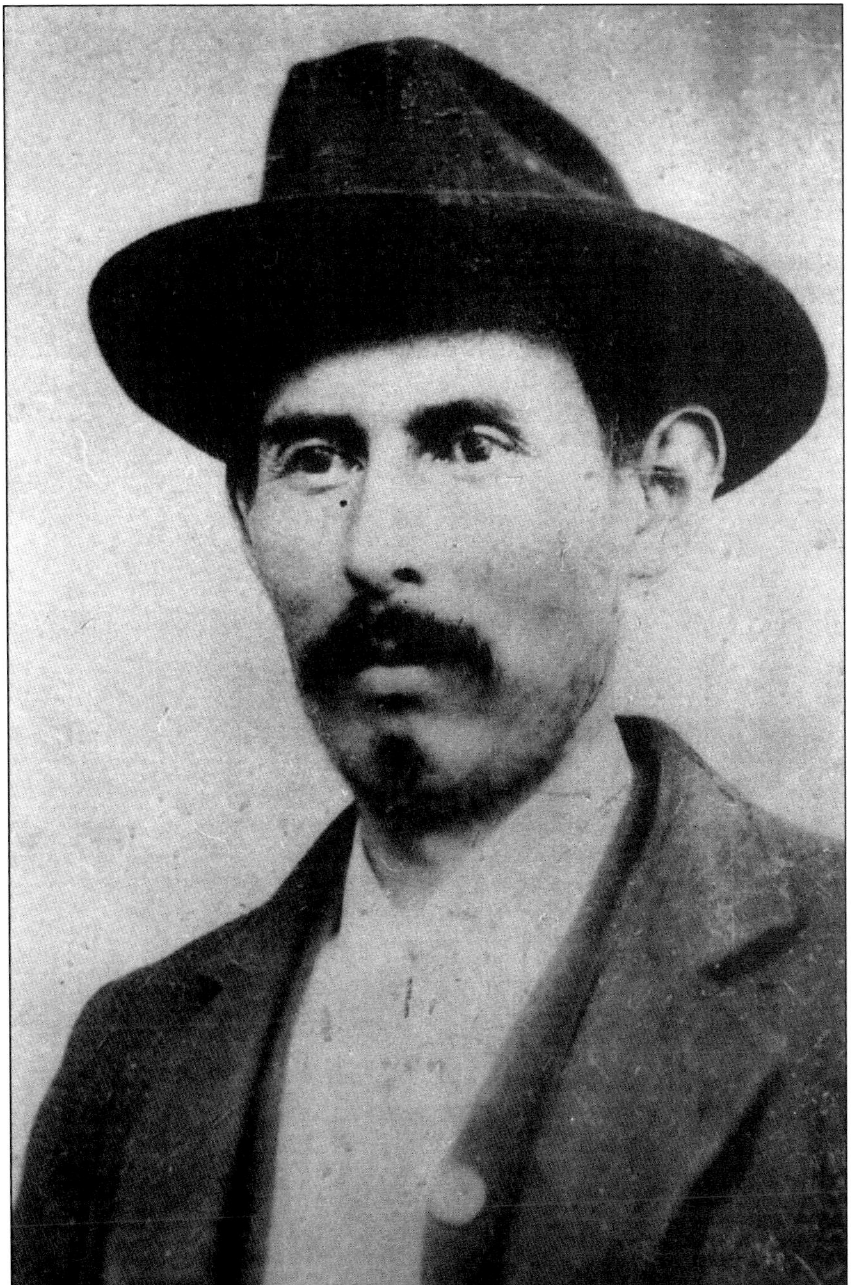

Jefferson Gardner was born and raised in the Wheelock area and was educated at Spencer and Norwalk Academies. He became treasurer of the Choctaw Nation, Apukshunnubbee district judge, and the postmaster of Eagletown. Gardner owned three general stores and a small sawmill. In 1884, he had a large house built near his store in Eagletown. Today, the large *T*-shaped house still stands and is used as a museum run by Dr. Lewis R. Stiles, who was himself raised in the house. Gardner was chief of the Choctaw Nation from 1894 until 1896. He spent his vast fortune fighting the allotment of individual lands and died penniless in 1906. He is buried at the Joe Christy Cemetery in Eagletown. (Courtesy of the McCurtain County Historical Society.)

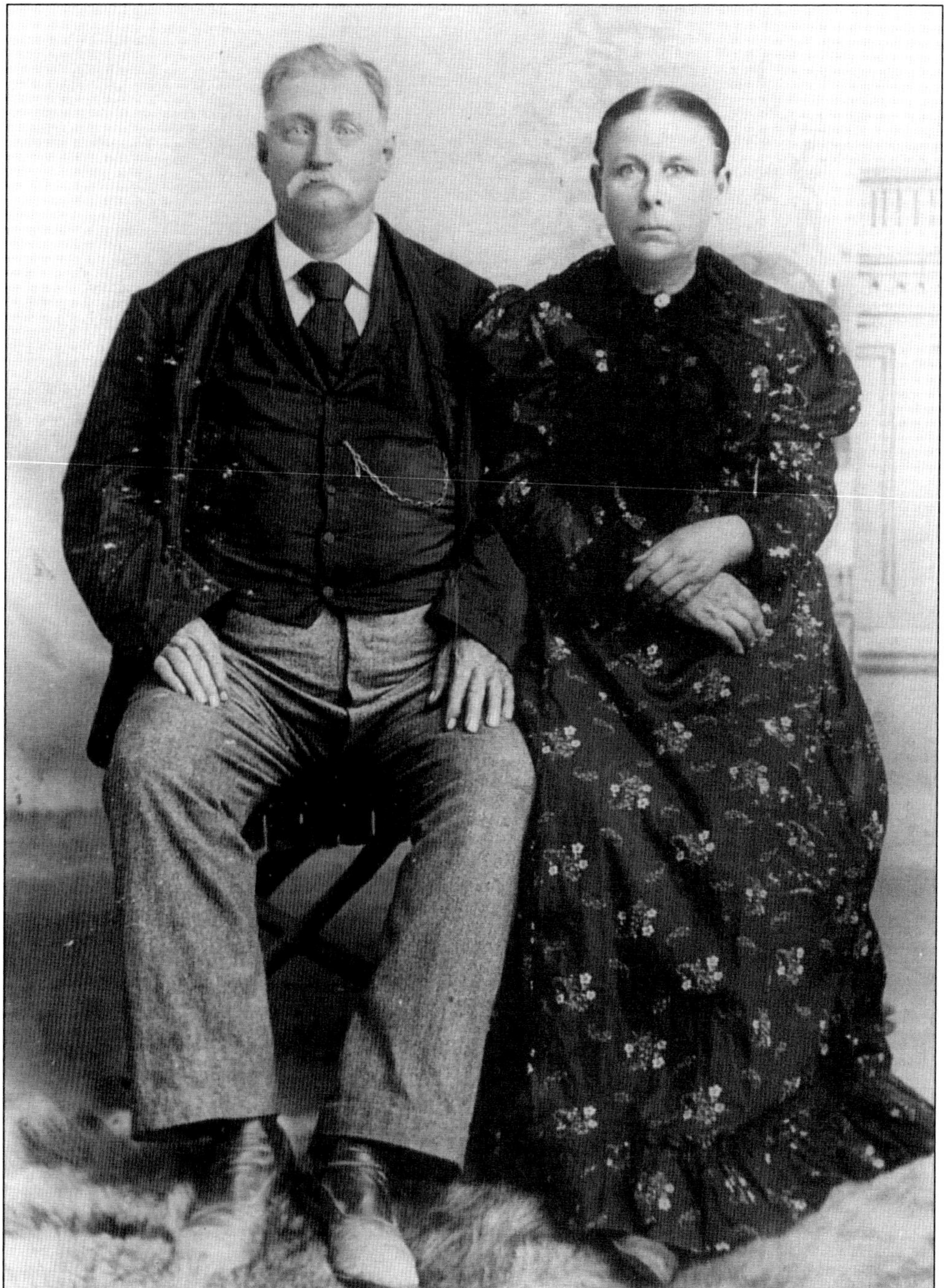

Henry Churchill Harris was a Supreme Court justice of the Choctaw Nation, made his first home in the Harris area in the early 1860s, and established a ferry on the Red River. Following a massive flood that destroyed much of Henry's property and crops, he moved his homesite to a place on higher ground and named it Pleasant Hill. The community that formed around it bears the name today. Henry is the namesake of the Harris community as well. (Courtesy of the McCurtain County Historical Society.)

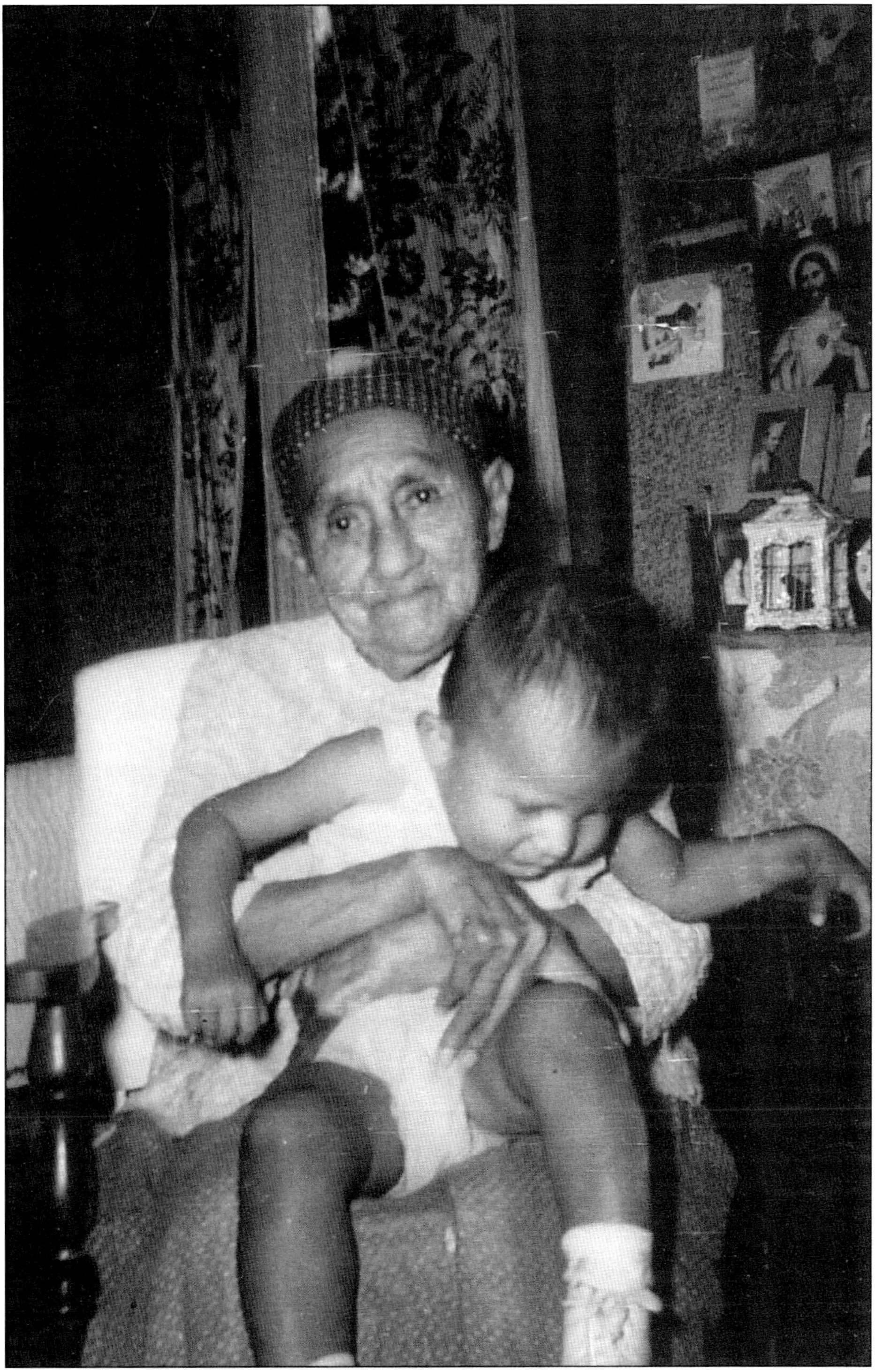

Mary Brandy made her home in the Kulli Tuklo vicinity, coming there from Louisiana. A full-blood Choctaw, Mary lived to be 117 years old and is buried in the Kulli Tuklo United Methodist Church Cemetery. (Kenneth Sivard Jr. collection.)

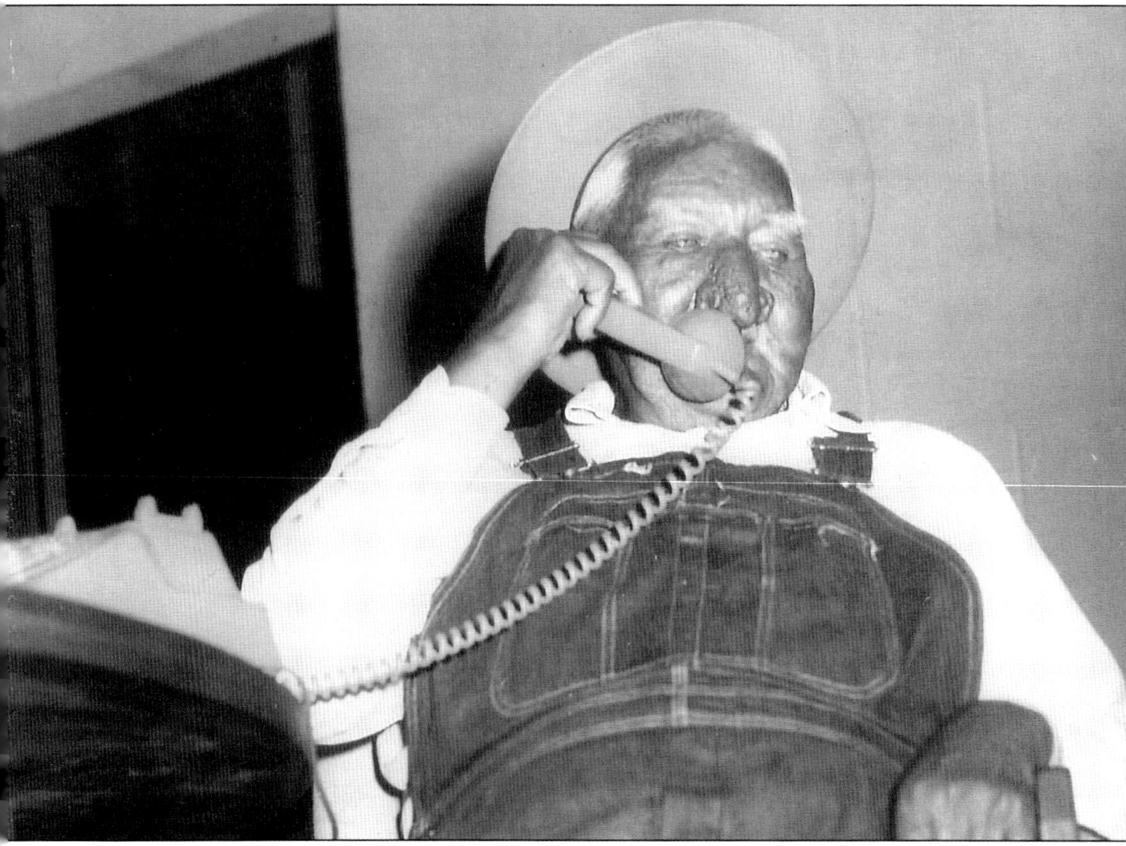

John Silas Tohnika was born in 1853 near Eagletown. He was well known in the Broken Bow area and owned a store in Eagletown in the 1910s and 1920s. Fluent in both the Choctaw and English languages, Tohnika had many friends from both the white and Choctaw races. He was the cousin of William Goings, the last man to be executed by the Choctaw Nation. Goings's body was released to Tohnika at the Alikchi Court Ground after the execution, and he buried Goings in an unmarked grave at the Tohnika Cemetery in Eagletown, where John himself was later buried after passing at his home in 1969 at the age of 116. (Kenneth Sivard Jr. collection.)

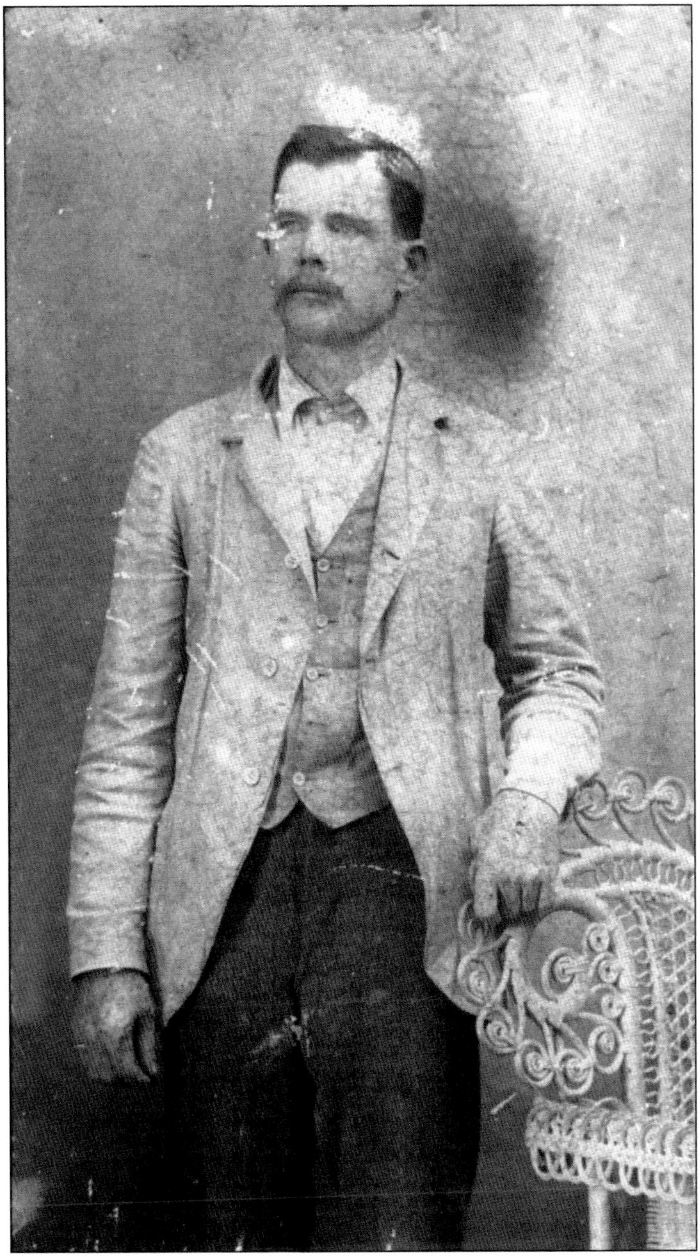

W.J. Whiteman was born northwest of Clarksville, Texas, in 1869. He received a diploma from the Little Rock Commercial College in 1890 and moved to the Goodwater community in 1893, building a house and store there; he ran a cotton gin and gristmill in the area as well. Whiteman also built stores in Haworth and Jadie. He served as a member of the county's first grand jury and was a charter director of the First National Bank in Idabel and the First National Bank of Haworth. He was also a founding member of the Southeastern Abstract Company in Idabel and the creator of the Whiteman Addition in Idabel. Whiteman was a charter member of the Goodwater Masonic Lodge and was instrumental in its establishment. He married Mattie Harris, daughter of Henry Harris, in 1896 and is buried alongside her and her family in the Harris Cemetery. (Kenneth Sivard Jr. collection.)

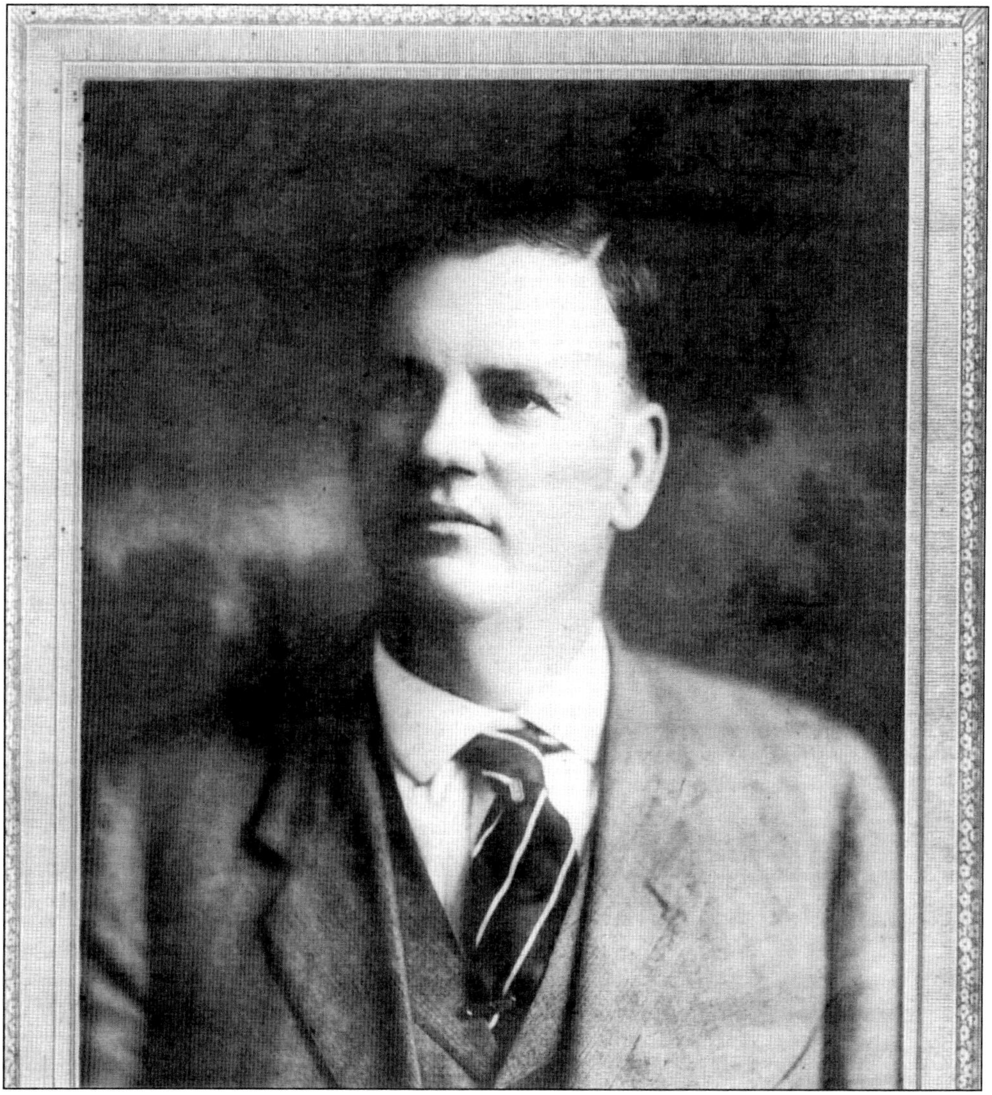

Thomas Jefferson Barnes came to the Goodwater community in 1902, setting up a tent on the W.J. Whiteman Cotton Gin yard. From this tent, Barnes would practice law in the Federal Commissioner's Court, which was then held in that community. After the court moved to Garvin later that year, Barnes followed by moving with his wife, Myrtle, by train to the bustling town. In 1907, with the coming of Oklahoma statehood, Barnes ran for the office of McCurtain County judge. He won by a heavy margin and took the oath of office on November 16, 1907, from Judge Spaulding in Idabel. Since Idabel was the new county's seat, Barnes again moved with his family, which now included a son and two daughters. In 1912, work was completed on the Barnes family's final home, a large, three-story mansion in the newly formed Whiteman Addition. Barnes was also a founding director of the First National Bank in Idabel and built many of the downtown buildings in Idabel. (Kenneth Sivard Jr. collection.)

William Reedy Morgan migrated to Broken Bow in the late 1910s, along with his little brother, in search of his parents, who had abandoned the boys and opened up a small café in the new town of Broken Bow. Billy, as he was often called, and his brother hitchhiked and hopped trains until they made it to the little sawmill town. Billy played quarterback for the Broken Bow Scouts football team from 1922 until 1924. In 1924, the school decided to change its mascot, and Billy came up with the idea of the Broken Bow Savages. He also submitted a drawing of the new mascot. Both were voted on by the student body and adopted as the school's new mascot. Billy served as a telephone lineman in the Civilian Conservation Corps (CCC) in the 1930s and in the US Navy during World War II. He made his home six miles east of Broken Bow and was a member of the Broken Bow Masonic Lodge. (Kenneth Sivard Jr. collection.)

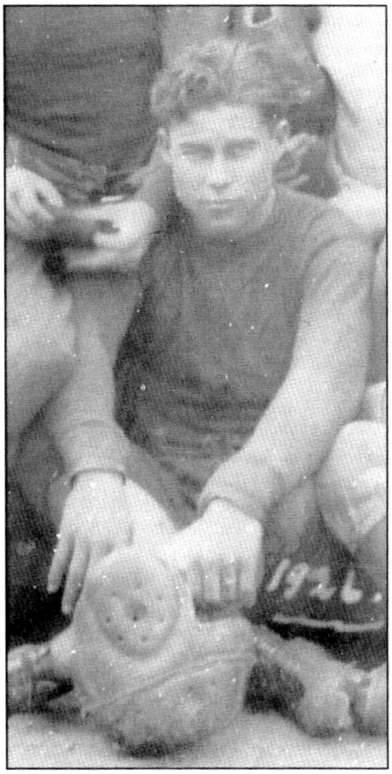

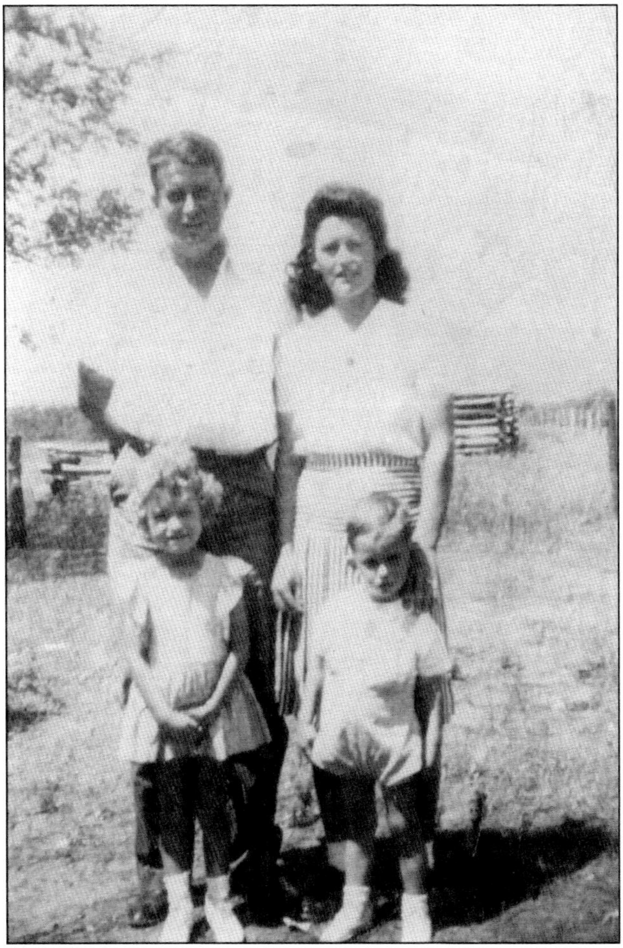

Howard Bunch ran several stores in the Broken Bow area. He is pictured here with his wife, Gladys, and his children Jerry and Shirley. (Courtesy of Gladys Bunch.)

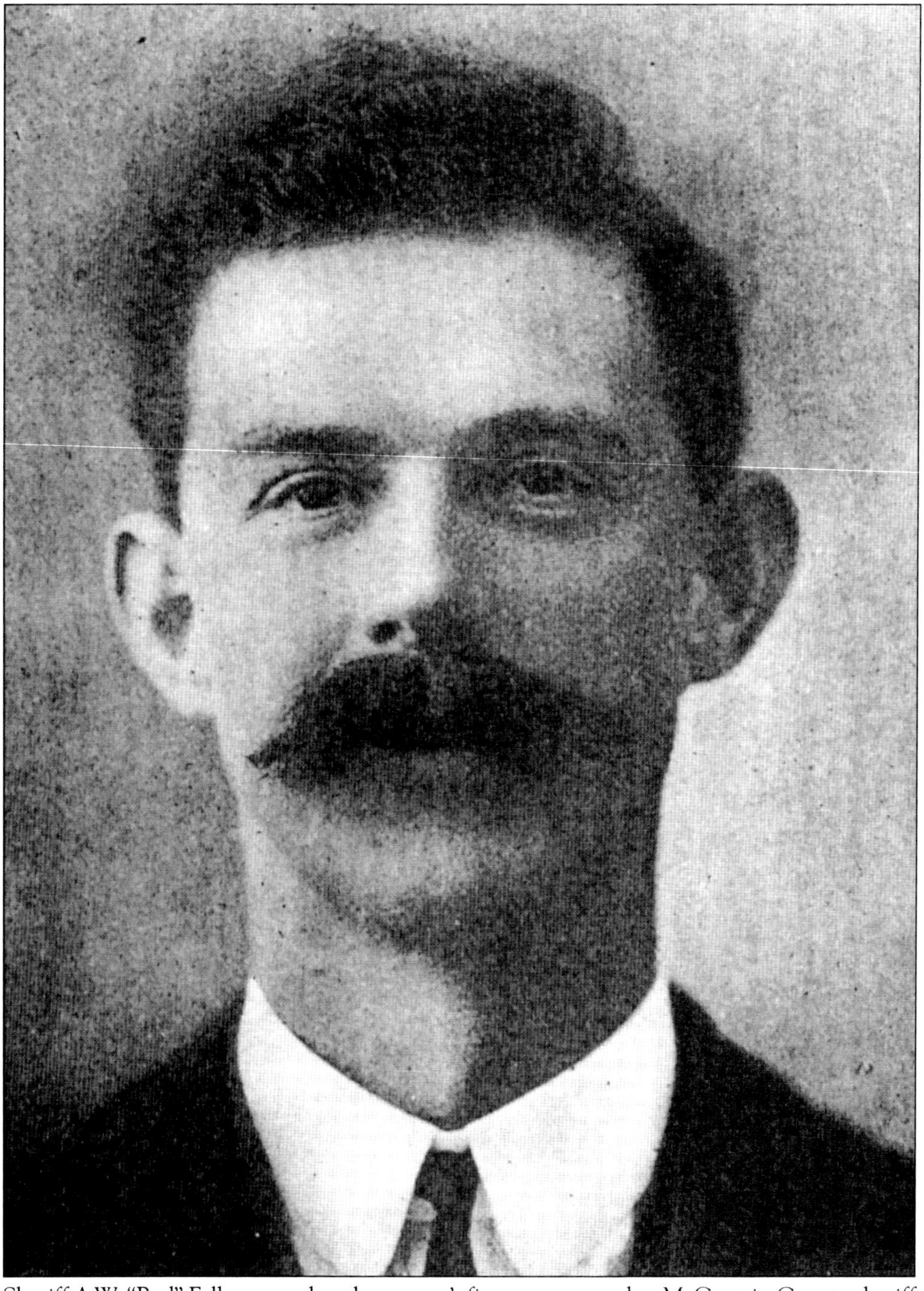

Sheriff A.W. "Bud" Felker served as the county's first surveyor and as McCurtain County sheriff from 1921 until August 14, 1922, when Clayton Thompson killed him while on duty in Wright City; Clayton shot two other people riding in a car with Felker. Clayton himself was later shot by Deputy Richard Jones, who was on the scene at the time of Sheriff Felker's murder. Felker was given a Masonic funeral and buried in the Wheelock Cemetery. Deputy Jones succeeded Felker as sheriff of McCurtain County. (Kenneth Sivard Jr. collection.)

Two

PICTURES OF OUR PAST

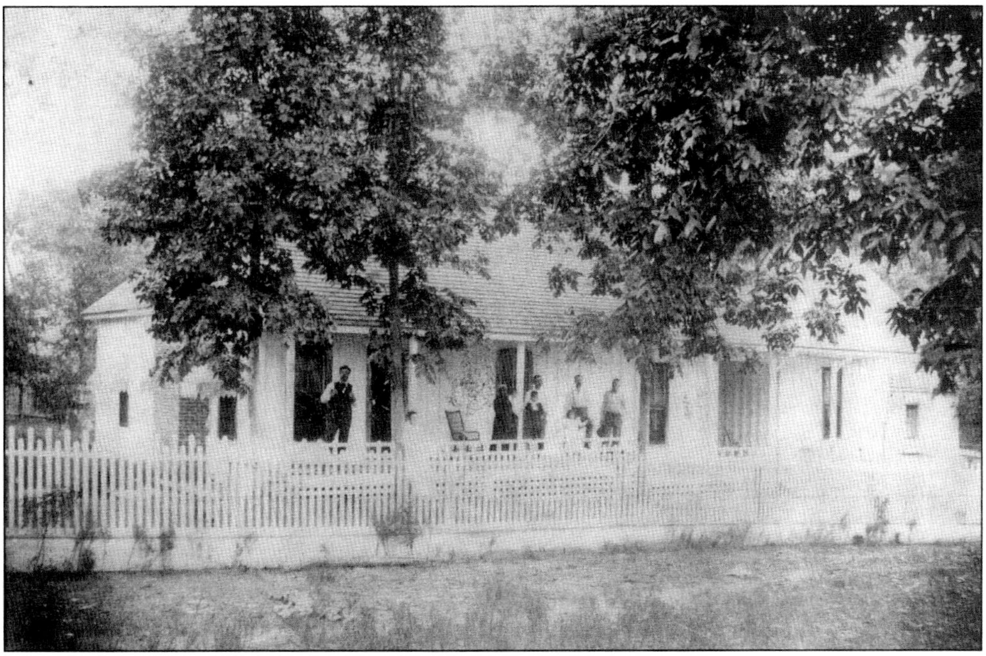

After settling in their new lands, Choctaws began to build small communities, usually consisting of a church, school, store, and perhaps a post office. These towns include Kulli Tuklo, Eagle Town, Wheelock, and Oka Achukma. Another such town, Shawneetown, was a large settlement even when the white inhabitants of Arkansas lived there in the late 1810s and early 1820s. Much of this settlement's success during the Choctaw years came from a store run by Robert M. Jones, the first millionaire in the Choctaw Nation. Often utilized as a hotel, the home of Robert Love in Shawneetown is seen here in 1895. (Courtesy of the McCurtain County Historical Society.)

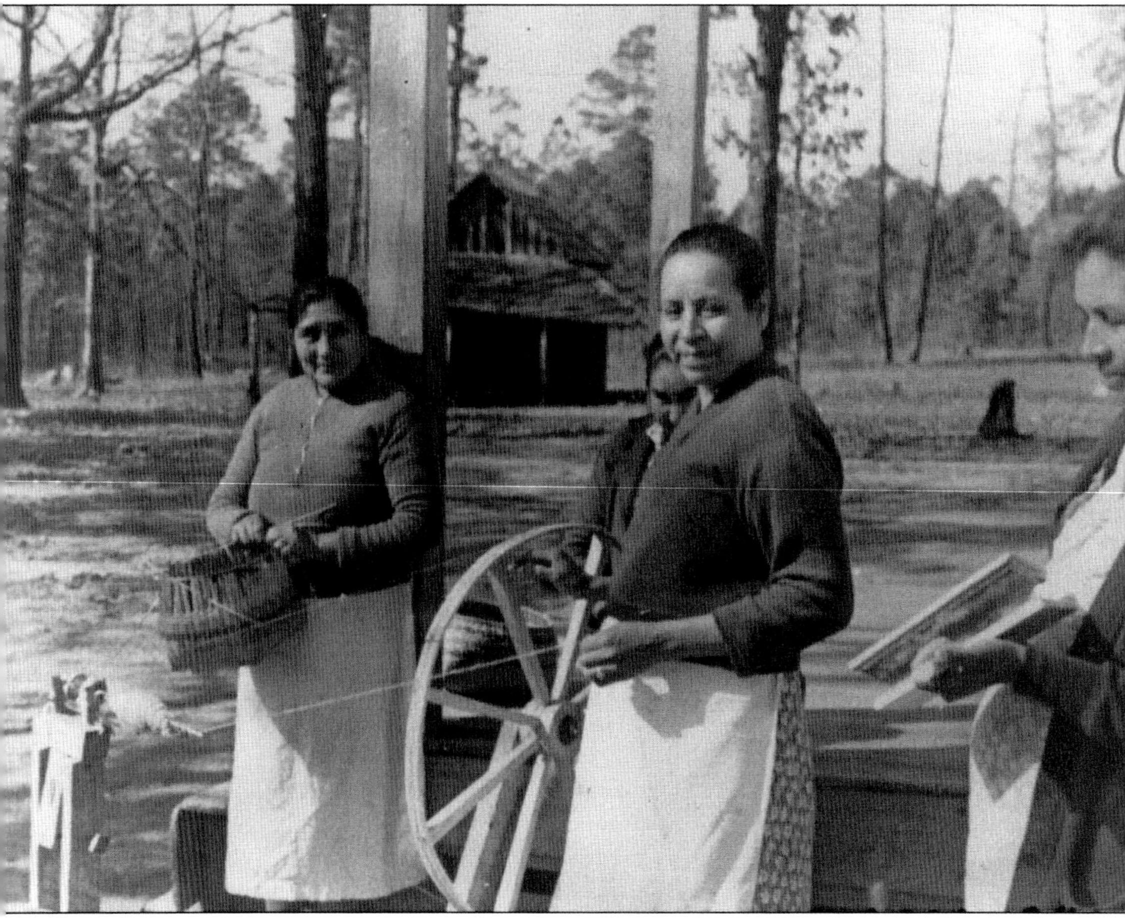

Weaving baskets was a valuable skill in the early days of Choctaw history. Baskets were used not only for transporting but also as sifters for cornmeal and flour. Weaving thread was also a necessary vocation. In the vast rural wilderness of the US western frontier, supplies were not always readily available. Shown is a group of women practicing these traditional arts on the steps of the St. Mathew Presbyterian Church in 1940. They are, from left to right, Mary Jessie, Fannie Wesley, Laura Willie, and Lestie Battiest. (Courtesy of the Oklahoma Historical Society Research Division.)

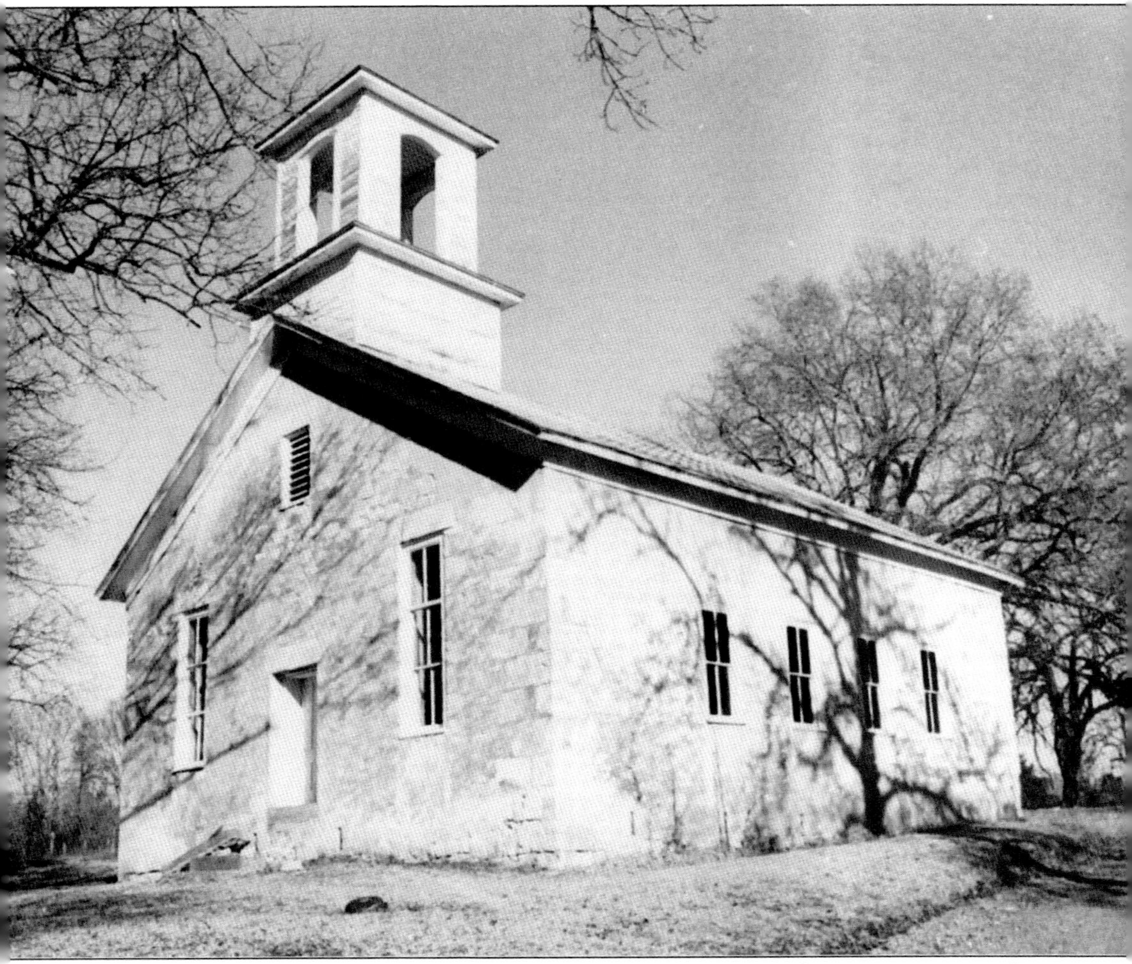

When the Choctaws traveled the Trail Of Tears beginning in 1831, many white missionaries made the journey with them, establishing churches and schools in the Choctaws' new home. Many great advances came from the tribe's partnerships with the missionaries, including the written Choctaw language and translated hymns and books of the Bible along with quality educations. Missions within what is now McCurtain County include Apekah, Stockbridge, Oka Achukma, and Wheelock. Alfred Wright, who established the Wheelock Mission, built the Wheelock Rock Church, formerly the Wheelock Presbyterian Church (pictured) in 1846. The church's 48-inch-thick walls are made of locally harvested stone. Today, it is the oldest church building in the state of Oklahoma. (Kenneth Sivard Jr. collection.)

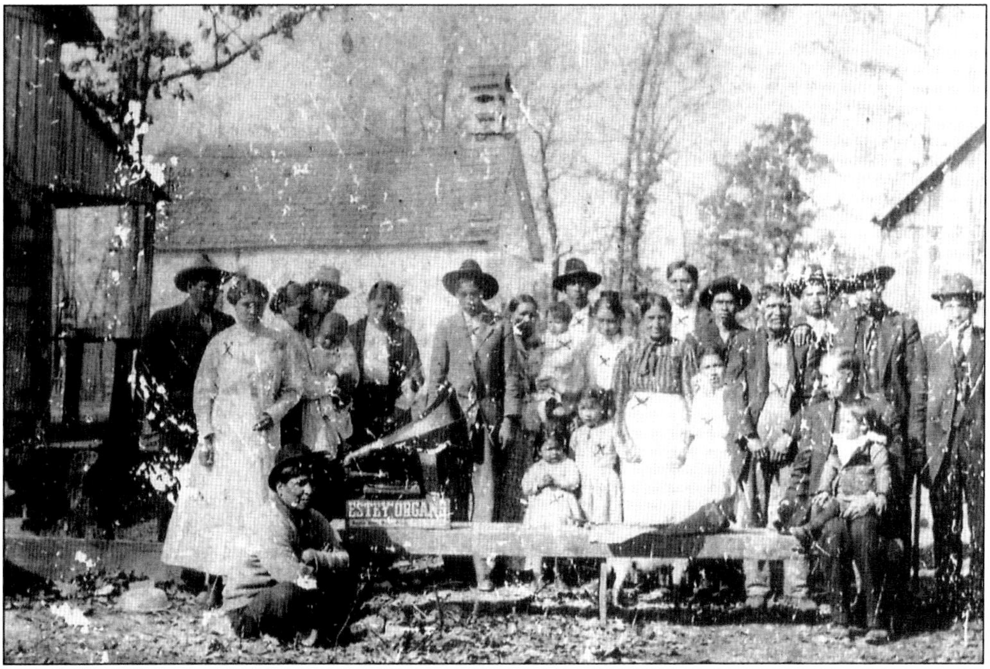

This 1921 picture depicts another Choctaw mission, the Mountain Fork Presbyterian Church, which was established in 1837 by Cyrus Byington. In this scene, members of the church gather to listen to a record player, which is seated on the bench in the foreground. (Kenneth Sivard Jr. collection.)

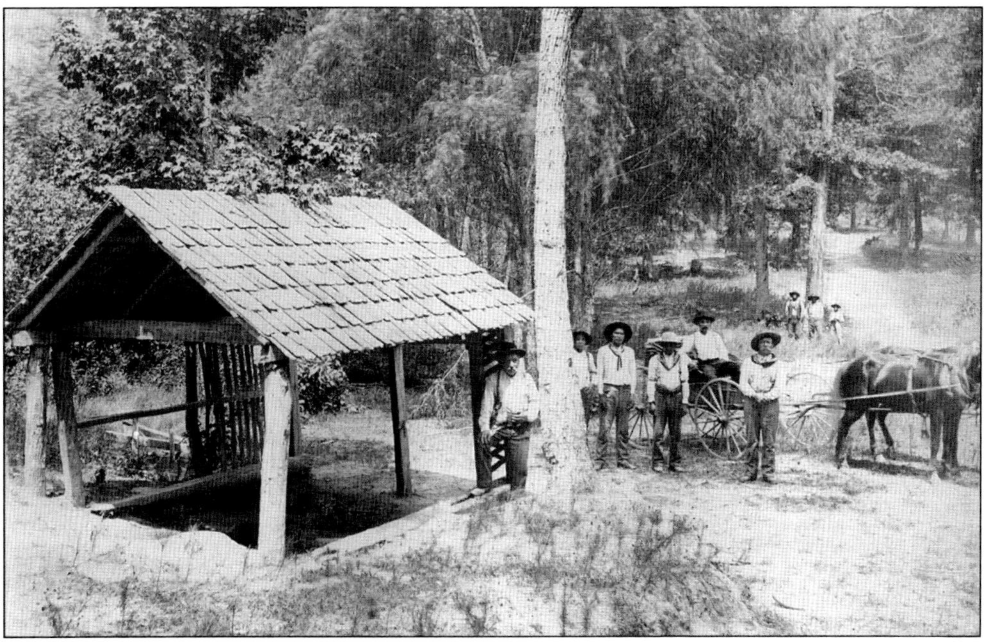

During the years before statehood, there were no water systems, and thus water was collected from wells or springs. Many springs served entire communities. Such was the case with Pero Springs, west of Eagletown. Here is a scene from the spring in the 1890s. Next the springhouse is James Dyer, and seated in the buggy is E.E. Dyer. (Courtesy of the McCurtain County Historical Society.)

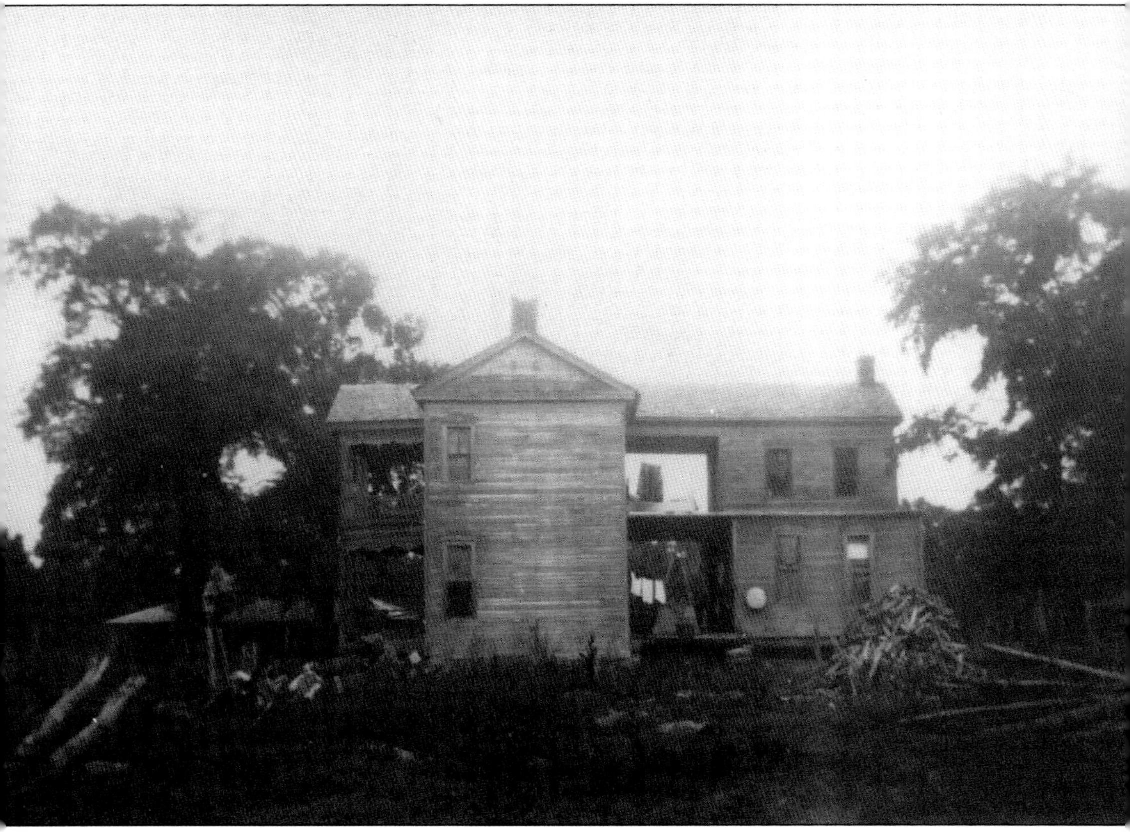

Soon after the Choctaw tribe's arrival as part of the Trail of Tears, members began to establish themselves in what is now McCurtain County. Most built small cabins and some later constructed lavish mansions. One such mansion was Choctaw chief Jefferson Gardner's house, which was built in 1884 by James and Noel Dyer. Gardner once owned a sawmill, a store, and ran the Eagletown Post Office. He died in April 1906, and the home was sold. In 1910, it was sold again and purchased by the Stiles family, which still owns the home today. (Kenneth Sivard Jr. collection.)

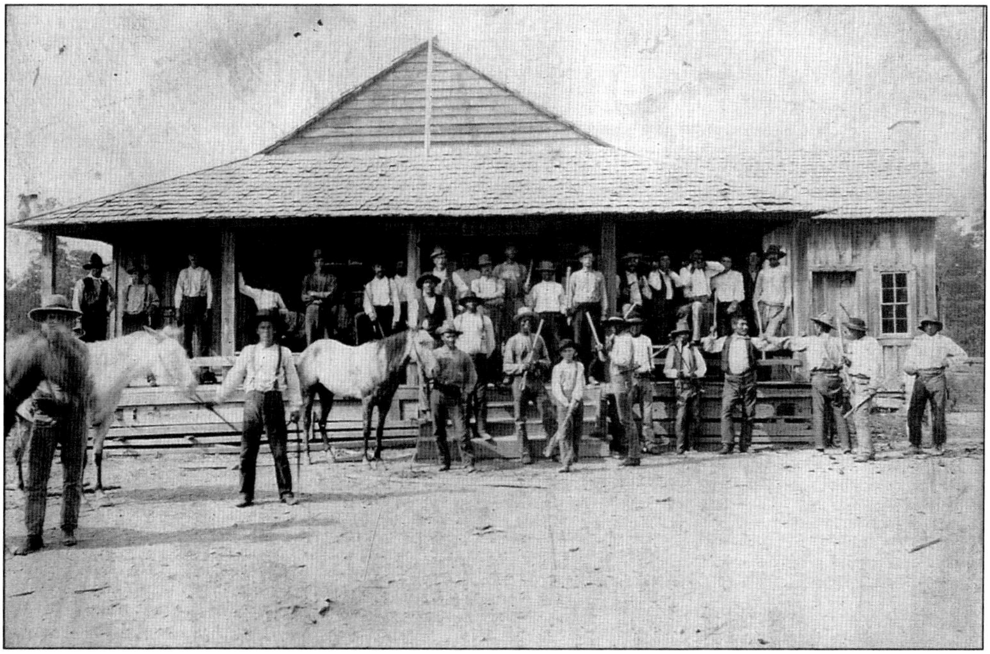

A group of men, with some holding stickball sticks and some shouldering rifles, has gathered in the 1890s outside the E.E. Dyer Store just west of the Mountain Fork River and the original site of Eagletown, six miles east of Broken Bow. This store once held the Eagletown Post Office, the oldest post office in Oklahoma. (Courtesy of the McCurtain County Historical Society.)

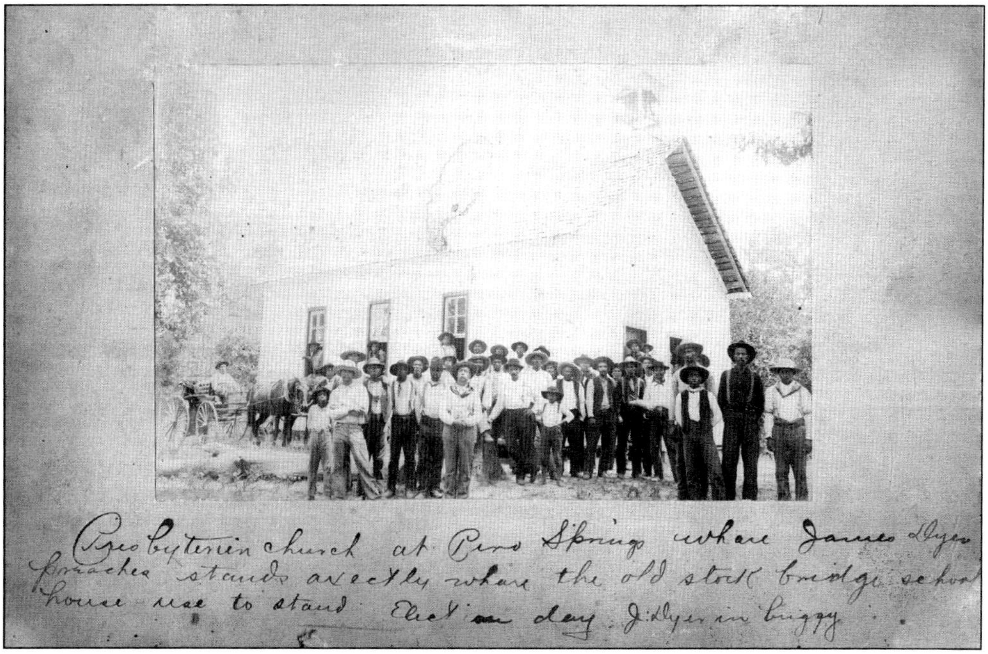

This is a picture taken on Election Day 1894 at the Pero Springs Presbyterian Church, where men have gathered to cast their votes. James Dyer, seen in the back left aboard a buggy, was the church's pastor. The church stood in the exact spot where the Stockbridge Mission School was west of Eagletown. (Courtesy of the McCurtain County Historical Society.)

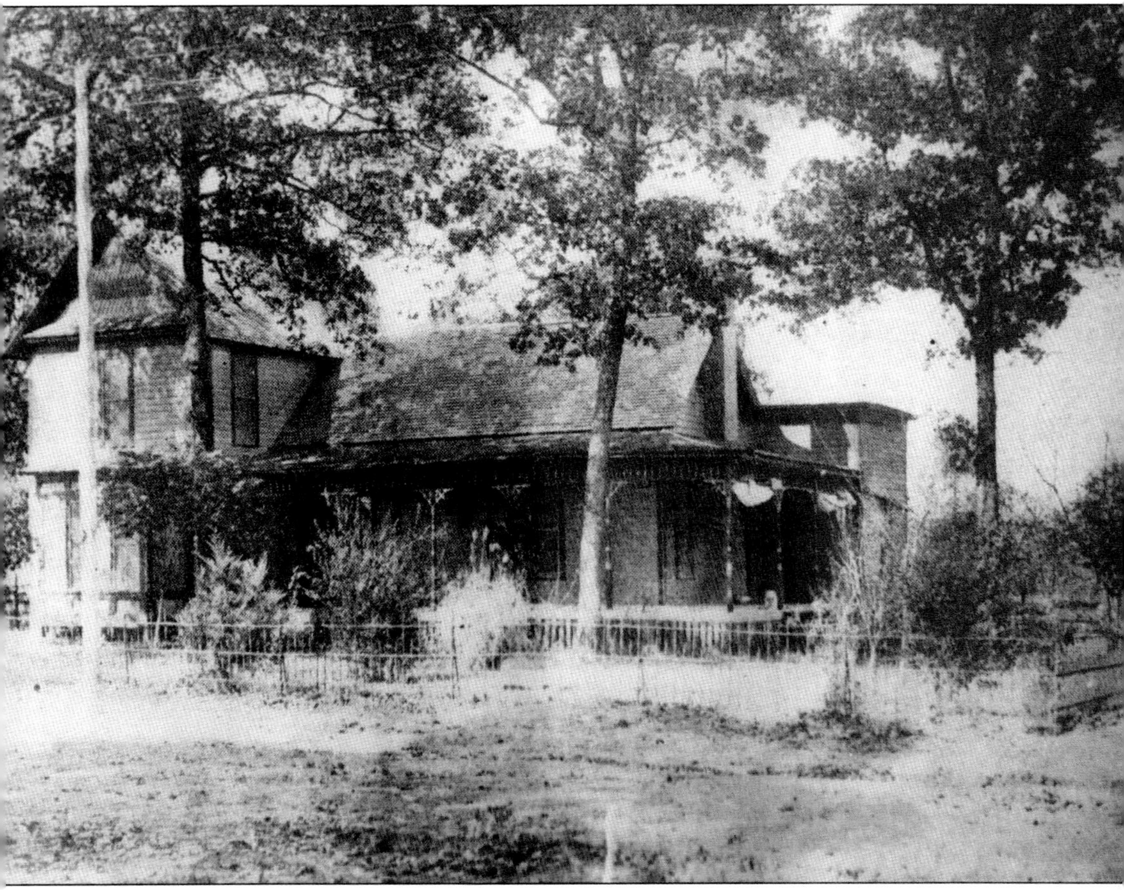

Before Oklahoma statehood, the federal government held a commissioner's court in what is now McCurtain County to try misdemeanor offences committed by whites or any American citizens living in this part of Indian Territory. The court was held in 1902 at Goodwater, near Haworth. It moved later that year to Garvin after the completion of the Frisco Railroad. Federal judge Spaulding presided over the court; his Garvin home is shown here in 1906. (Kenneth Sivard Jr. collection.)

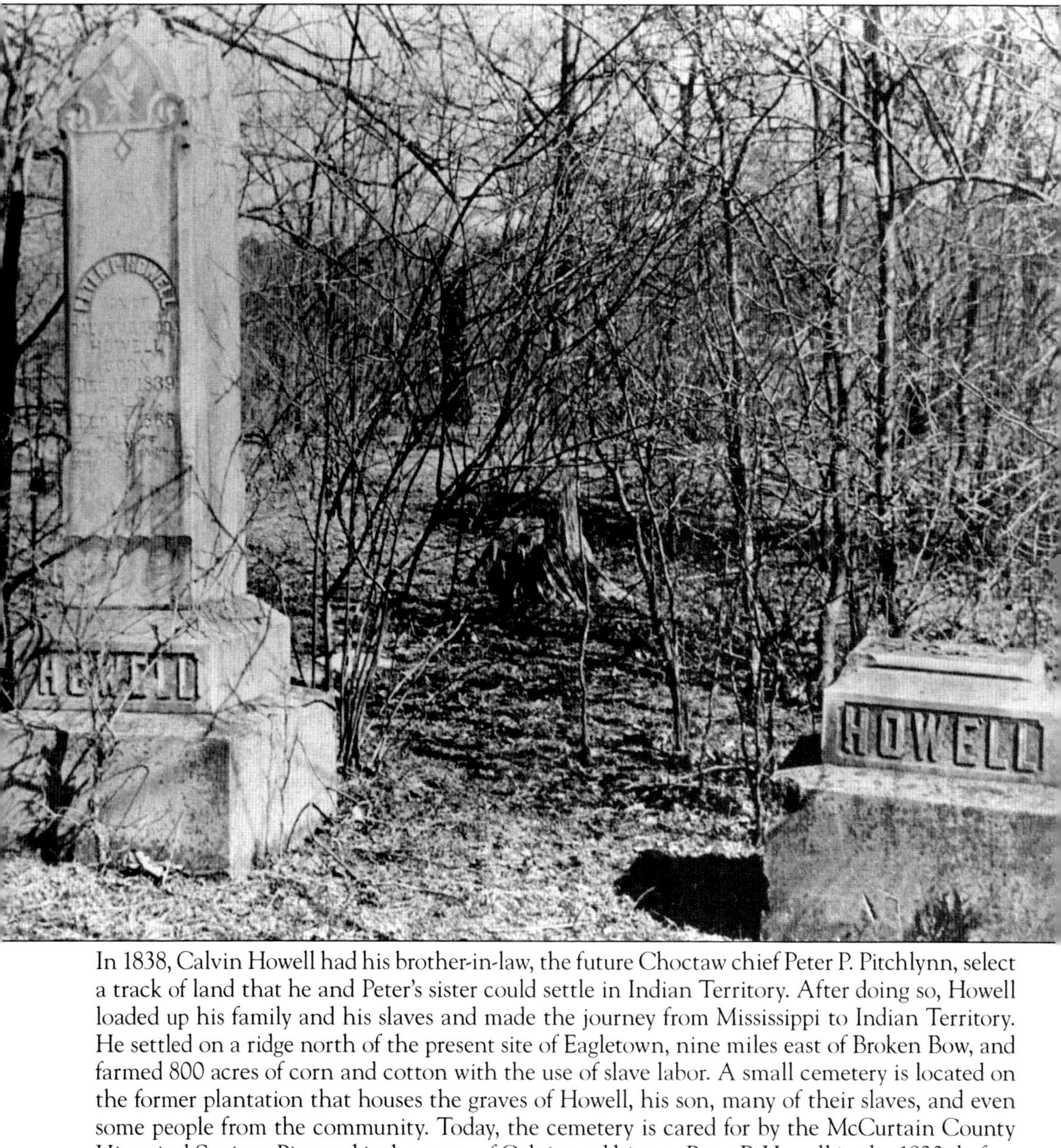

In 1838, Calvin Howell had his brother-in-law, the future Choctaw chief Peter P. Pitchlynn, select a track of land that he and Peter's sister could settle in Indian Territory. After doing so, Howell loaded up his family and his slaves and made the journey from Mississippi to Indian Territory. He settled on a ridge north of the present site of Eagletown, nine miles east of Broken Bow, and farmed 800 acres of corn and cotton with the use of slave labor. A small cemetery is located on the former plantation that houses the graves of Howell, his son, many of their slaves, and even some people from the community. Today, the cemetery is cared for by the McCurtain County Historical Society. Pictured is the grave of Calvin and his son Peter P. Howell in the 1920s before restoration work was performed by the historical society. (Kenneth Sivard Jr. collection.)

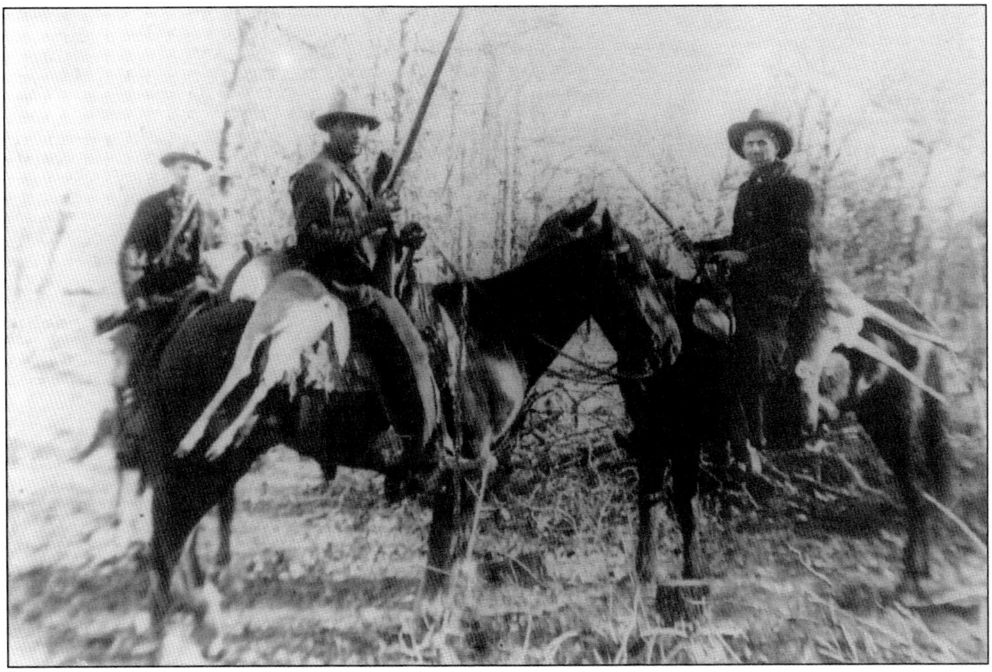

Hunting was a very important task in the years before, and even after, statehood. Shown are Clayton Wilson, Bunk Galloway, and James Kirk on a deer hunt north of Millerton in 1901. Kirk was the son-in-law of Choctaw Chief Isaac Garvin and is credited with establishing the town of Garvin. (Kenneth Sivard Jr. collection.)

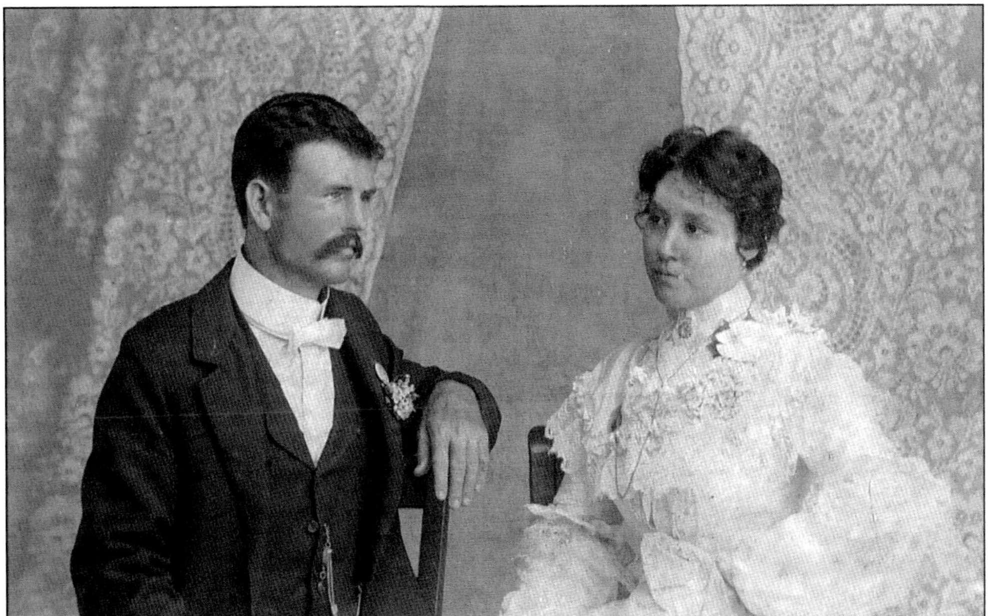

Thomas J. Barnes came to Indian Territory in 1902 as a lawyer to the federal commissioner's court at Goodwater. Barnes moved with the court to Garvin later that year and lived there until becoming the county's first judge in 1907. He is seen here with his wife, Myrtle, on their wedding day of August 12, 1900. (Kenneth Sivard Jr. collection.)

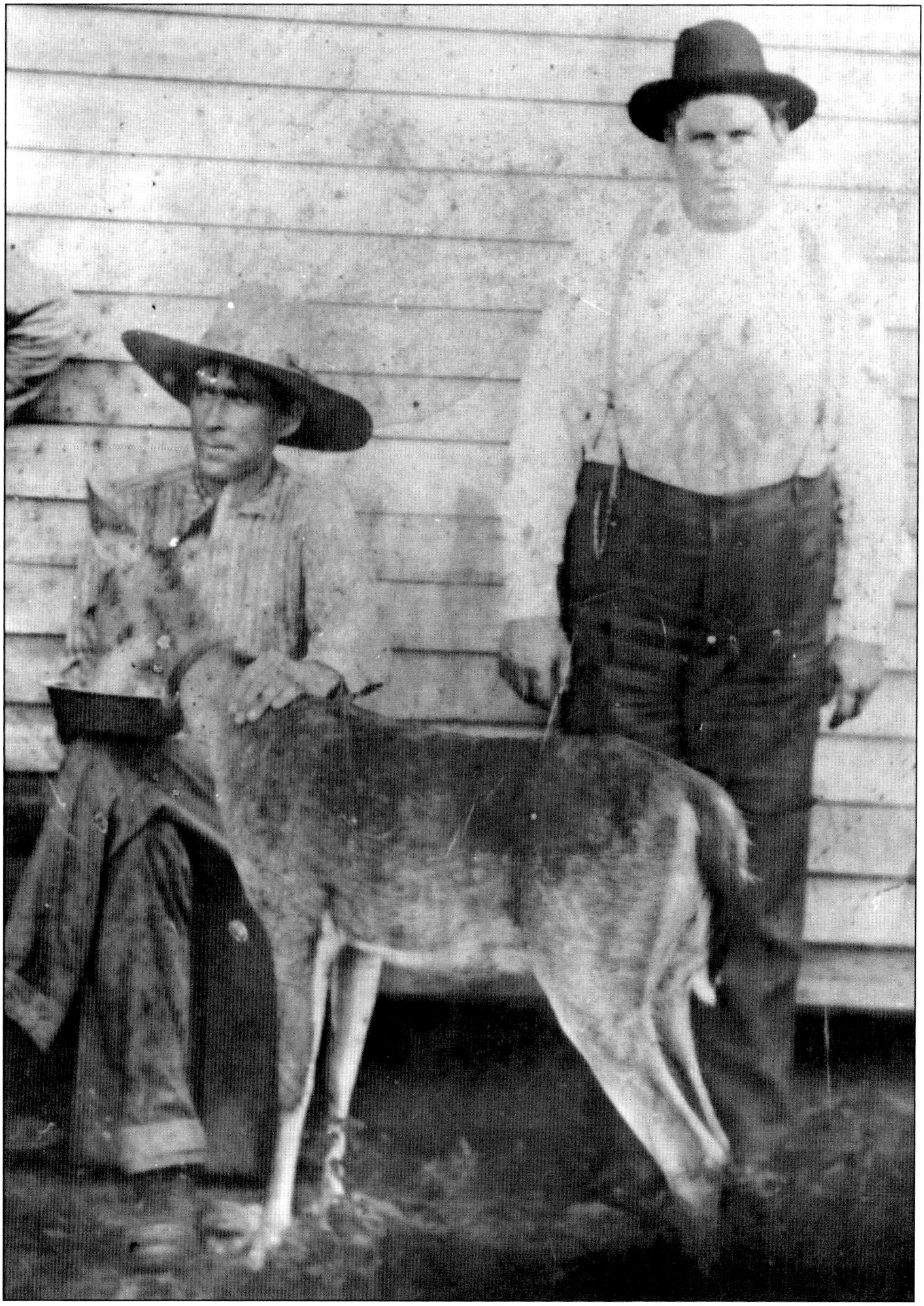

McCurtain County has always had an abundance of wildlife. When the Choctaws first arrived in the county in 1831, they found a large, natural salt lick on the western bank of the Mountain Fork River near Eagletown. A corral was built around the lick, and when deer, wild horses, or even wild cows would enter, they would be trapped to be harvested for food or domestication. Two unidentified men are shown feeding a deer near Moon in 1905. (Kenneth Sivard Jr. collection.)

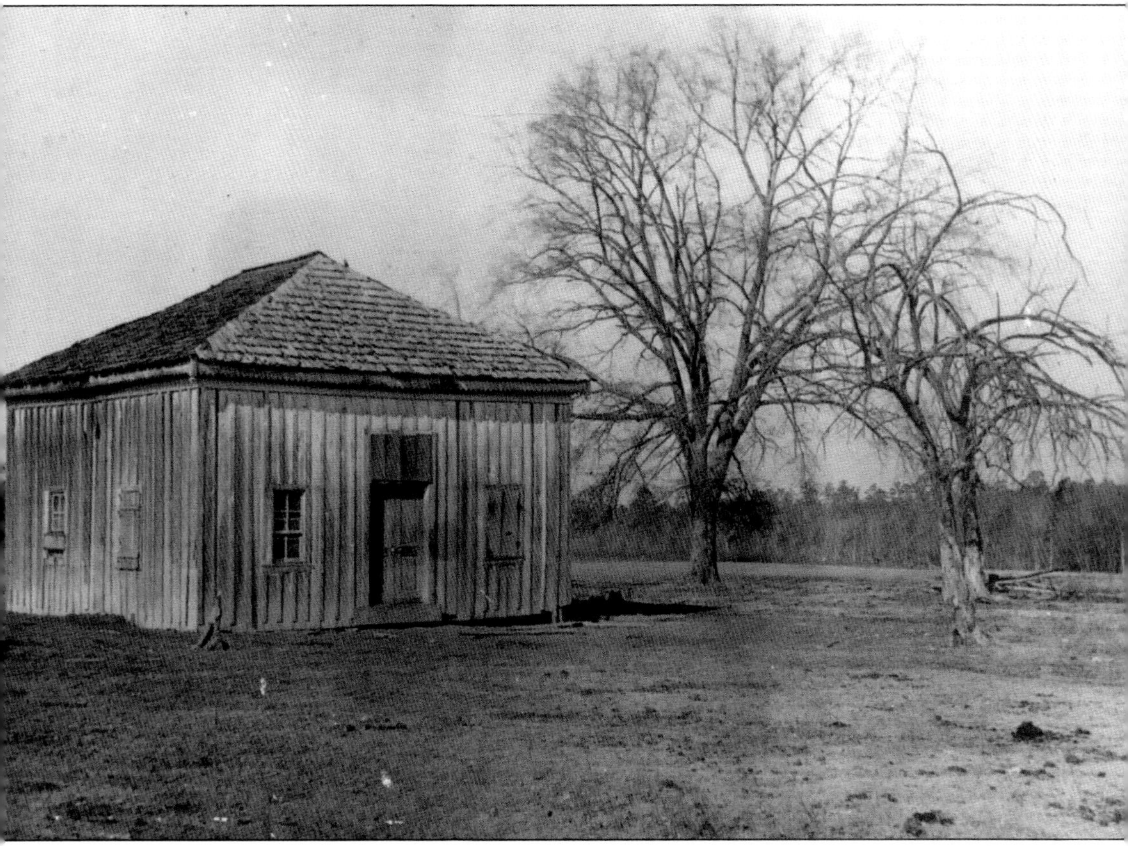

The Choctaw Constitution of 1855 established the Choctaw Nation's county court system. Five counties made up what is now McCurtain County: Nashoba, Eagle, Bok Homma, Bok Tuklo, and Towson. Each county had a courthouse and "whipping tree" where criminals were punished. The Eagle County Courthouse and whipping tree are seen in this post-1899 photograph. (Courtesy of the Oklahoma Historical Society Research Division.)

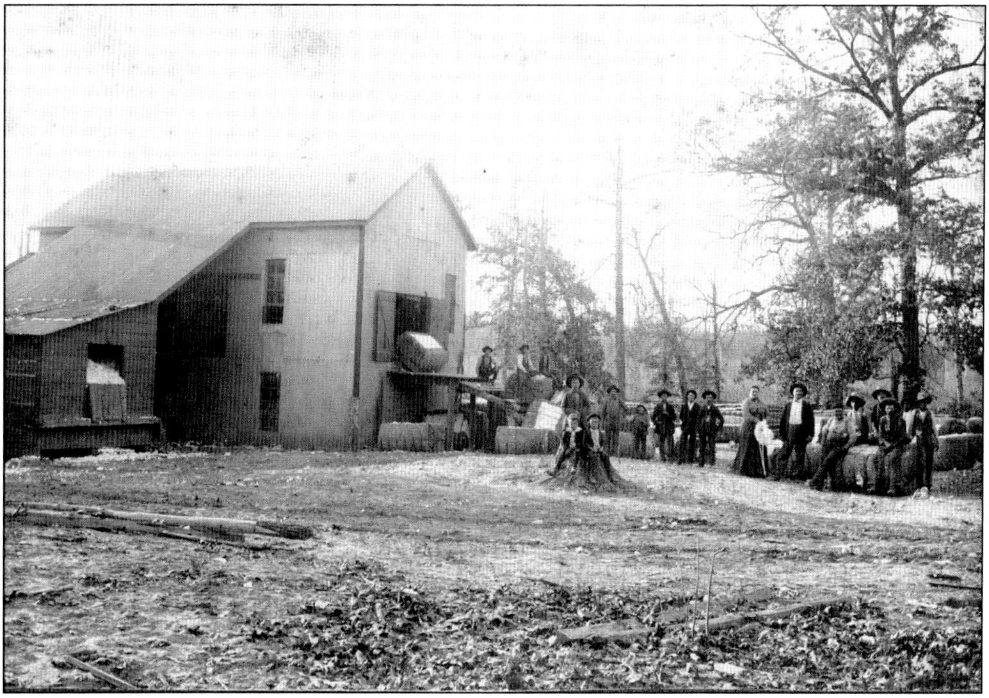

After the coming of statehood, things certainly changed in McCurtain County, but some things stayed the same as far as everyday life. Many businesses already existed in the county for years and continued to do so, some lasting until the economic disaster of the 1930s. One such business was the Kirk Cotton Gin in Garvin, seen here around 1900. (Kenneth Sivard Jr. collection.)

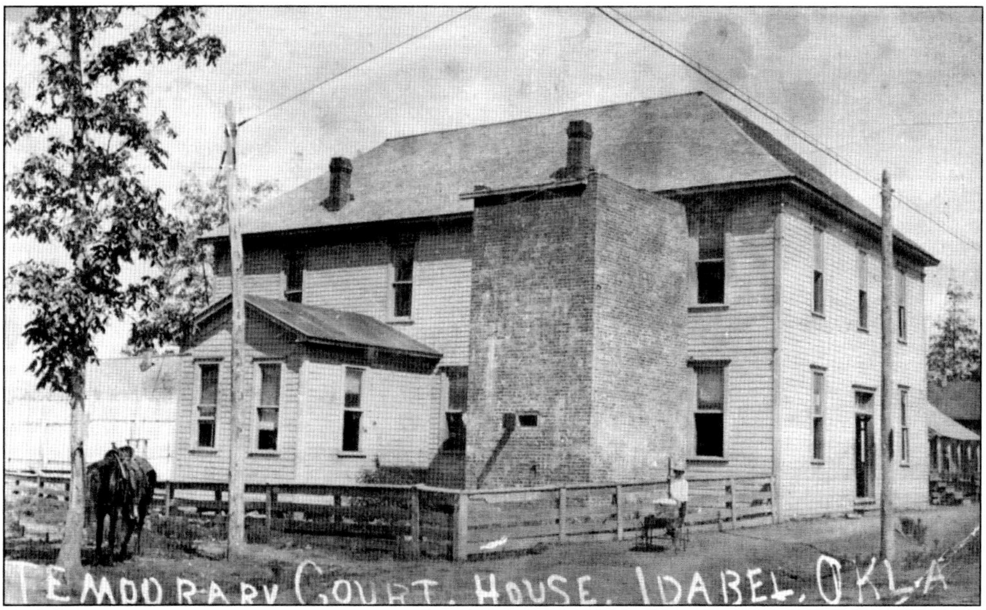

For almost a half of a year after Oklahoma became a state, McCurtain County had no courthouse. This building on South Central Street in Idabel was constructed in 1908 to serve as a temporary fix to that problem. The young boy on the sidewalk is C.A. Jeter with his hot tamale cart. (Kenneth Sivard Jr. collection.)

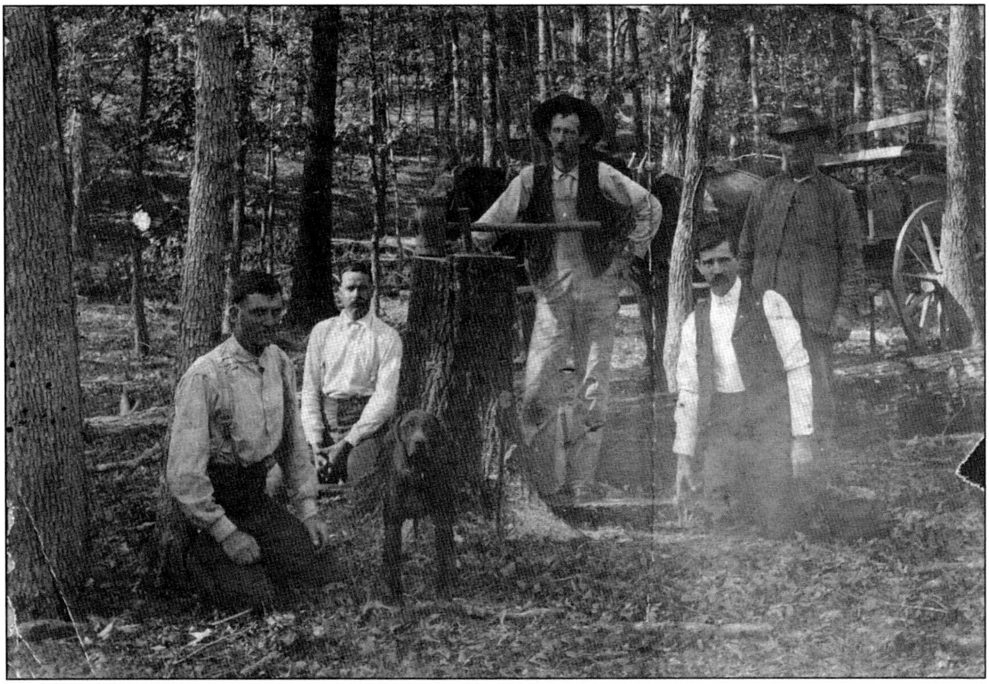

Pictured here is a group of loggers in 1910. Soon after statehood, there were lumber mills in Newton and later Broken Bow, Bismark, Wright City, as well as in towns such as Garvin and Millerton. Clearing the virgin timber was big business. (Kenneth Sivard Jr. collection.)

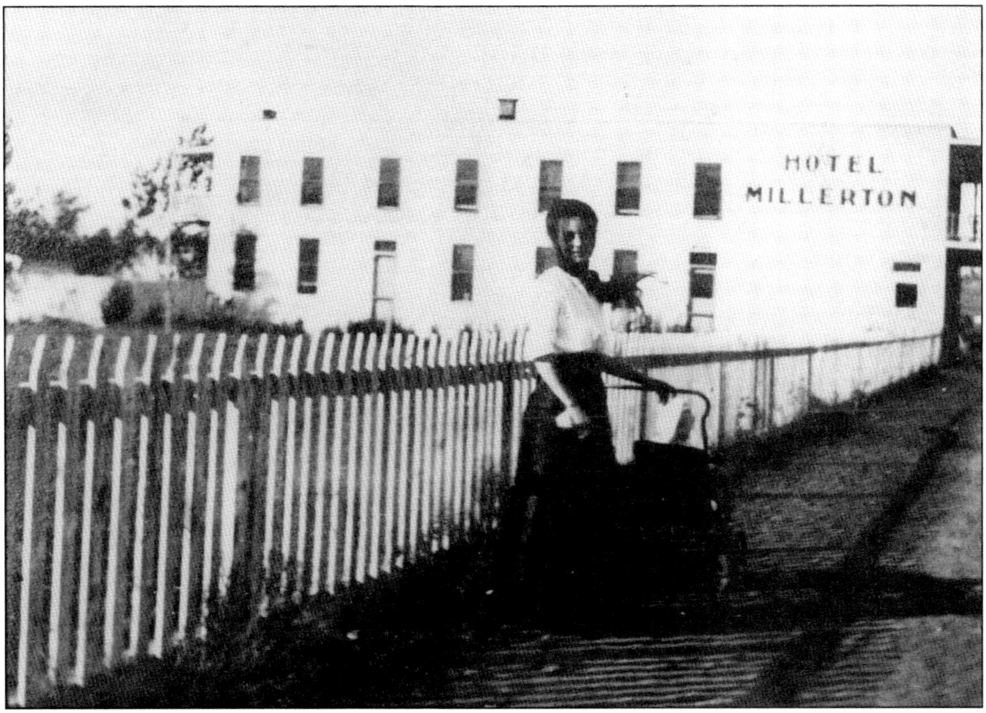

In the early days of Oklahoma, the town of Millerton flourished because of the lumber market. At one time it even had a hotel, pictured here around 1910, and a bank. (Kenneth Sivard Jr. collection.)

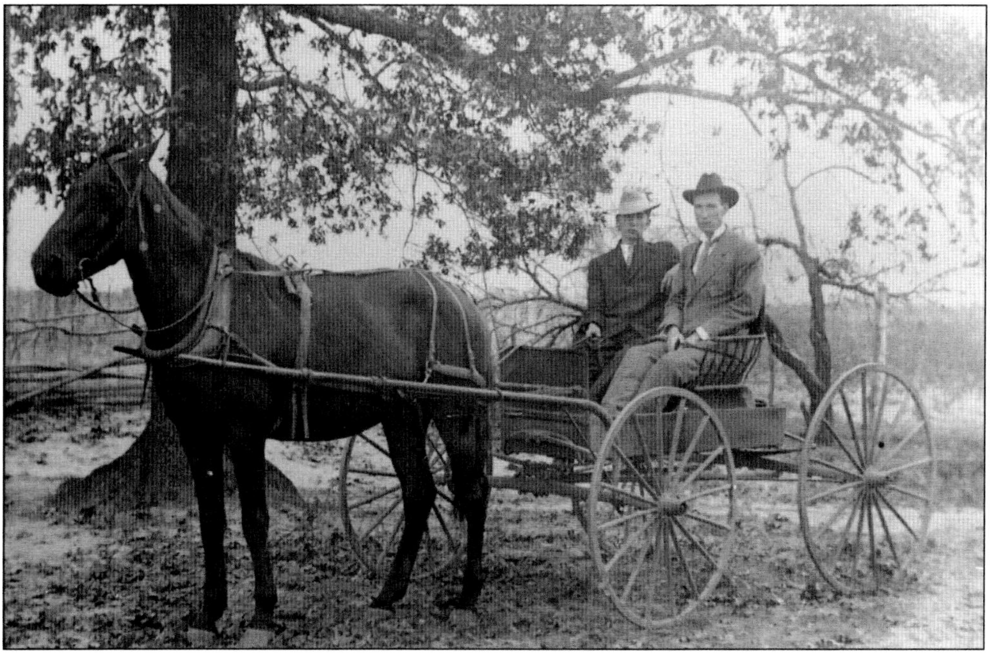

Today's roads were nonexistent in the early development of the county. Transportation was done on muddy or dusty roads that were commonly unusable during wet weather. Cars did not appear in the county until the late 1910s. Shown are two young men in a one-horse buggy. (Kenneth Sivard Jr. collection.)

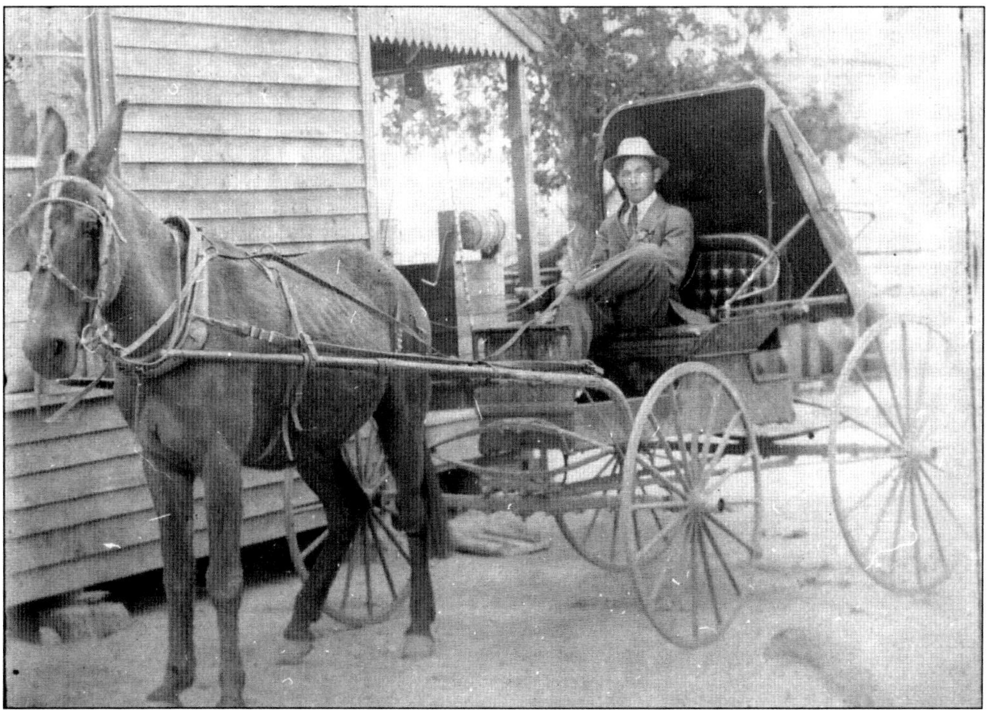

This is another example of a buggy, this time with an alternate mode of transportation, the mule. Note the well on the back porch of the house in the background. (Kenneth Sivard Jr. collection.)

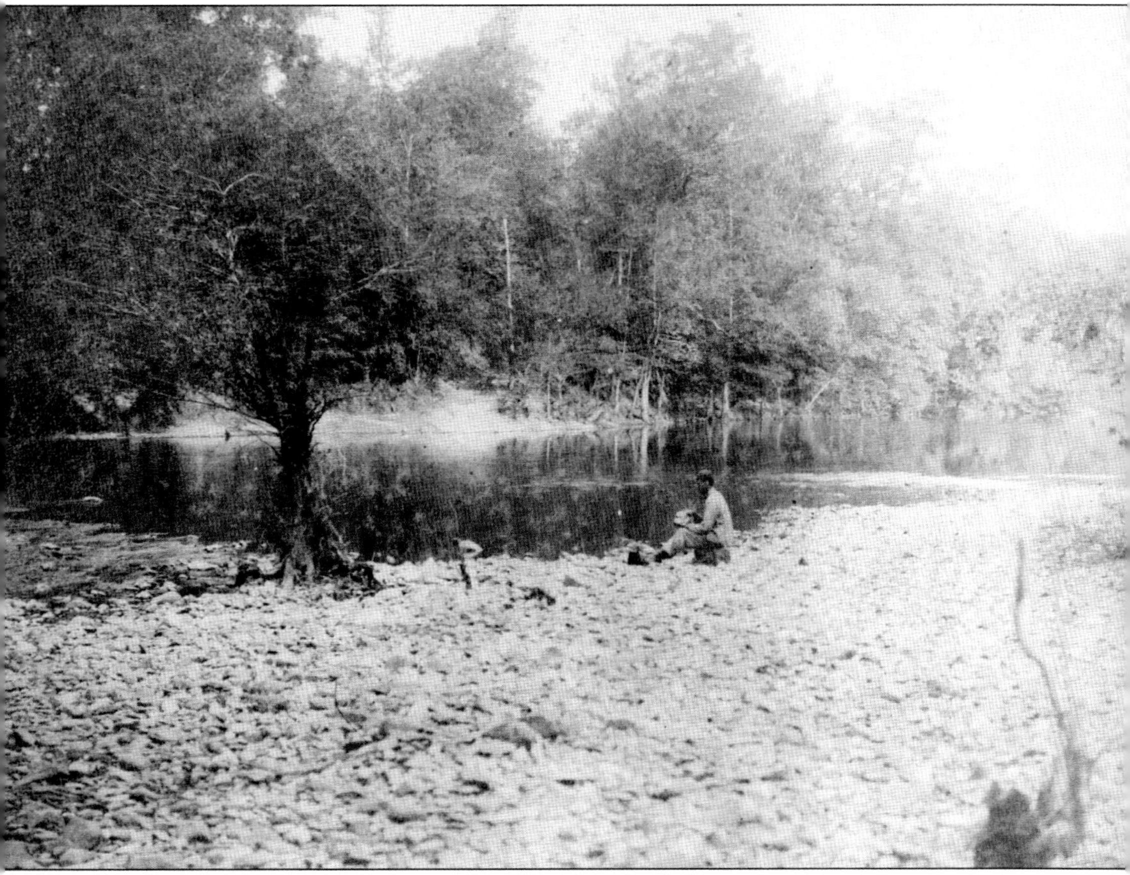

The abundance of rivers and streams posed another obstacle while traveling in McCurtain County. Many roads would go miles out of the way just so that a river could be crossed. This crossing on the Mountain Fork River, known as the Tonhika Crossing, was used on the road from Ultima Thule, Arkansas, to the Tonhika settlement, southwest of Eagletown, on the western bank of the river. (Kenneth Sivard Jr. collection.)

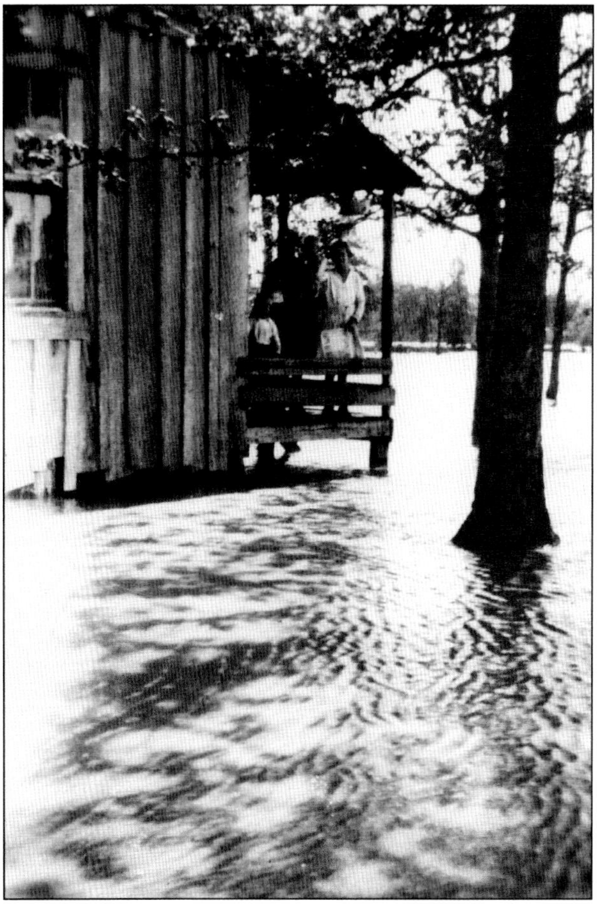

Flooding was a great danger in the early 1900s before any dams were built on the streams and rivers of the county as seen with this family stranded in the 1927 flood of Smithville. (Kenneth Sivard Jr. collection.)

Church services were held with great reverence in the beginning days of statehood. Many newly formed towns and communities sought to build beautiful sanctuaries as a means of hometown pride and also to offer a monument to their religion. This is the Garvin Presbyterian Church in 1909, the year it was constructed. The church was made of native limestone and hosted massive stained-glass windows. The church was sold to the Baptists in 1932. (Kenneth Sivard Jr. collection.)

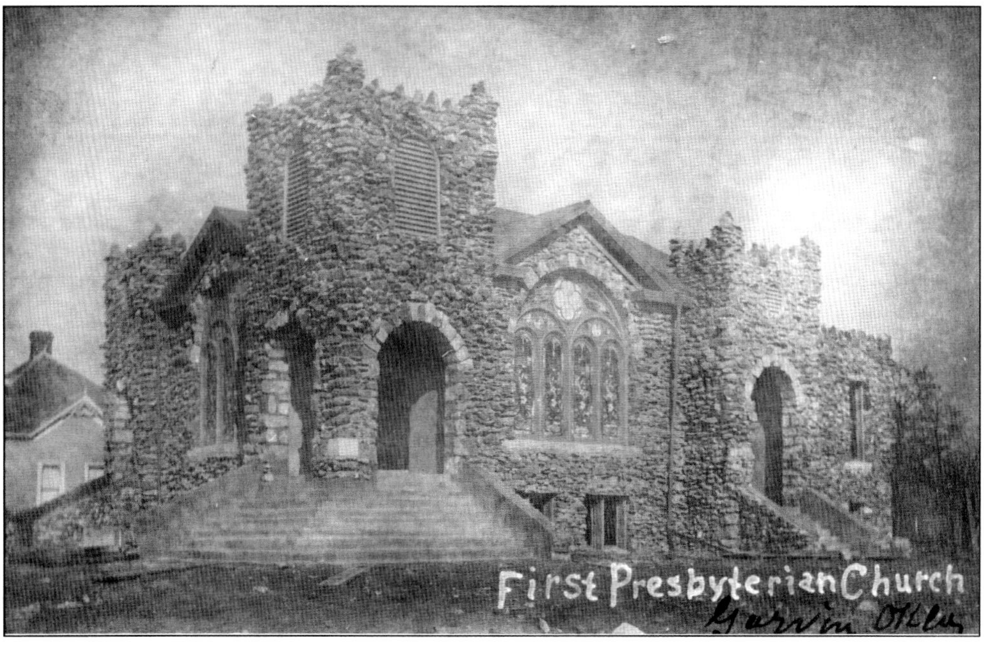

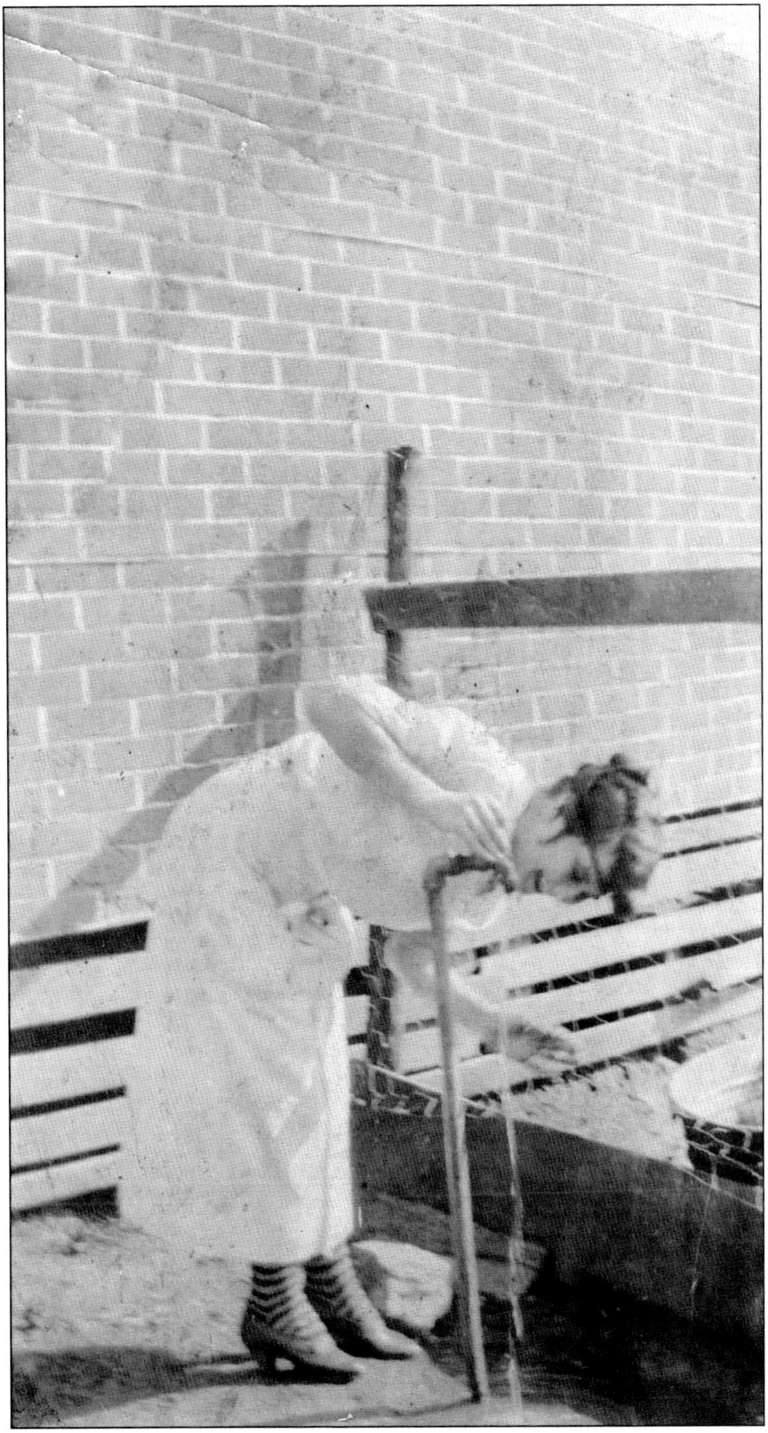

After statehood, towns such as Valliant, Garvin, and Idabel endeavored to develop city water systems. Many of the citizens of those towns never lived in an area that offered running water in or outside the home such as what is seen with this young lady trying out an outside water faucet in 1910. (Kenneth Sivard Jr. collection.)

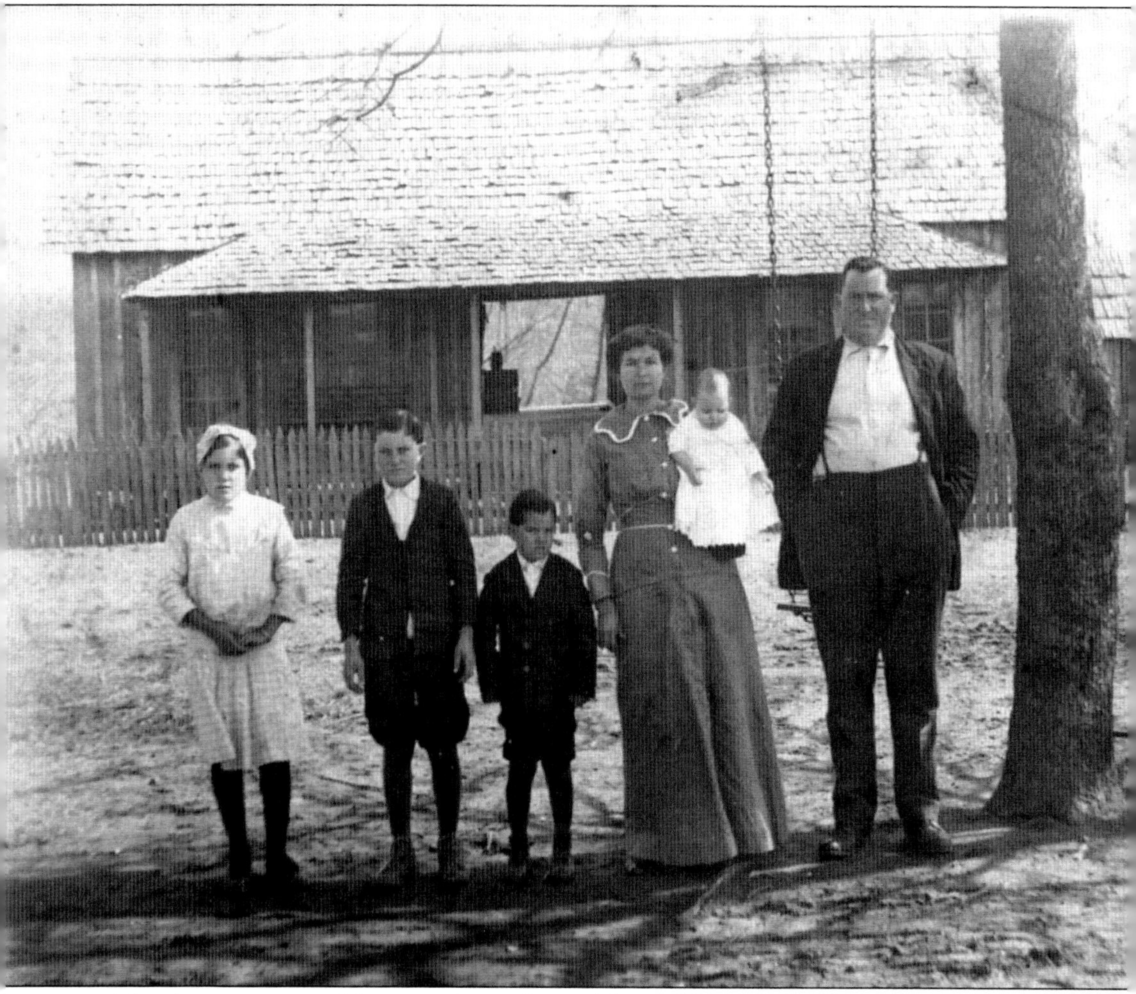

A family poses in period dress standing in front of their home, typical of the era, in the community of Ida, which later became Battiest. As white settlers started to make new homes in McCurtain County after statehood, some struggled to establish a foothold. Most started out with simple homes on harsh, untamed land. These resilient people grew to establish families and new lives on what was then America's frontier. (Kenneth Sivard Jr. collection.)

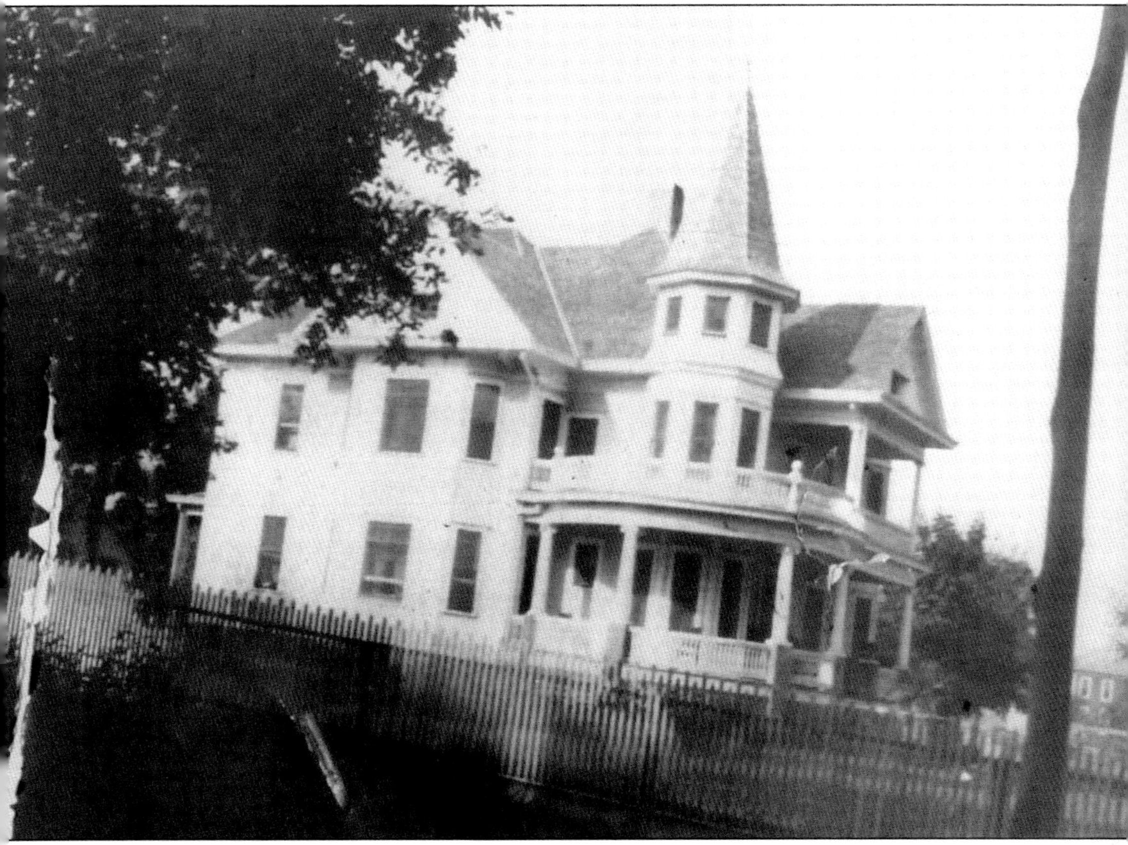

During the early 1910s, many of the fine homes in Idabel were built, which set the standard for luxury in the county. Here is the T.J. Barnes home as it looked when its construction was finished in 1912. It was wired for electricity before electricity was offered in Idabel and was fitted for indoor plumbing even though the house was outside of Idabel city limits at the time. (Kenneth Sivard Jr. collection.)

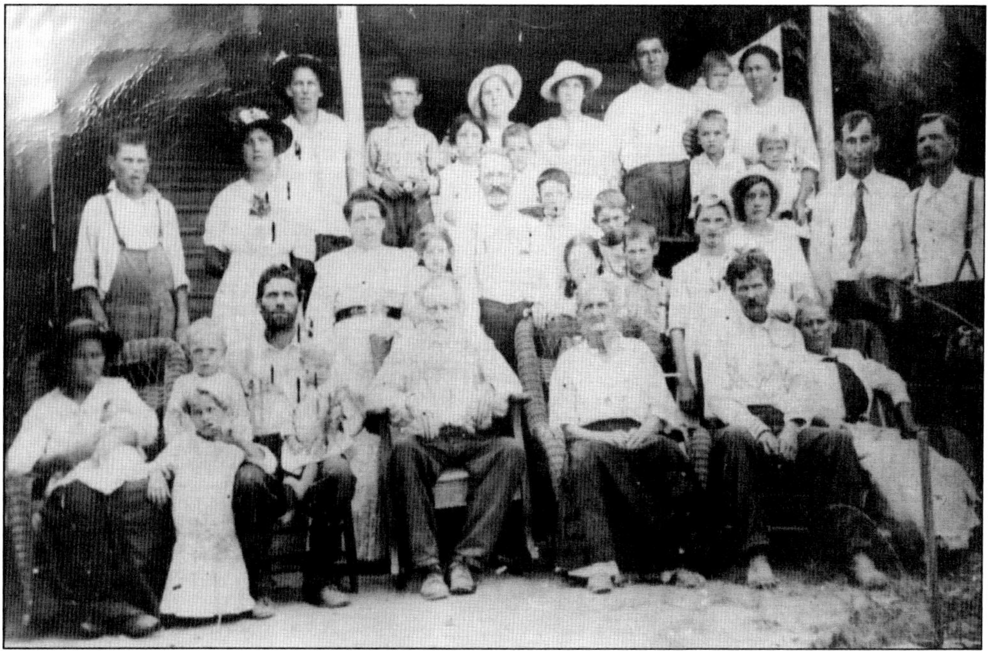

Family reunions were popular occasions after statehood as was settler's reunions. The D.C. Whiteman family reunion is shown here in Haworth in 1916. The Whiteman family was instrumental in bringing industry and business to the Haworth area in the years shortly before and after Oklahoma statehood. (Kenneth Sivard Jr. collection.)

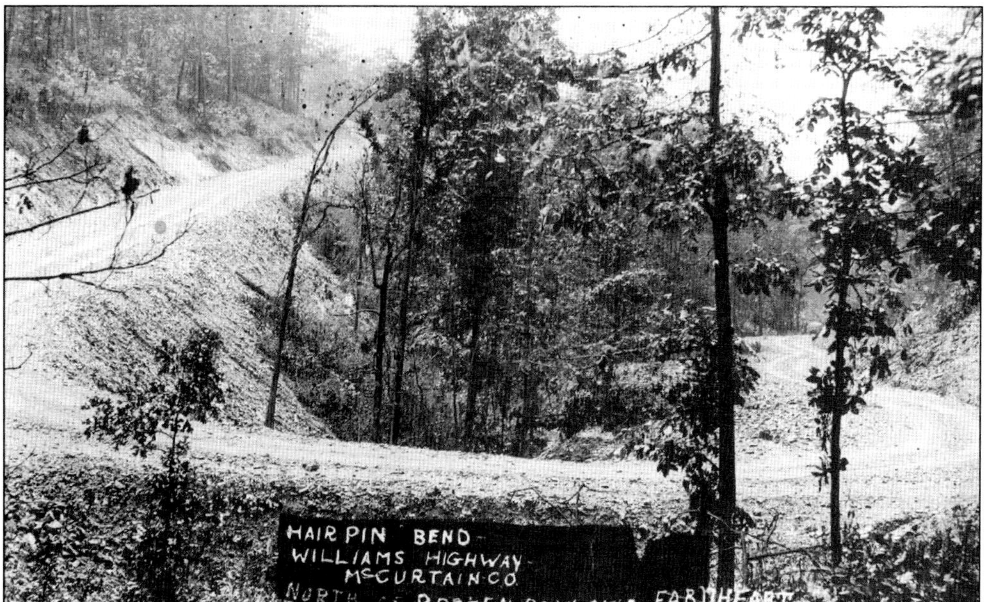

The early 1920s saw great advances in McCurtain County in terms of transportation when the Williams Highway, Highway 21, and the Bankhead Highway were built. The Williams Highway connected the towns of Smithville, Bethel, and Battiest with the rest of the county. Travel on the highway was dangerous as shown in this picture of Hairpin Bend north of Hochatown. (Kenneth Sivard Jr. collection.)

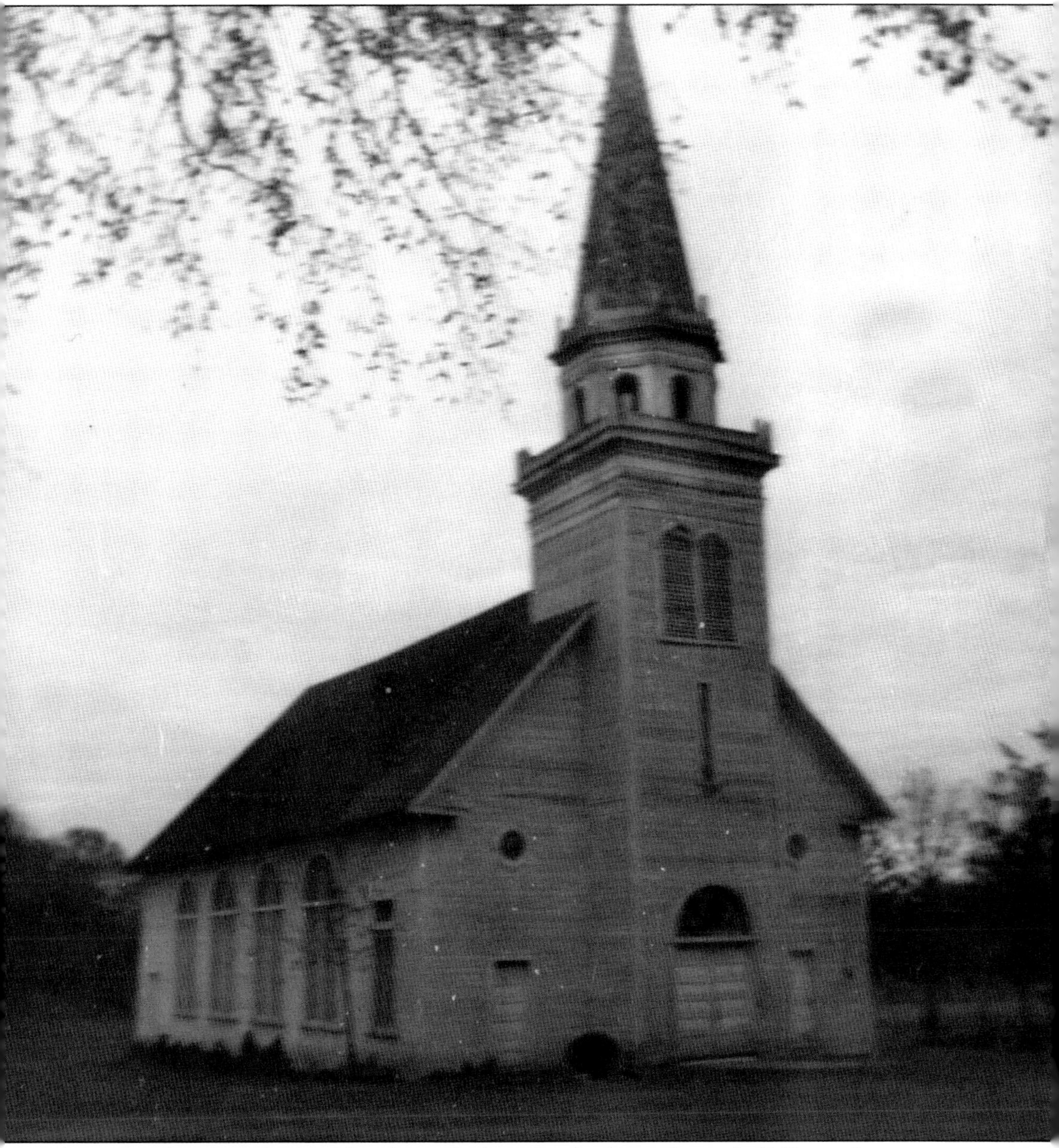

The Sealy Chapel Methodist Church was built in Smithville in the early 1920s on the campus of the Folsom Training School to serve the school's students and staff. It was later used as the Smithville Methodist Church and hosted the Mountain Fork Singing Convention for many years. The church is shown here in November 1960 after a few years of sitting vacant. (Kenneth Sivard Jr. collection.)

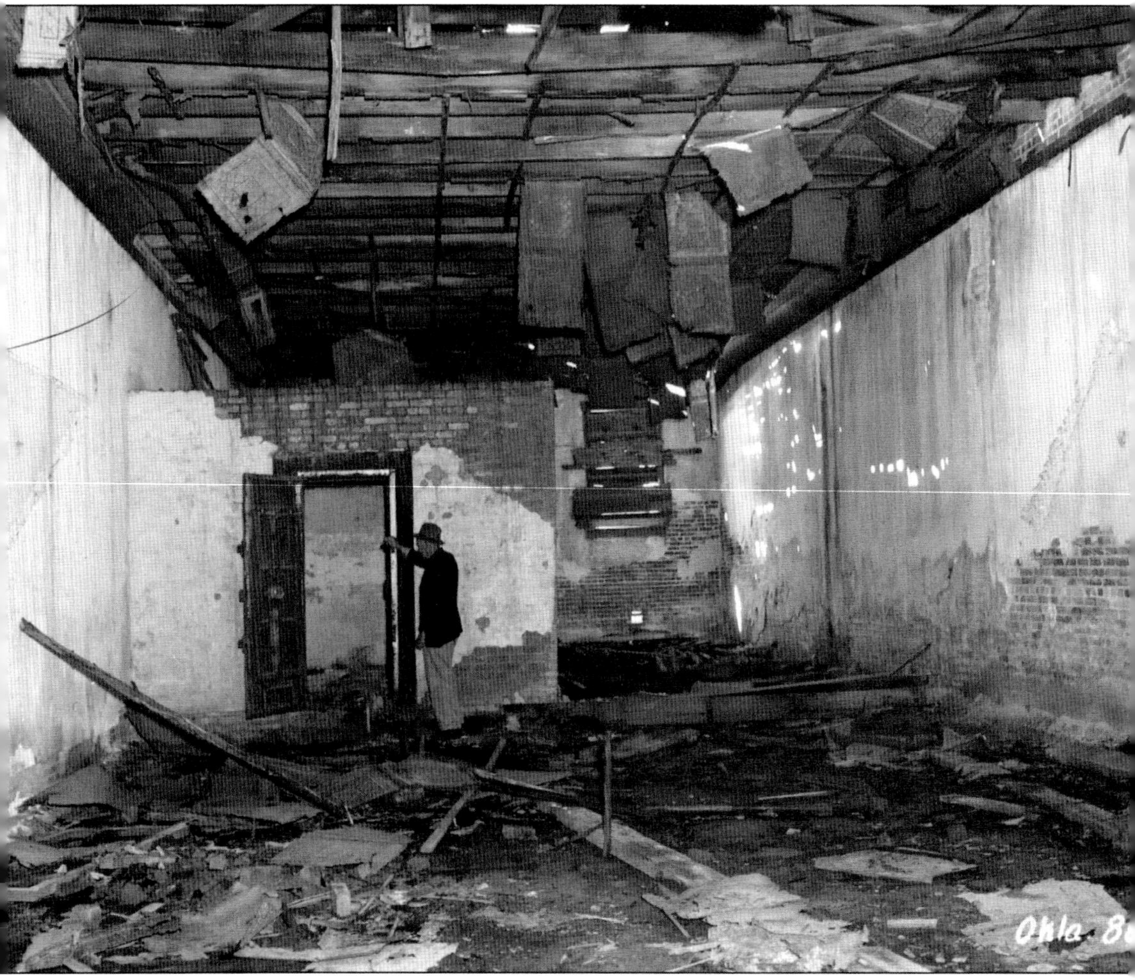

With the oncoming of the Great Depression, the county, like everywhere else in the nation, experienced an unimaginable decline in industry and economy. The Depression saw the descent of McCurtain County towns such as Haworth, Garvin, Millerton, America, Bok Homma, and Eagletown. These towns all lost stores, hotels, lumber mills, schools, cotton gins, and even banks. For some, it was the end of the towns as they knew them. This is a picture of the interior of the Citizens State Bank in Haworth in 1939 fourteen years after its close. (Kenneth Sivard Jr. collection.)

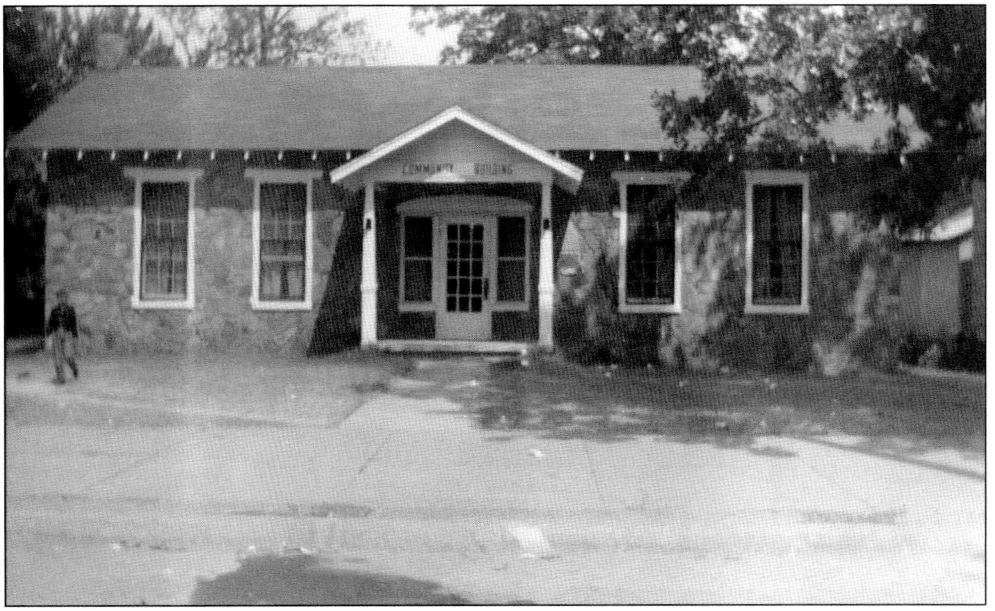

McCurtain County benefited greatly from Franklin Roosevelt's "alphabet soup programs." The WPA constructed many buildings in the county, including this one, the Broken Bow Community Center, on Main Street. The building still stands today in nearly original condition. (Kenneth Sivard Jr. collection.)

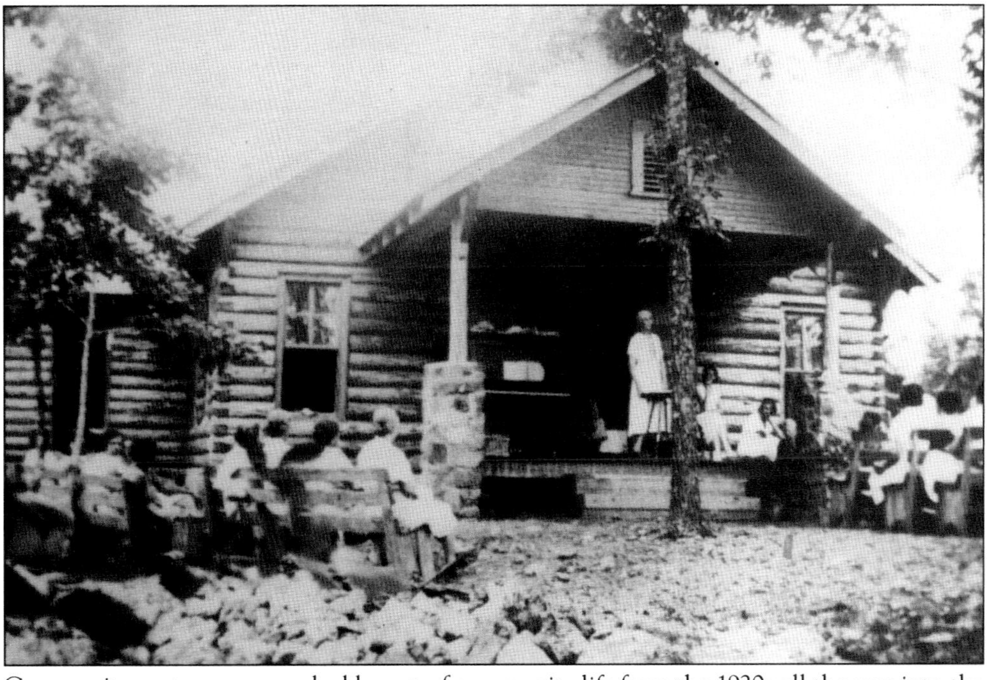

Community centers were a valuable part of community life from the 1920s all the way into the 1950s. Small communities that did not have community centers often used schools as meeting places. In these centers, a wide range of activities took place, from Bible studies to cakewalks. Shown is a Home and Community Education meeting taking place at the Sweet Home Community Center in the 1930s. (Kenneth Sivard Jr. collection.)

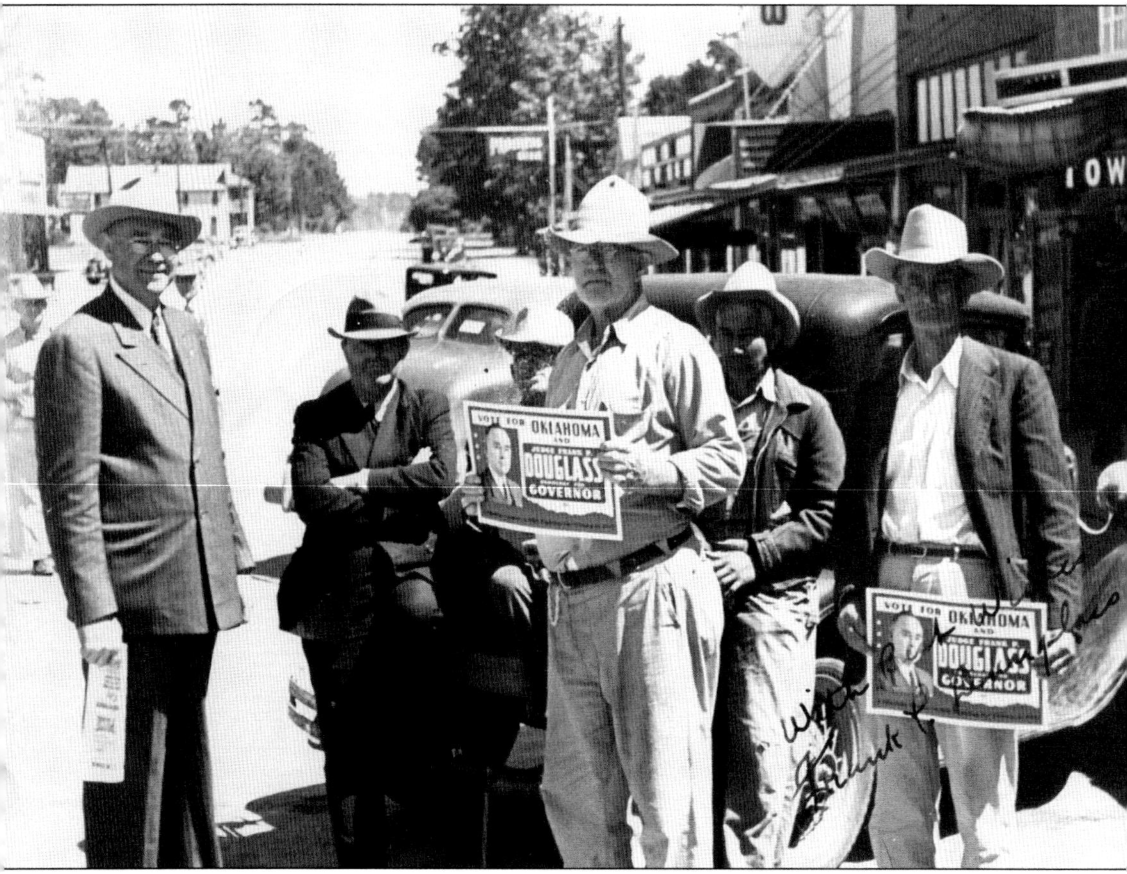

During the Great Depression, downtown areas were also a center point of community activity. In towns such as Valliant, Idabel, and Broken Bow, people would come usually on Saturday to do their shopping and to catch up on community happenings in a world with no telephones. It was not unusual to see more than 500 people on Central and Main Streets in Idabel on any given Saturday alone. Here, a group of men visit on Main Street in Broken Bow with Frank Douglas during his campaign for governor of Oklahoma in the late 1930s. (Kenneth Sivard Jr. collection.)

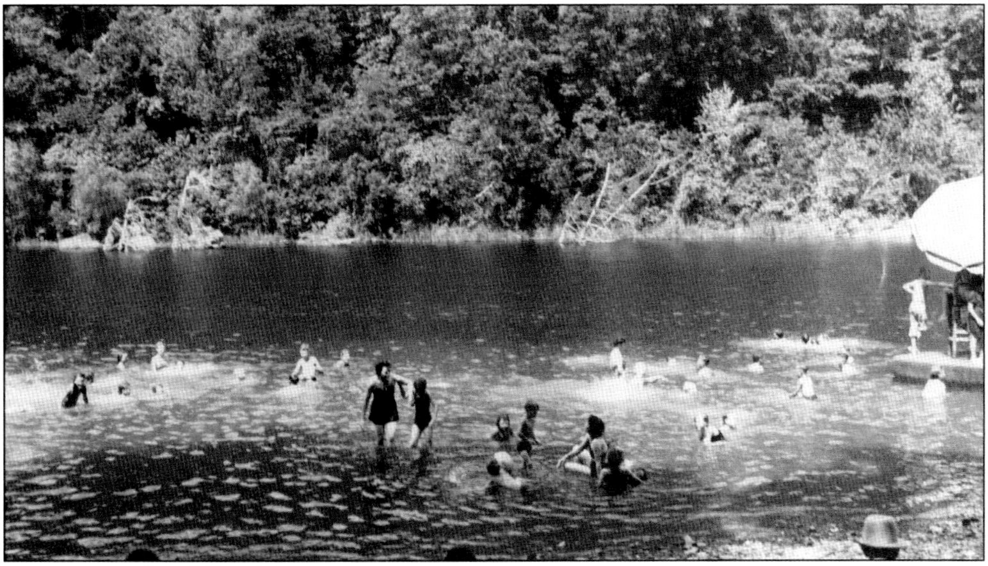

The Rivers of McCurtain County have always been popular gathering places for the people of McCurtain County. Ever since the 1930s, Beavers Bend on the Mountain Fork River has been a favorite recreation spot for locals and tourists alike, such as these swimmers in the 1940s. (Kenneth Sivard Jr. collection.)

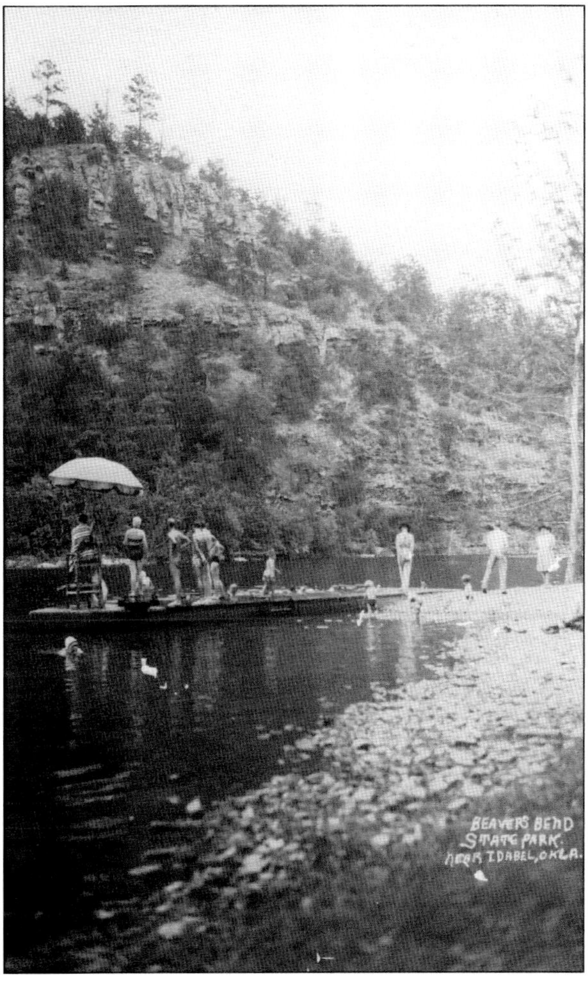

Beavers Bend swimming hole is pictured in the late 1930s. Note the lifeguard under the umbrella. (Kenneth Sivard Jr. collection.)

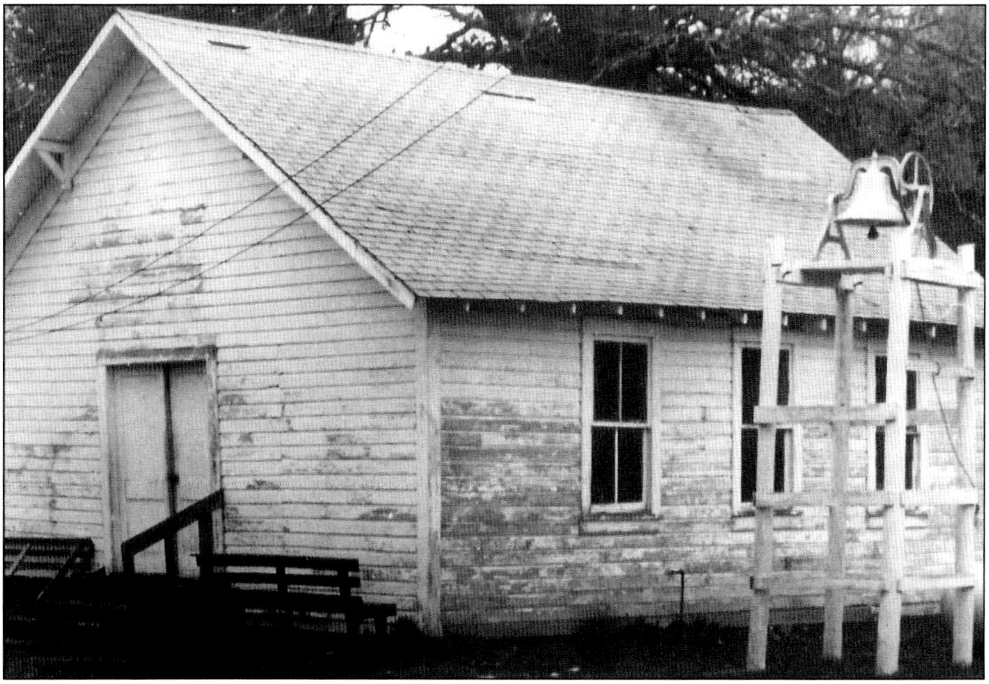

This is Mountain Fork Presbyterian Church near Eagletown as it appeared in the 1950s. Many of the county's small rural churches in the 1930s were small, one-room frame buildings. (Kenneth Sivard Jr. collection.)

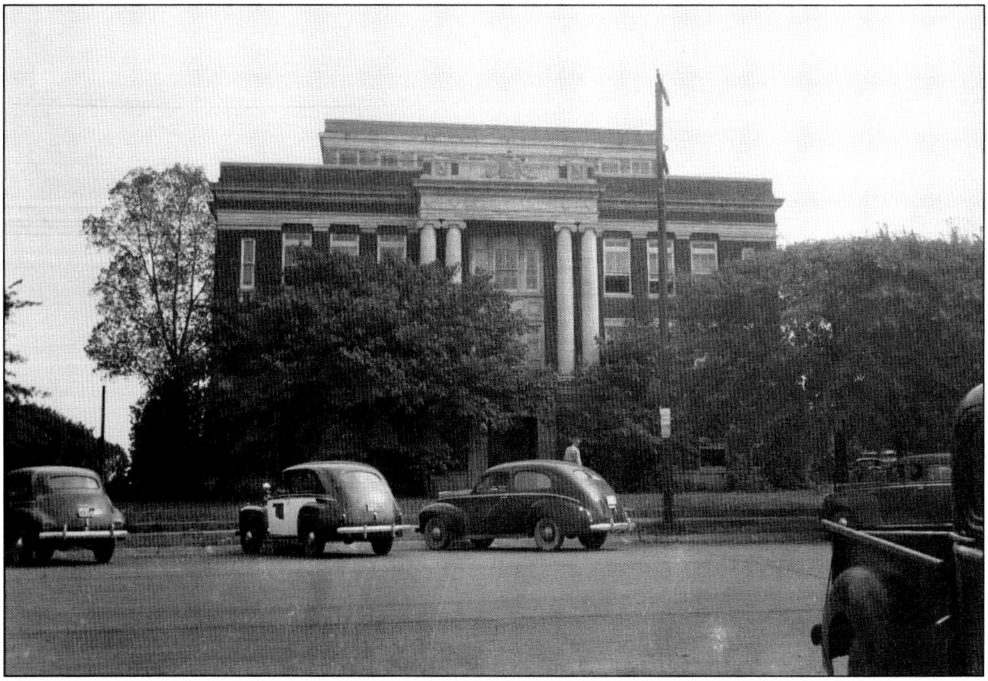

The Manhattan Construction Company of Muskogee, Oklahoma, built McCurtain County's third courthouse, shown here in 1945, at a cost of $118,936 in 1920. The building stood on North Central Street on the site of the current McCurtain County Jail. (Kenneth Sivard Jr. collection.)

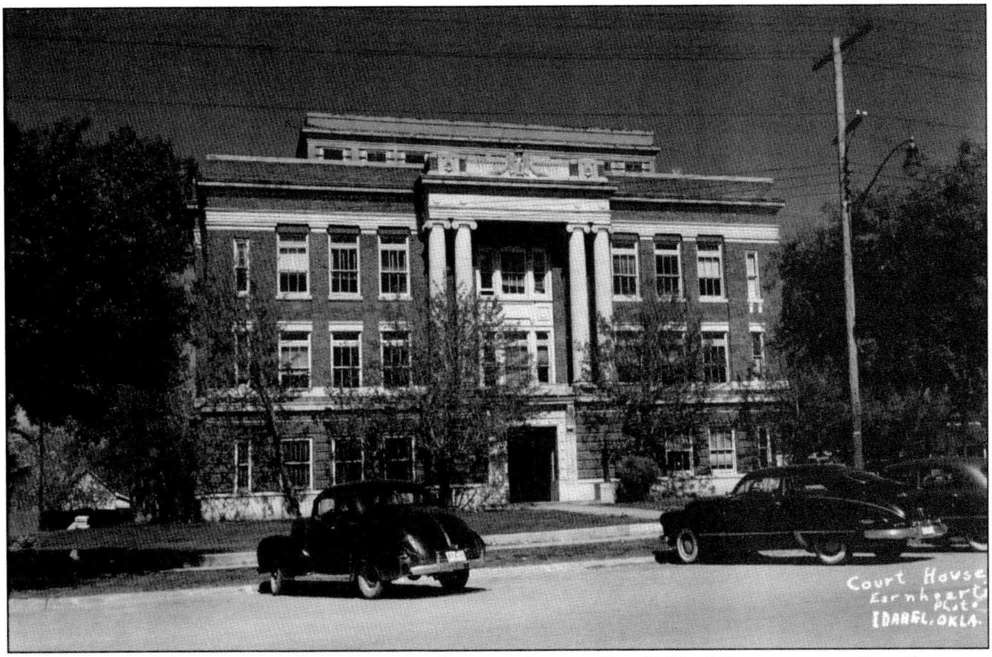

Pictured is another view of the 1920 courthouse taken in the 1950s. The county jail at the time sat atop the courthouse. (Kenneth Sivard Jr. collection.)

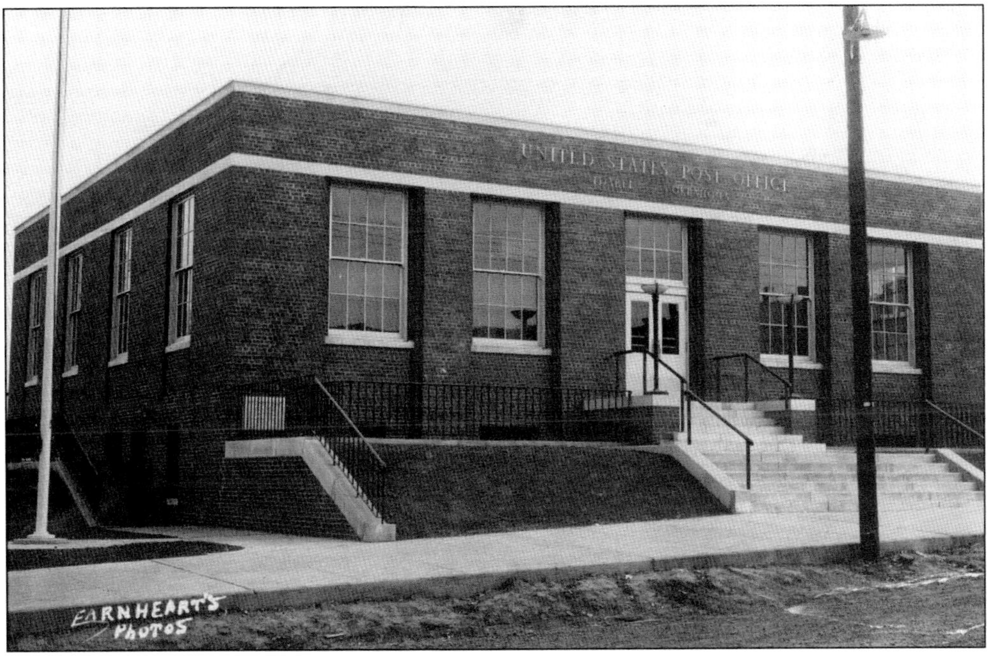

This beautiful post office was built in Idabel in 1939 on the southwest corner of the intersection of Avenue A and East Main Street. It was torn down in the 1970s to make room for a parking lot after the post office moved into a new building on South Central Street across the street from the county courthouse. (Kenneth Sivard Jr. collection.)

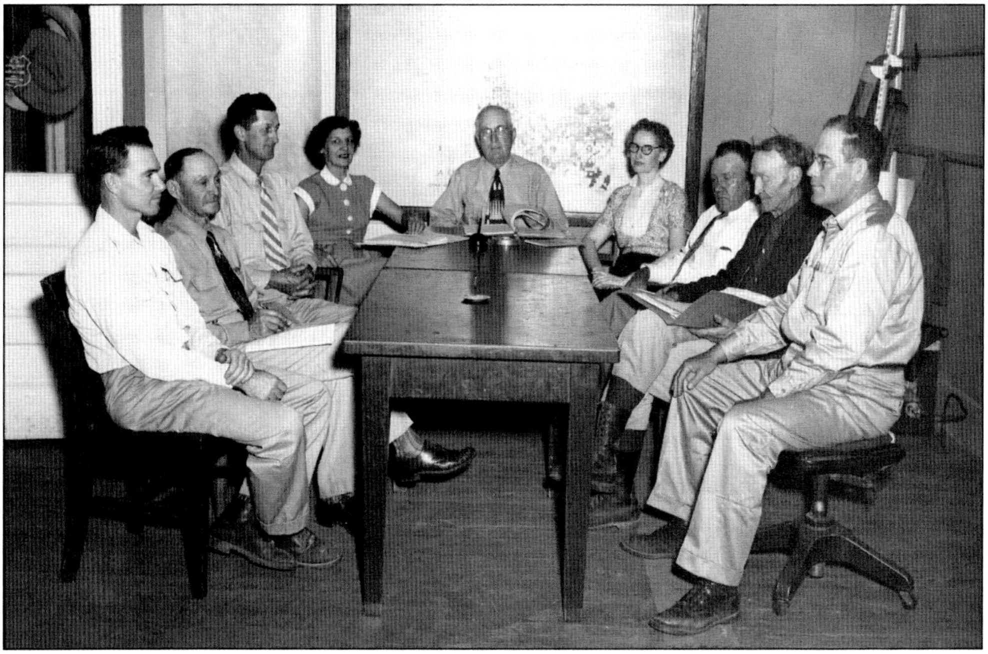

With the agricultural reform of the 1930s, the county became much more cautious of how it managed its farmland with meetings such as this, a Soil Conservation Service Agriculture Board meeting in the McCurtain County Courthouse in the 1940s. Pictured are, from left to right, G.F. Parsons, Luther DeBerry, J.A. Rone, Doris Thomas, C.F. Cornelius, Josephine Frazier, H.F. Marshal, H.C. Walker, and Earl Hayes. (Kenneth Sivard Jr. collection.)

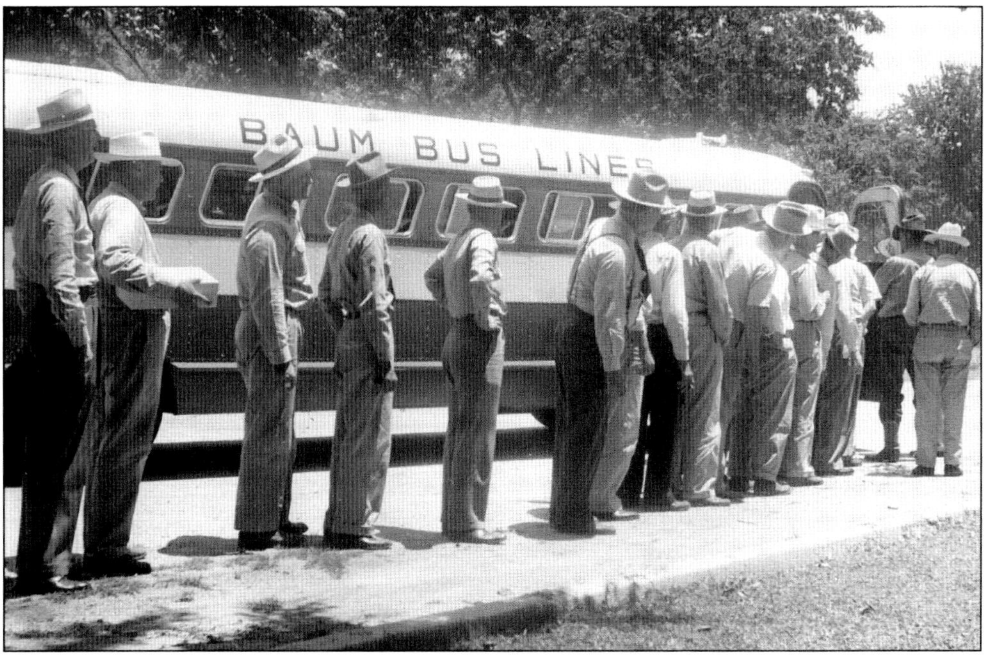

With the many bodies of water in McCurtain County, flood control is a very important issue. Shown is a group of county men boarding a bus headed for a flood-control camp in Mill Creek, Oklahoma, on May 16, 1949. (Kenneth Sivard Jr. collection.)

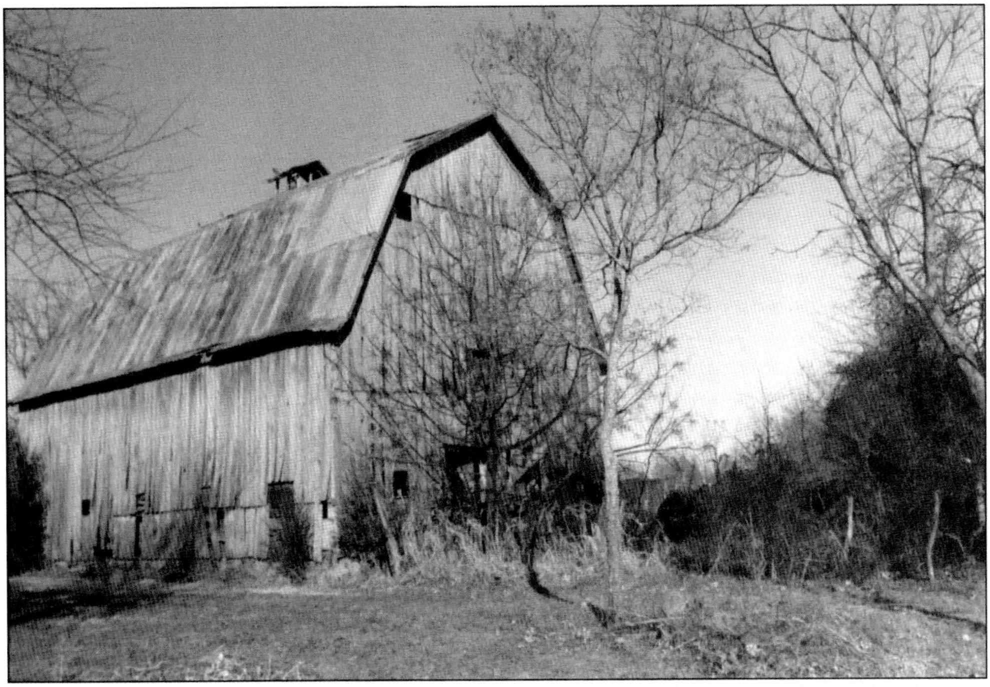

This large barn stood on Lynn Lane in Idabel for years and was the subject of many local artists work, and it came to represent the end of an era in the Idabel area when it was destroyed in the early 1980s. (Kenneth Sivard Jr. collection.)

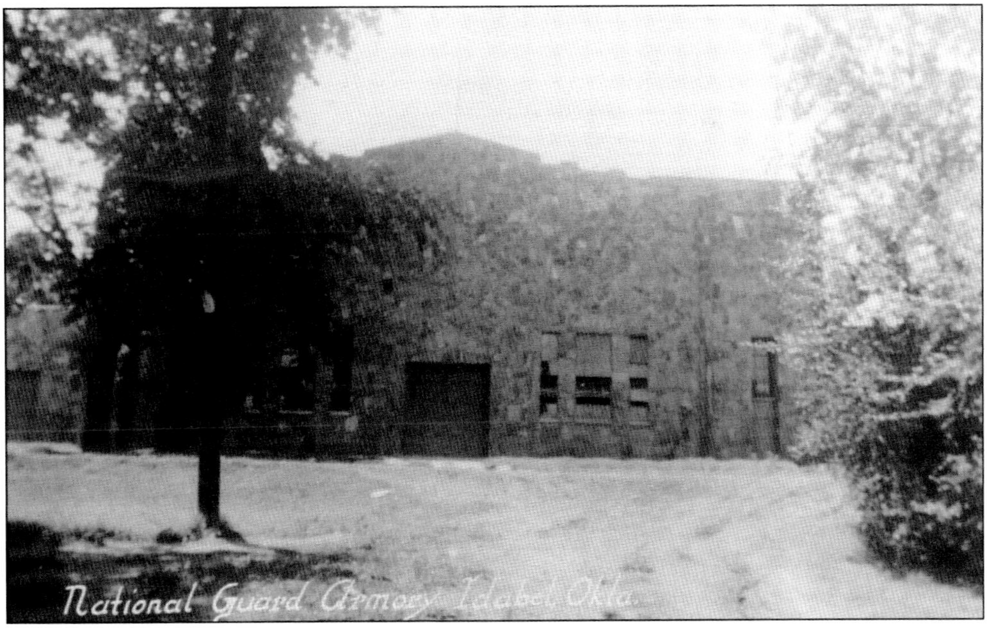

The Idabel Armory was constructed in 1939 on Washington Street by the WPA. It served as an armory for many years and as the McCurtain County Courthouse while the present courthouse was being built in 1964. In this picture, Washington Street is only a dirt trail in front of the armory building. Today, the building serves as the Idabel School System's bus barn. (Kenneth Sivard Jr. collection.)

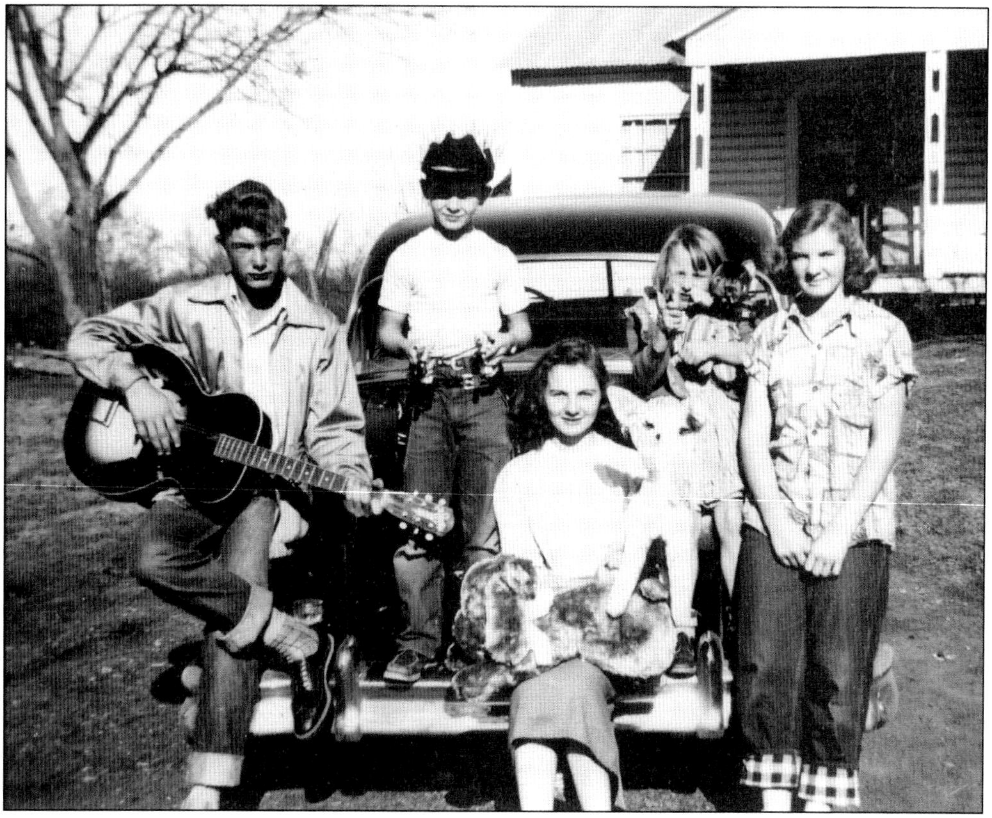

Clothes and toys typical of the early 1950s are shown in this picture of the Cochran children in front of their home in the Iron Stobb community. From left to right are Curtis, Johnny, Ann, Carol, and Nona Cochran. Johnny ran a store out of the Cochran home from 1989 to 1991. (Kenneth Sivard Jr. collection.)

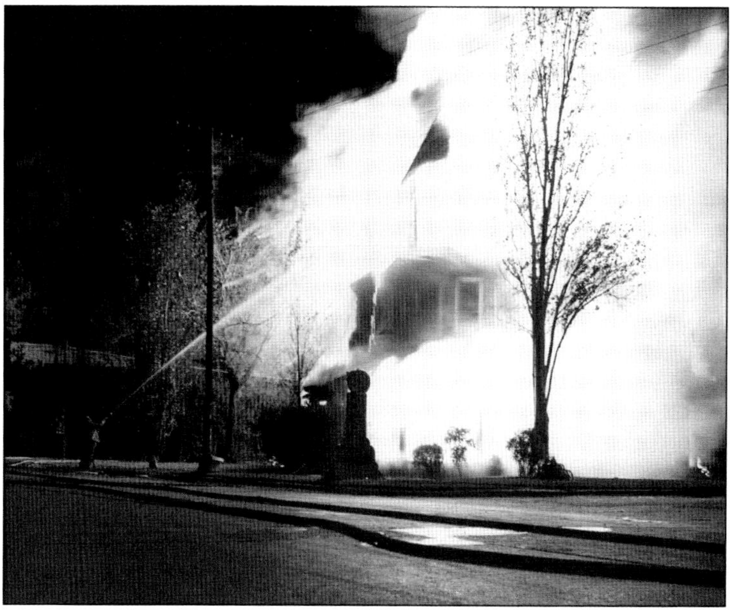

Over the years, many of McCurtain County's great historic properties have been lost to fire. Such was the case on Halloween night in 1959 when the Coffey Funeral Home, formerly McCurtain County's first hospital, Graydon Hospital, burned to the ground. The fire was so massive that it could be seen from miles away. (Kenneth Sivard Jr. collection.)

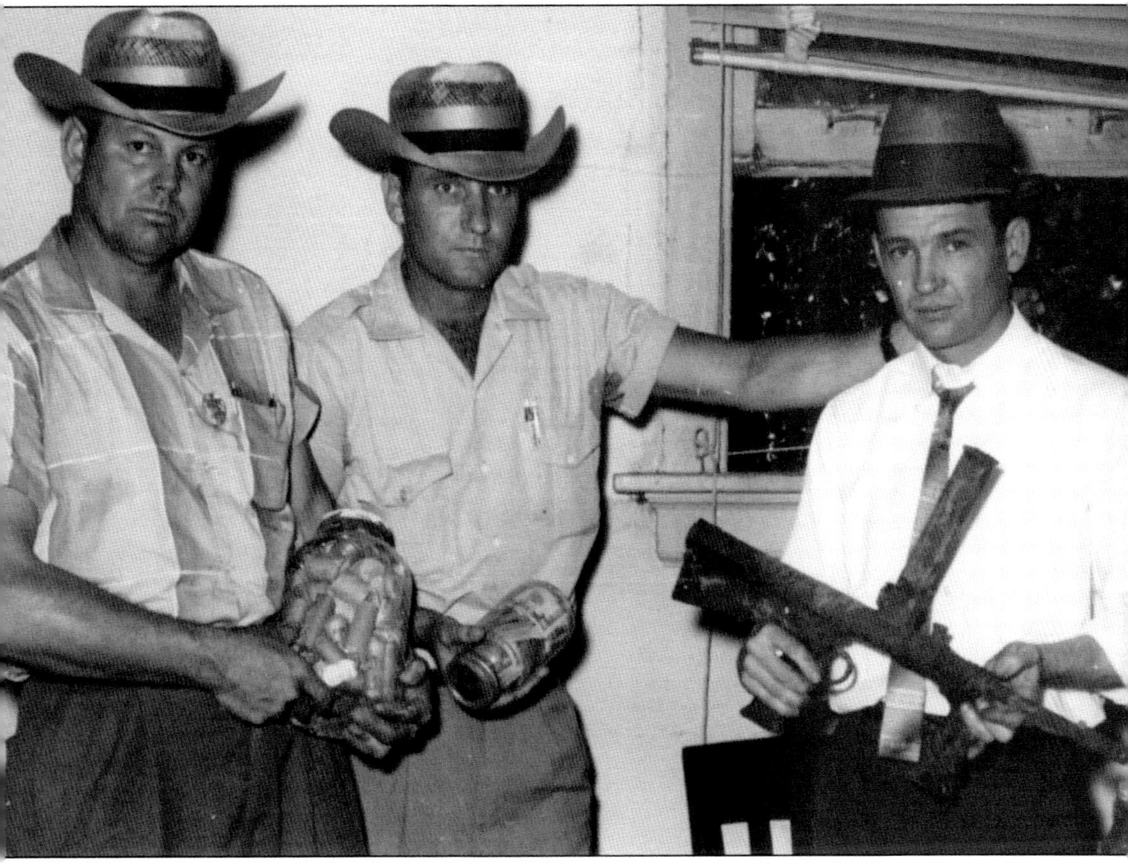

McCurtain County has had its share of bank robberies in the past, such as in Valliant, Haworth, Idabel, and Millerton. One such incident took place in March 1960 when three young men robbed a bank at Valliant. The money and a weapon retrieved from Little River, where the men dumped them after the robbery, are shown being held by McCurtain County sheriff's deputies. (Kenneth Sivard Jr. collection.)

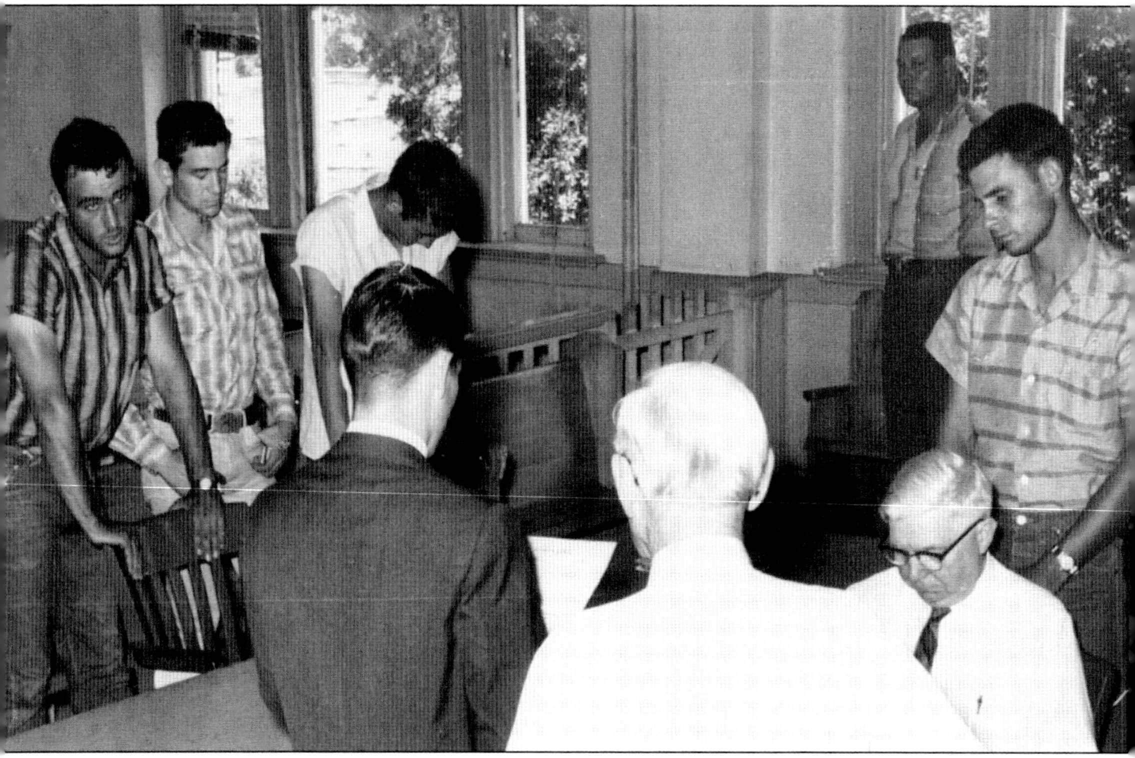

The three suspects in the Valliant bank robbery stand for their preliminary hearing before a judge in the county courthouse. (Kenneth Sivard Jr. collection.)

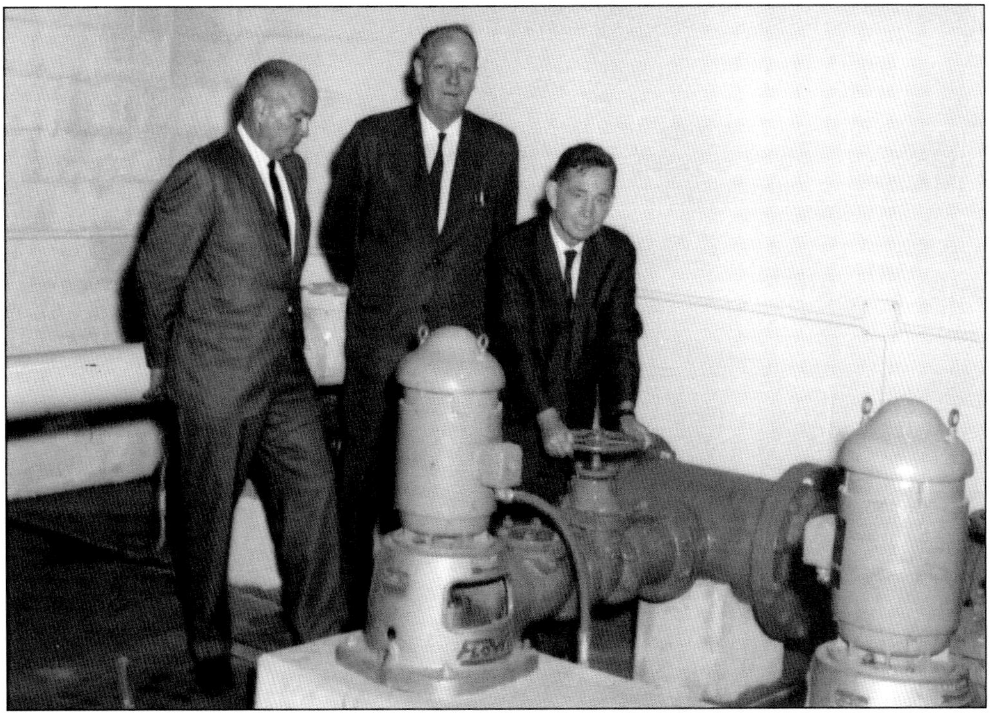

Congressman Carl Albert is seen turning on the water to Rural Water District No. 1 in 1967. The county's rural water systems were a great advance in the progress of the county. (Kenneth Sivard Jr. collection.)

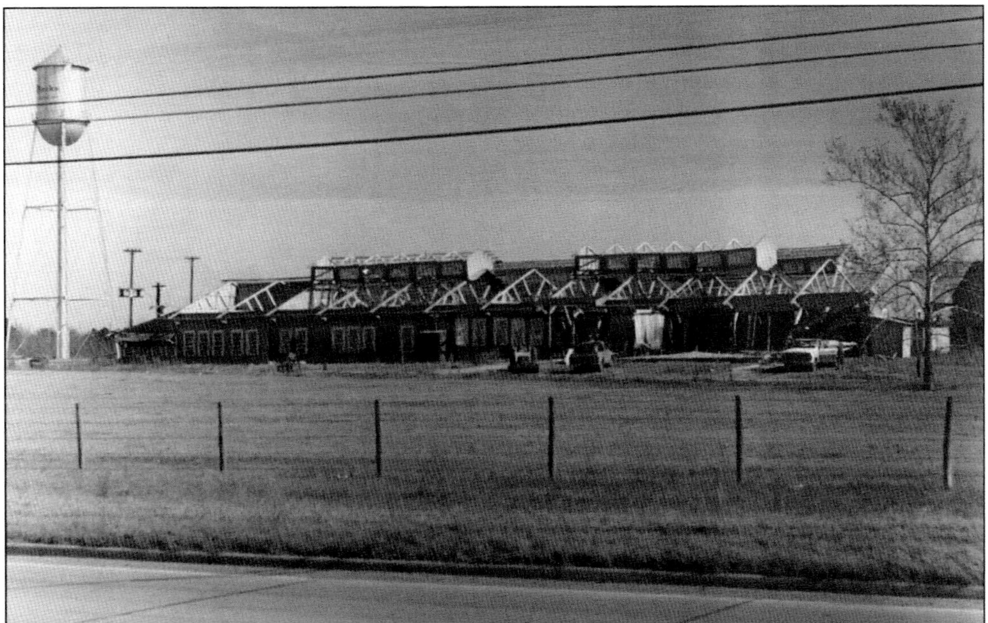

After Weyerhaeuser bought the Dierks properties within the county in 1969, it decided to discontinue the Dierks Lumber Mill. This signaled the end of an era for Broken Bow when demolition began in 1970. (Kenneth Sivard Jr. collection.)

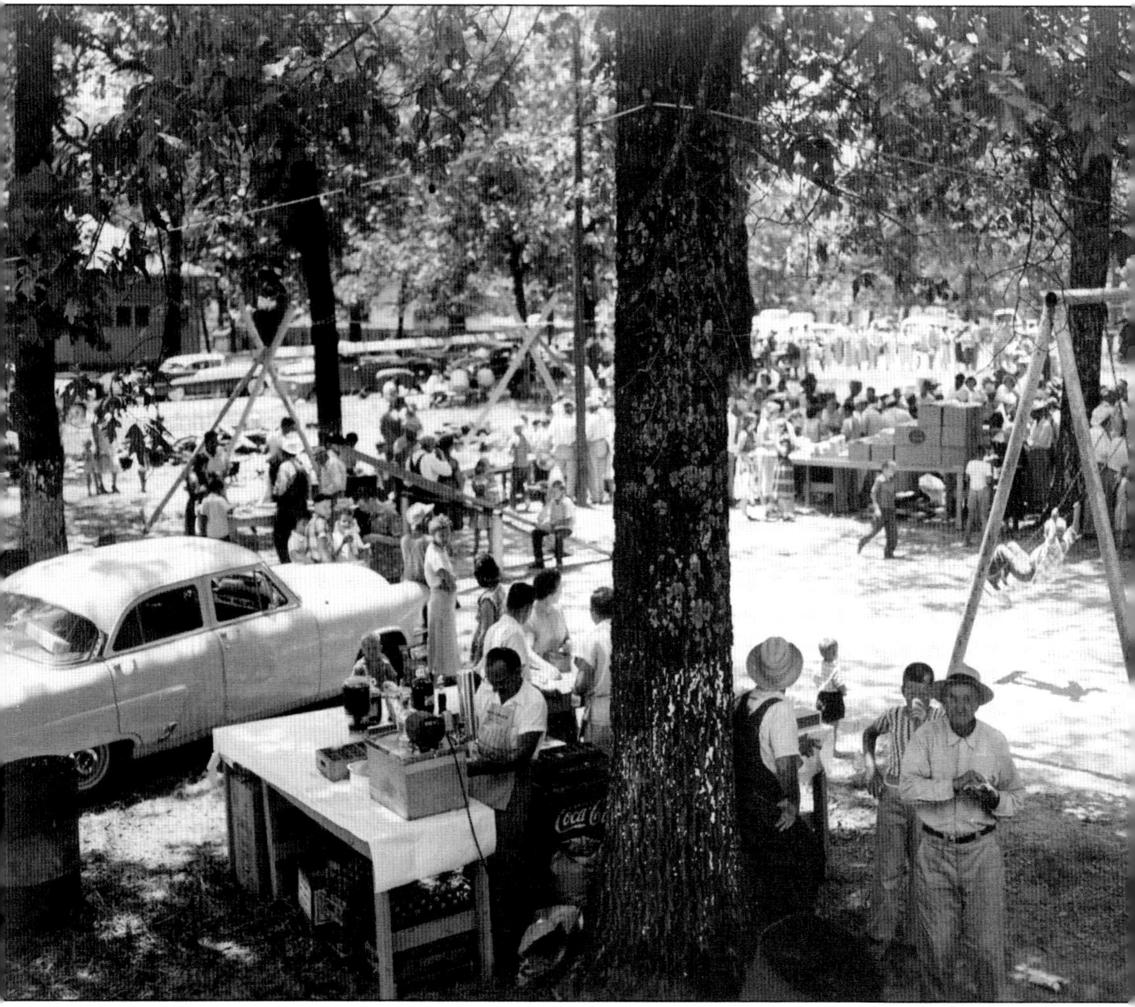

Picnics have been a popular social function in McCurtain County in the past, such as the church picnic shown here at Beavers Bend in 1959. (Kenneth Sivard Jr. collection.)

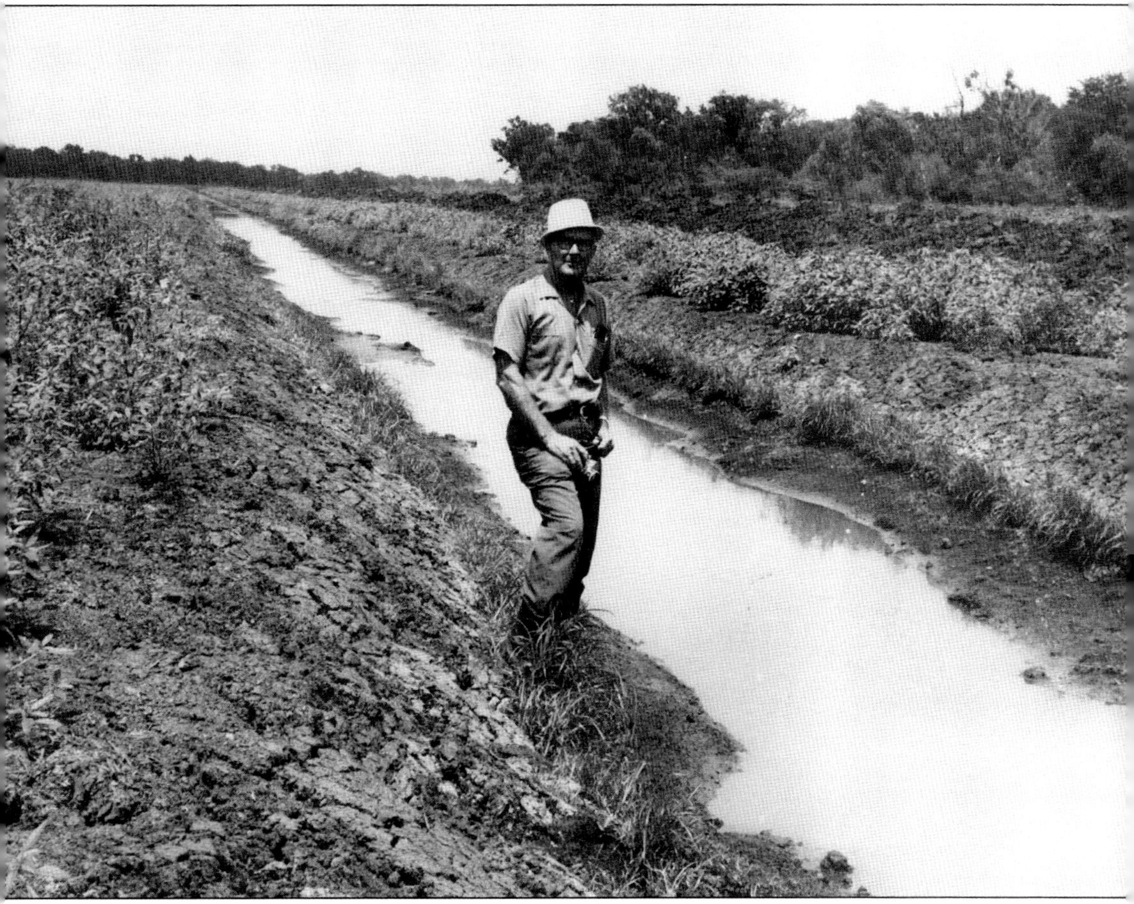

The Soil Conservation District built a drainage line in 1970 in the Pecan Grove community. Drainage lines allowed proper drainage for agricultural fields, allowing farmers to utilize more of their lands while also helping to control flooding. Seen here is Dean Foster of the Forest Hill community. Foster was a World War II veteran and a former president of the McCurtain County Historical Society. (Kenneth Sivard Jr. collection.)

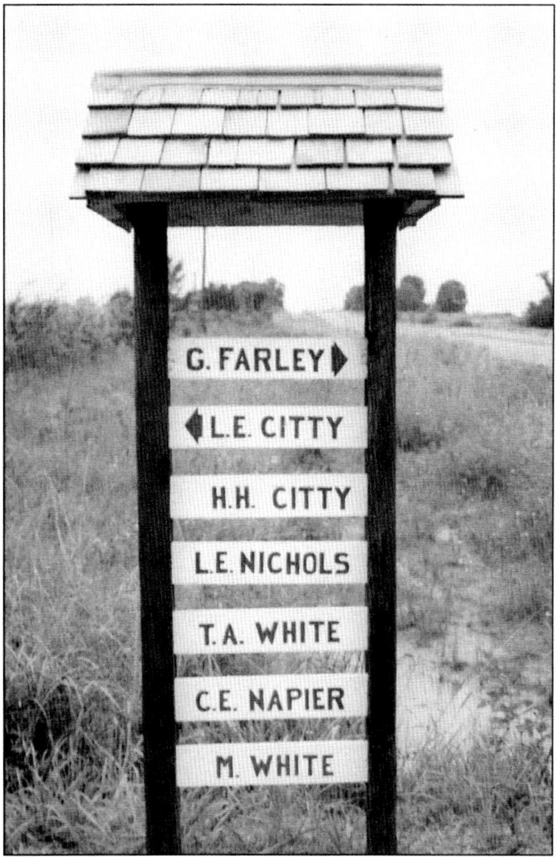

This sign, which gave directions to area homes, stood on Oklahoma State Highway 3 near Redland in the 1970s and shows the community atmosphere that still exists in McCurtain County. (Kenneth Sivard Jr. collection.)

In a stark contrast to the sign at Redland, this sign erected by the Idabel Chamber of Commerce shows the rowdy side of county residents as it greeted visitors into the city for nearly 10 years. (Kenneth Sivard Jr. collection.)

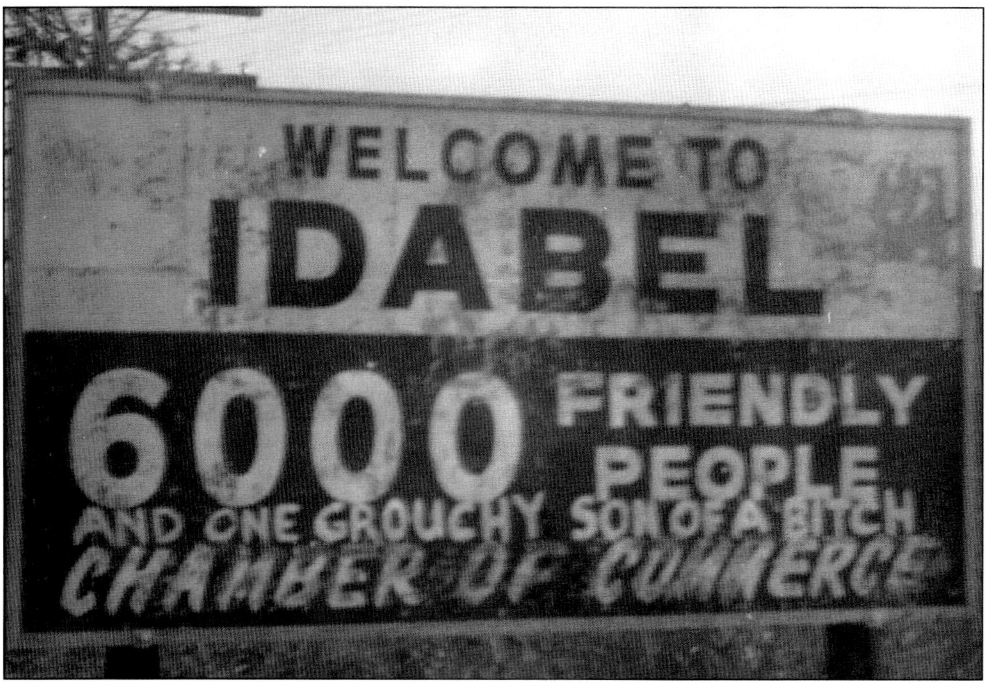

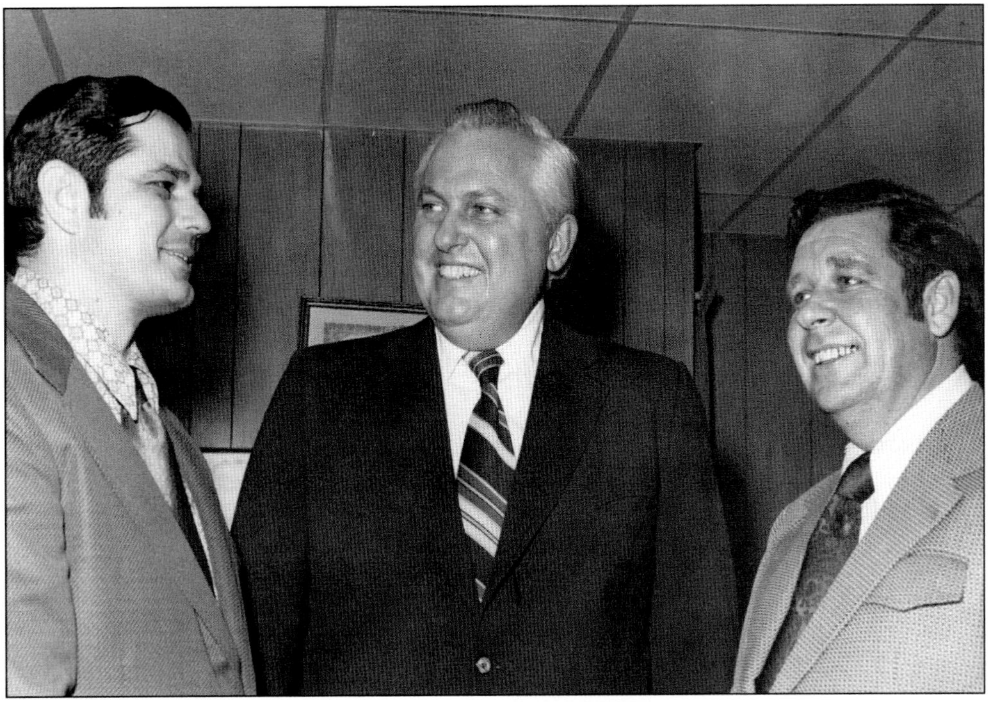

McCurtain County has long been a favorite visiting place for the state's government officials. Gov. "Alfalfa Bill" Murray lived here for a time, and Governor Williams even had a vacation cabin in the northern portion of the county during the 1920s. Another frequenting governor was David Hall, seen here in 1970 along with state senator Jim Lane and state representative Mike Murphy. (Kenneth Sivard Jr. collection.)

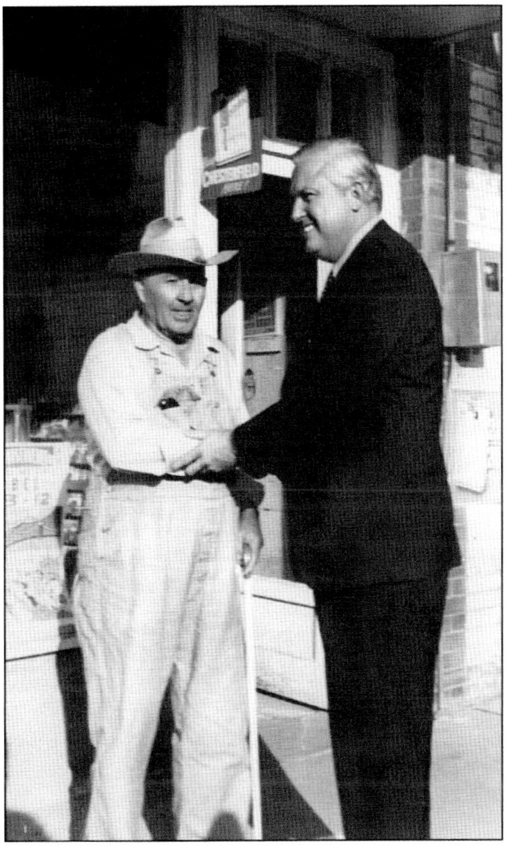

Gov. David Hall visits with a man in downtown Idabel in March 1970. (Kenneth Sivard Jr. collection.)

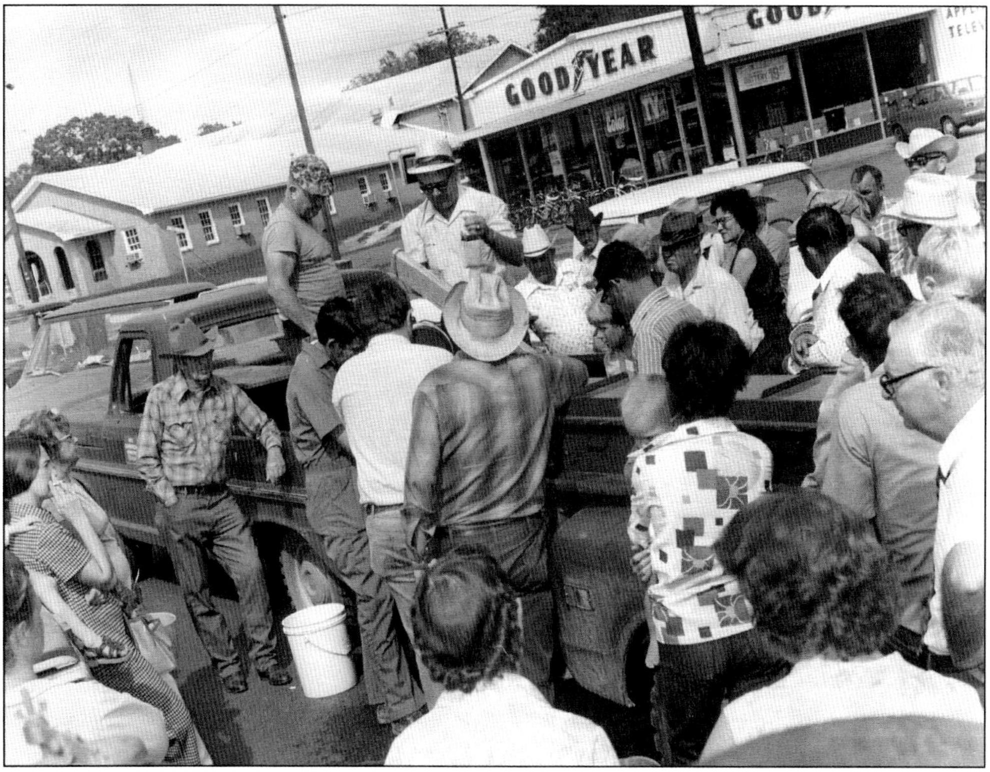

Fishing has long been a pastime for county residents. With the building of many government flood-control ponds in the county, as well as the construction of many private ponds, there was a need to stock fish in the new ponds. Shown is Dean Foster with the Soil Conservation Service in 1974 distributing bass fingerlings to locals in the Jumper Shopping Center in Idabel. (Kenneth Sivard Jr. collection.)

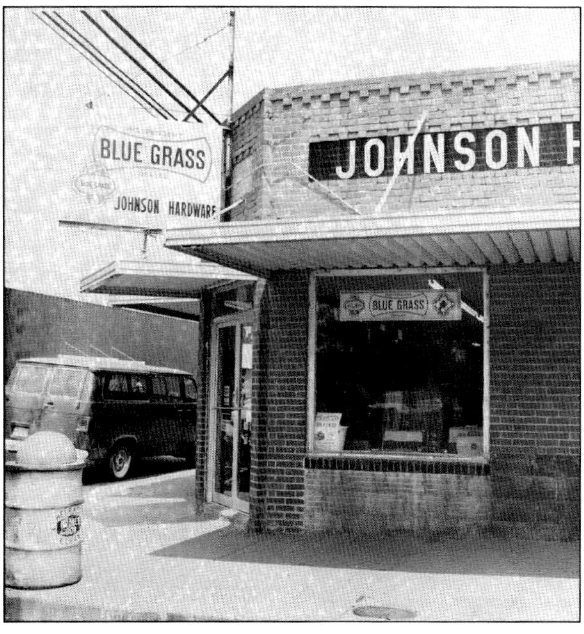

Hardware stores have always been a necessity in McCurtain County. Johnson Hardware, seen here in 1979, served the Broken Bow area for many years with its location on Main Street. (Kenneth Sivard Jr. collection.)

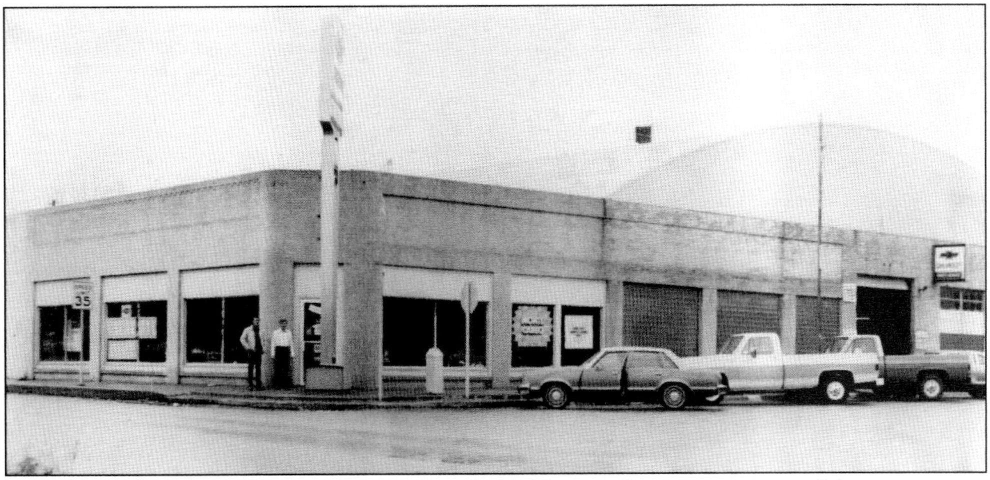

The Broken Bow Chevrolet dealership occupied a building on the western corner of the intersection of Main and Martin Luther King Streets and is shown here in the mid-1980s. Today, the Broken Bow Fire Department inhabits the building. (Kenneth Sivard Jr. collection.)

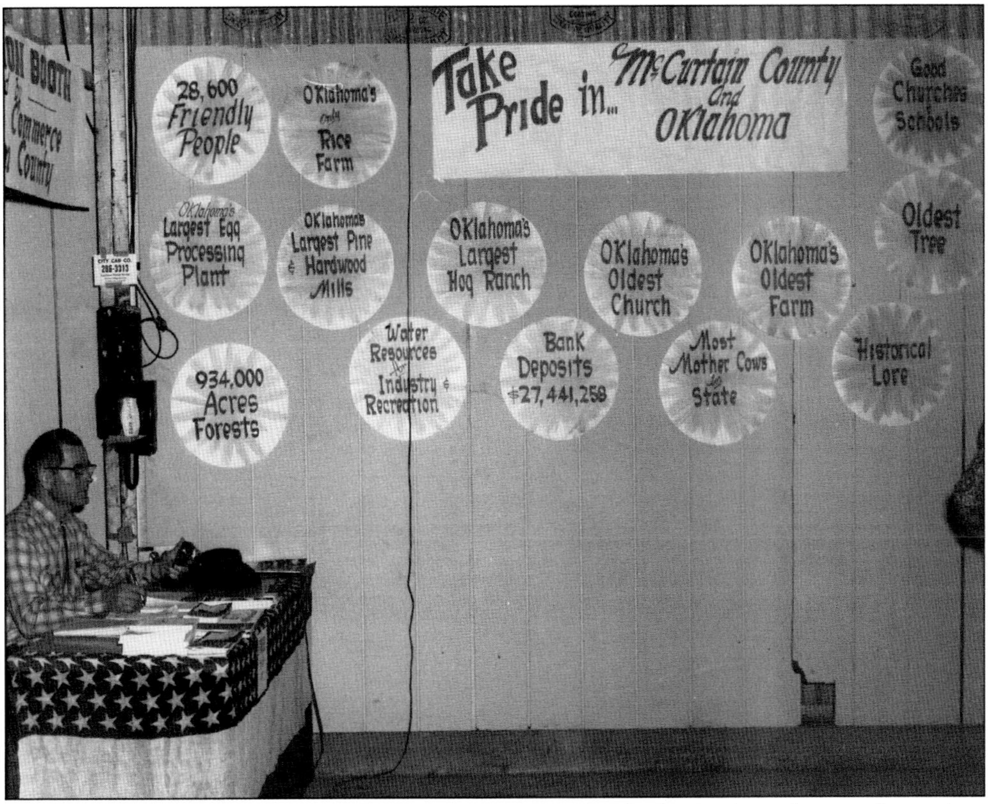

The people of McCurtain County have a great sense of pride about where they are from. At a McCurtain County Free Fair booth in 1989, information about the county is shown laid out by county chamber of commerce groups. (Kenneth Sivard Jr. collection.)

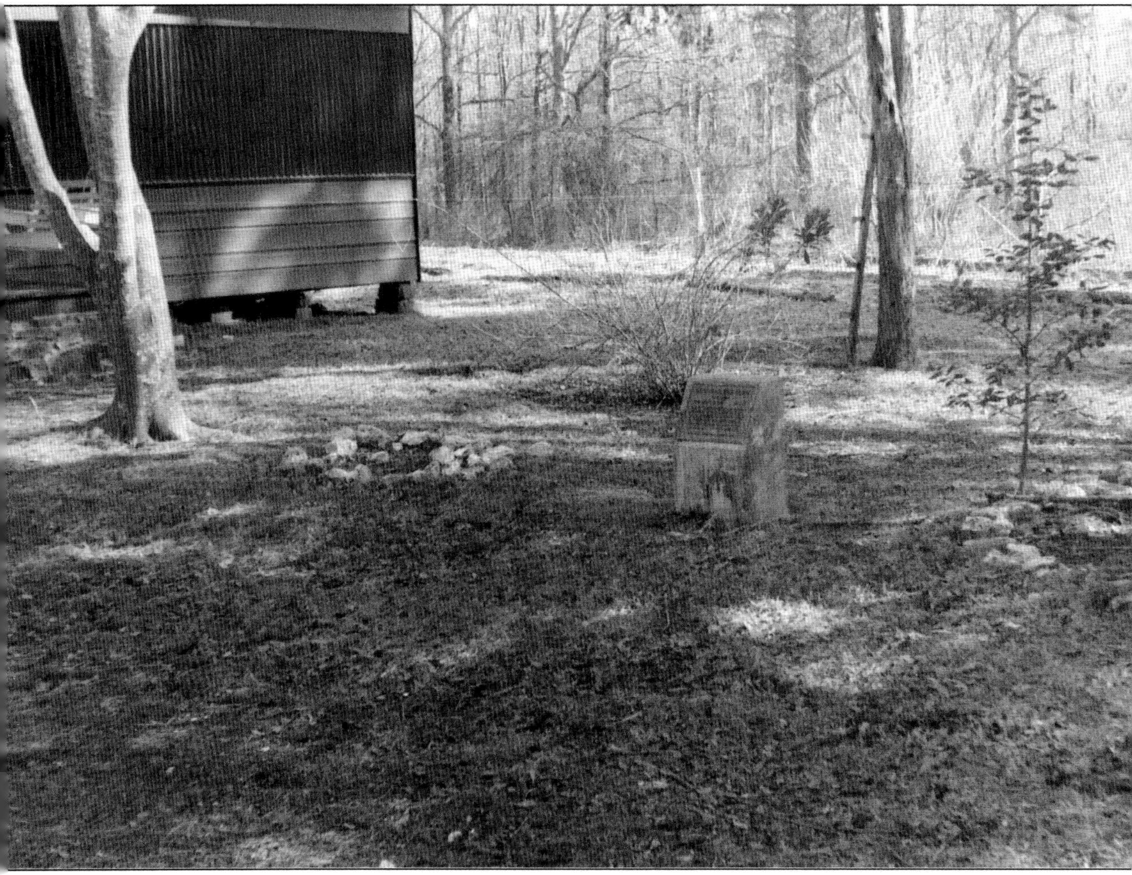

Chito Harjo was a Creek Indian leader who led a rebellion against the allotment policies of the US government in what is known as the Crazy Snake Rebellion. Chief Crazy Snake, as Harjo was called, was fatally injured in a confrontation with US forces. He was brought to the home of Daniel Bobb of Smithville, where he later died and is buried. This is the historical bronze marker representing the grave site of the Creek leader that was erected in 1959. (Kenneth Sivard Jr. collection.)

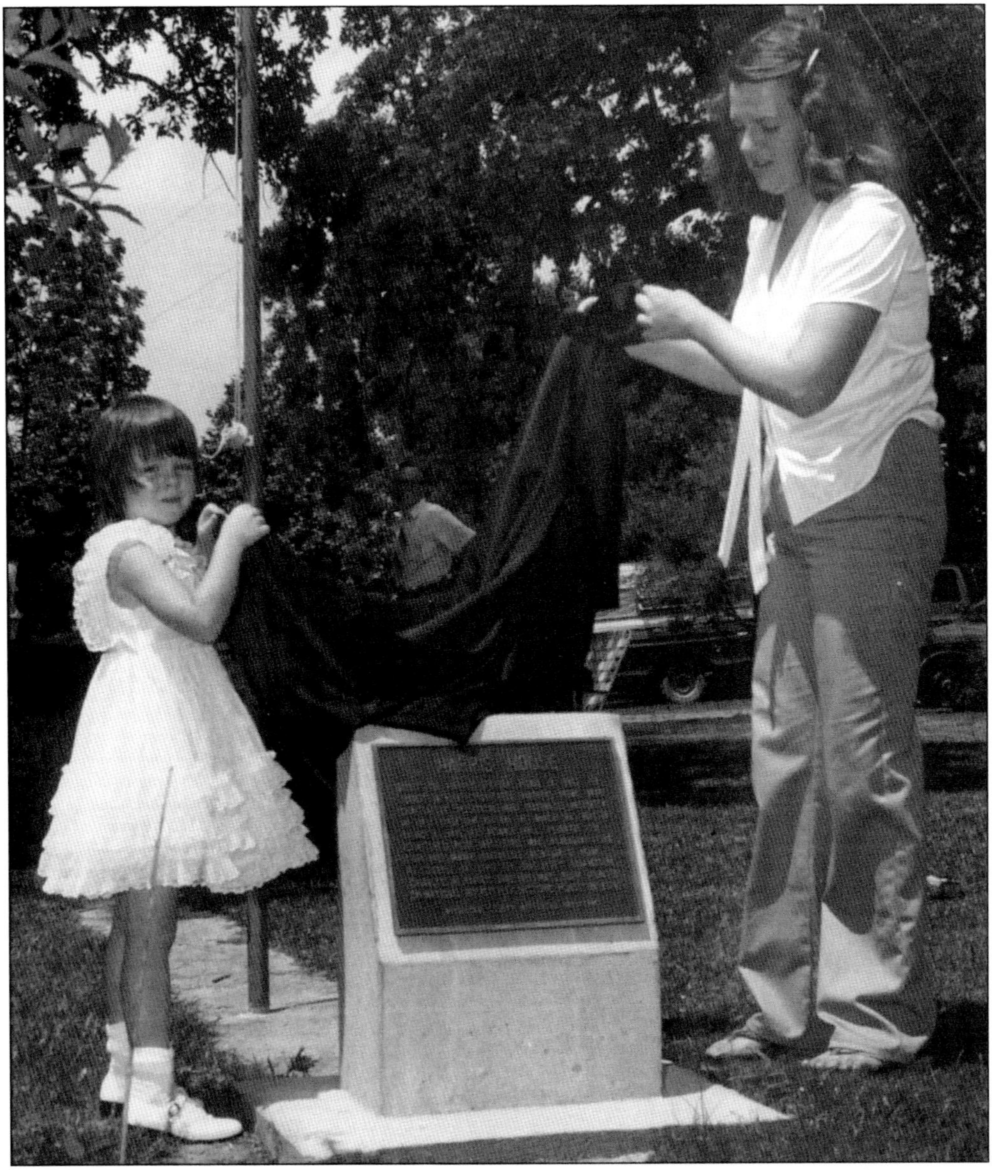

In the 1970s, an interest grew within McCurtain County about the county's diverse history. As a result, the McCurtain County Historical Society was formed. The society set out on a mission to preserve, protect, and educate others about the history of the county. As a result, many historical markers were erected in the area. Shown is the unveiling of the Harris House site marker in the Pleasant Hill community. Built in 1867, the Harris House is the oldest home standing in the county. (Kenneth Sivard Jr. collection.)

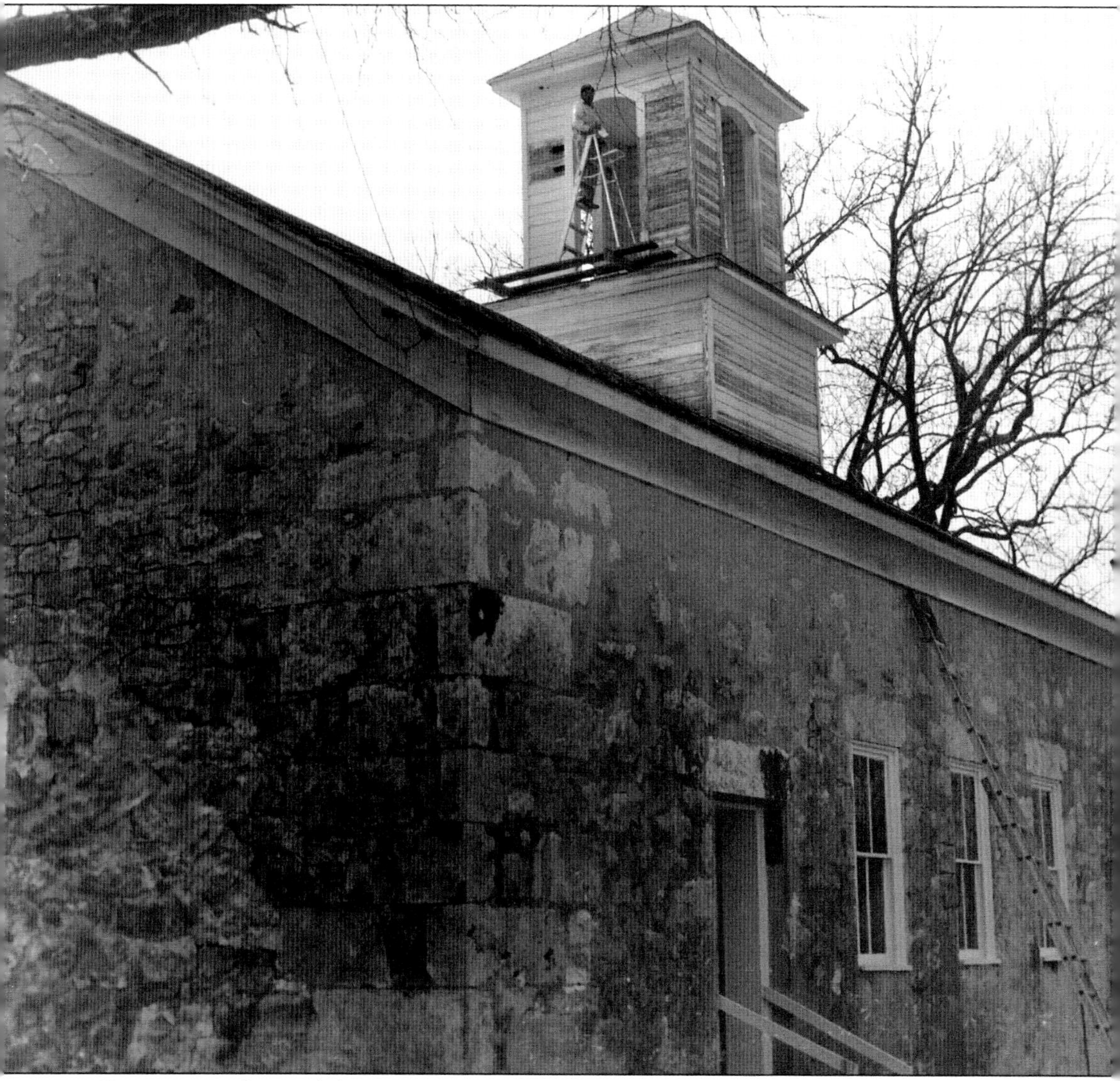

Repainting of one of the county's favorite historic landmarks in the 1980s, Wheelock Rock Church, built by Alferd Wright in 1846, is the oldest standing church in Oklahoma. Today, the church is cared for by an independent group that has gone great lengths to make sure that the church has been preserved for future generations.

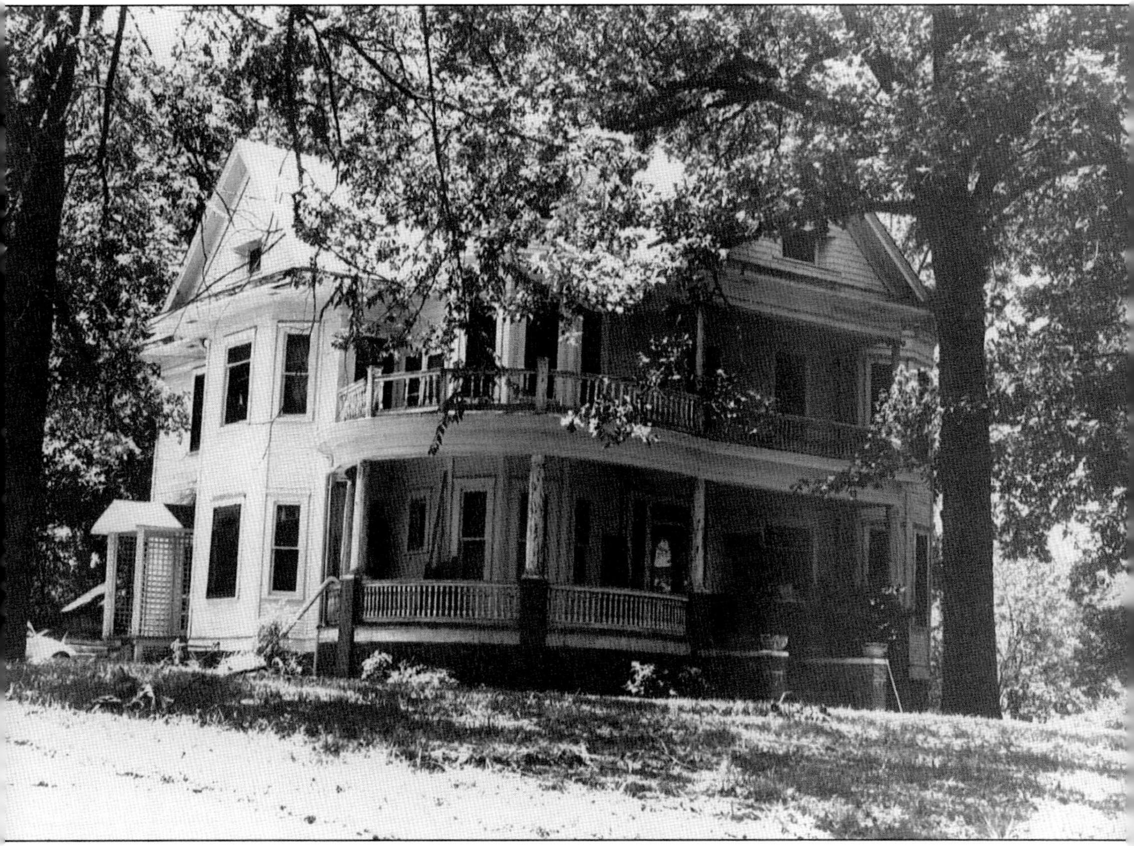

Here is a picture of the Barnes Mansion in Idabel as it appeared in the mid-1970s after years of vacancy. World-famous painter and Idabel native Harold Stevenson purchased the house from the Barnes estate and endured great expense restoring it. Stevenson sold the house to the McCurtain County Historical Society in 1987. The Barnes-Stevenson House now serves as the county historical society's headquarters and is operated as a museum. (Kenneth Sivard Jr. collection.)

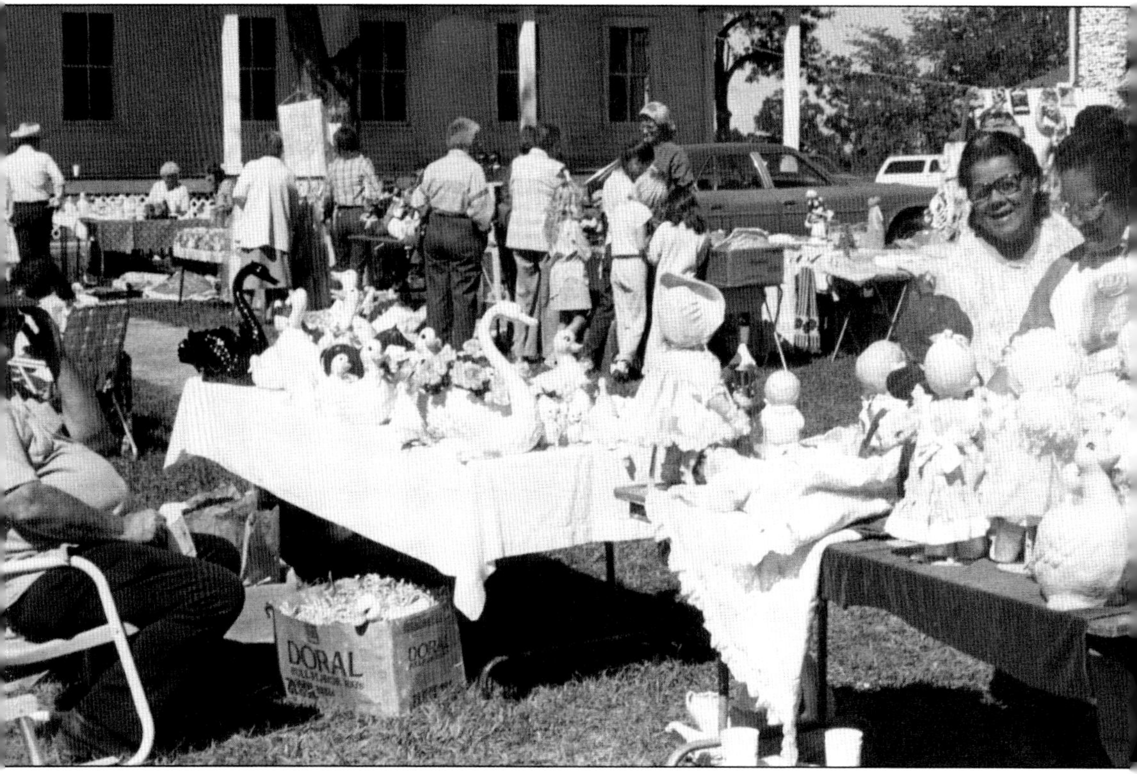

When the McCurtain County Historical Society was formed in 1972, a list was made by the society of the top sites of historical interest and importance. At the top of that list was the Wheelock Academy, which sat vacant for nearly 27 years. The society formed an annual arts and crafts fair, such as the one shown here in 1981 on the lawn of Pushmataha Hall, at the academy to draw attention to the site. (Kenneth Sivard Jr. collection.)

The rodeo has been a favorite pastime in McCurtain County since 1931. Tony Nelson of Idabel is shown here on a Coffey Rodeo Company bull at the Wright City Junior Rodeo in the early 1980s. (Kenneth Sivard Jr. collection.)

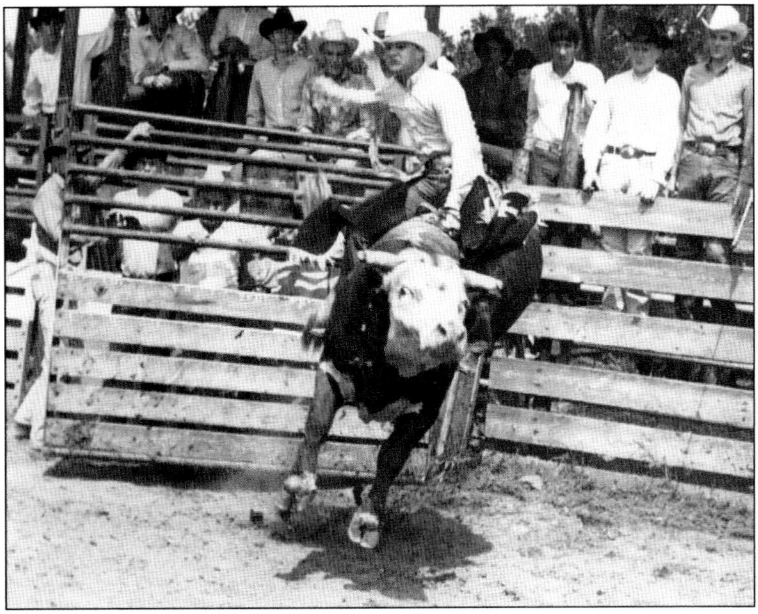

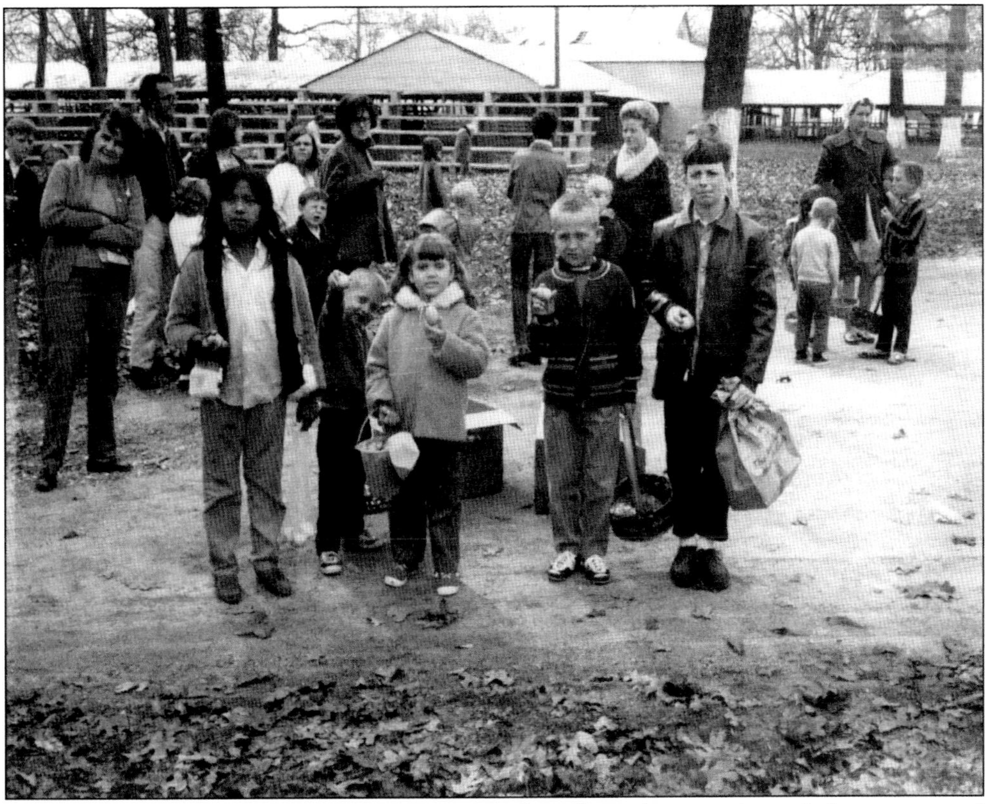

The sense of community in McCurtain County has always been evident. A favorite annual community event is the Jaycees Easter egg hunt shown here at the McCurtain County Fair Grounds in the late 1970s. (Kenneth Sivard Jr. collection.)

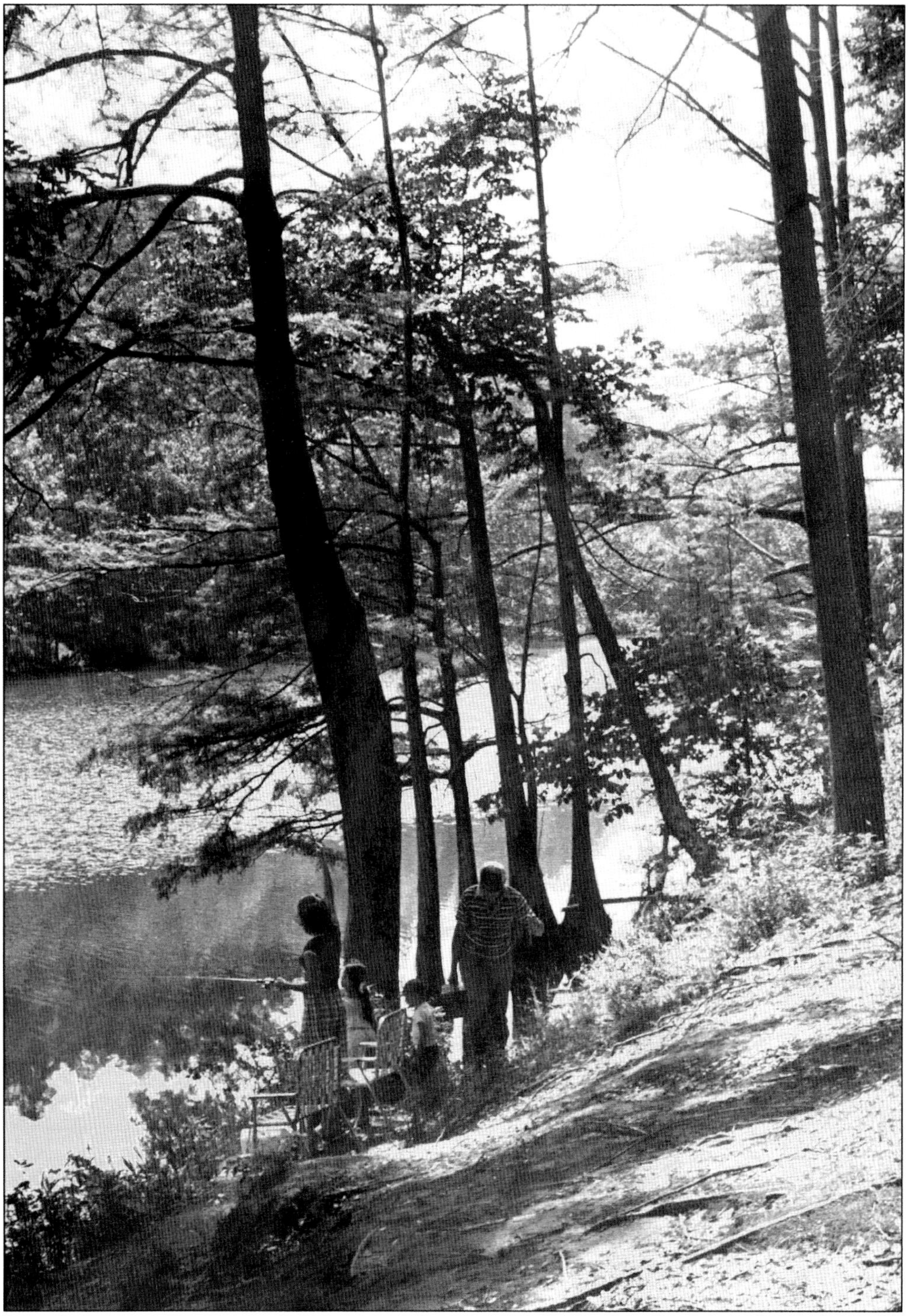

A family looks to be having fun fishing in the Mountain Fork River near Hochatown in 1982. The picturesque scenery of the McCurtain County wilderness offers endless adventure and family-friendly activities to all who visit. (Kenneth Sivard Jr. collection.)

Three

Education

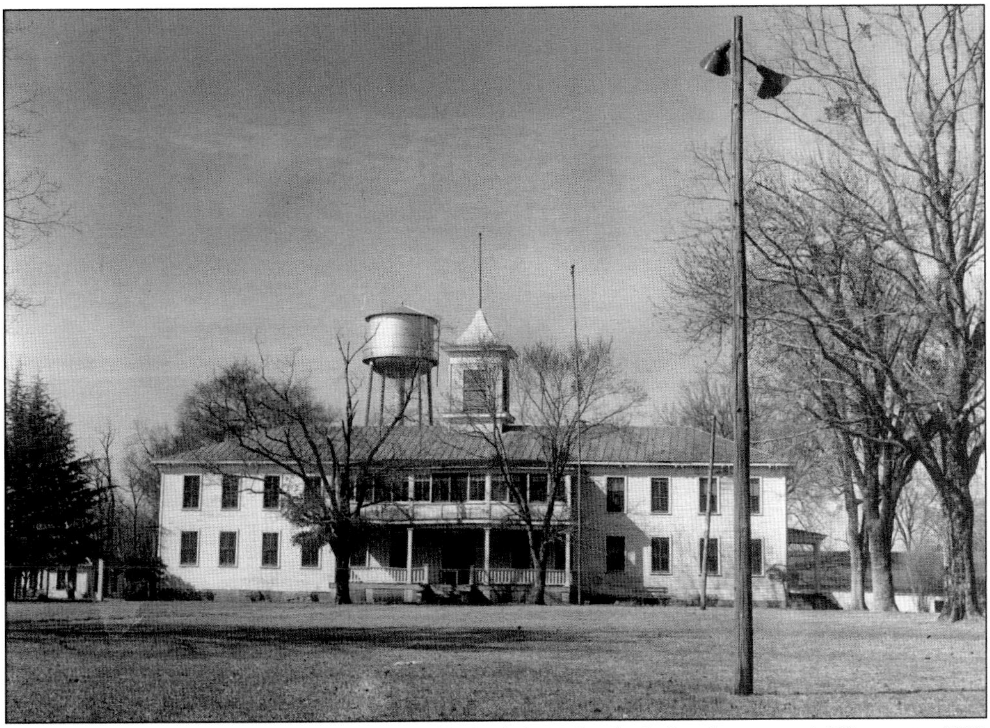

Presbyterian missionary Alferd Wright established the Wheelock Academy near Millerton in 1833 as a day school for Choctaw boys and girls. Later, it evolved into a boarding school for Choctaw girls. In 1884, the school was under the management of the US government and was moved a short distance from the original location, and girl's dormitory Pushmataha Hall and a small, one-room school building were added. By the time the school closed in 1955, it was self-sufficient with a dairy and chicken yard as well as an abundance of agricultural crops. Pushmataha Hall is seen here in 1965, ten years after the school's close. (Kenneth Sivard Jr. collection.)

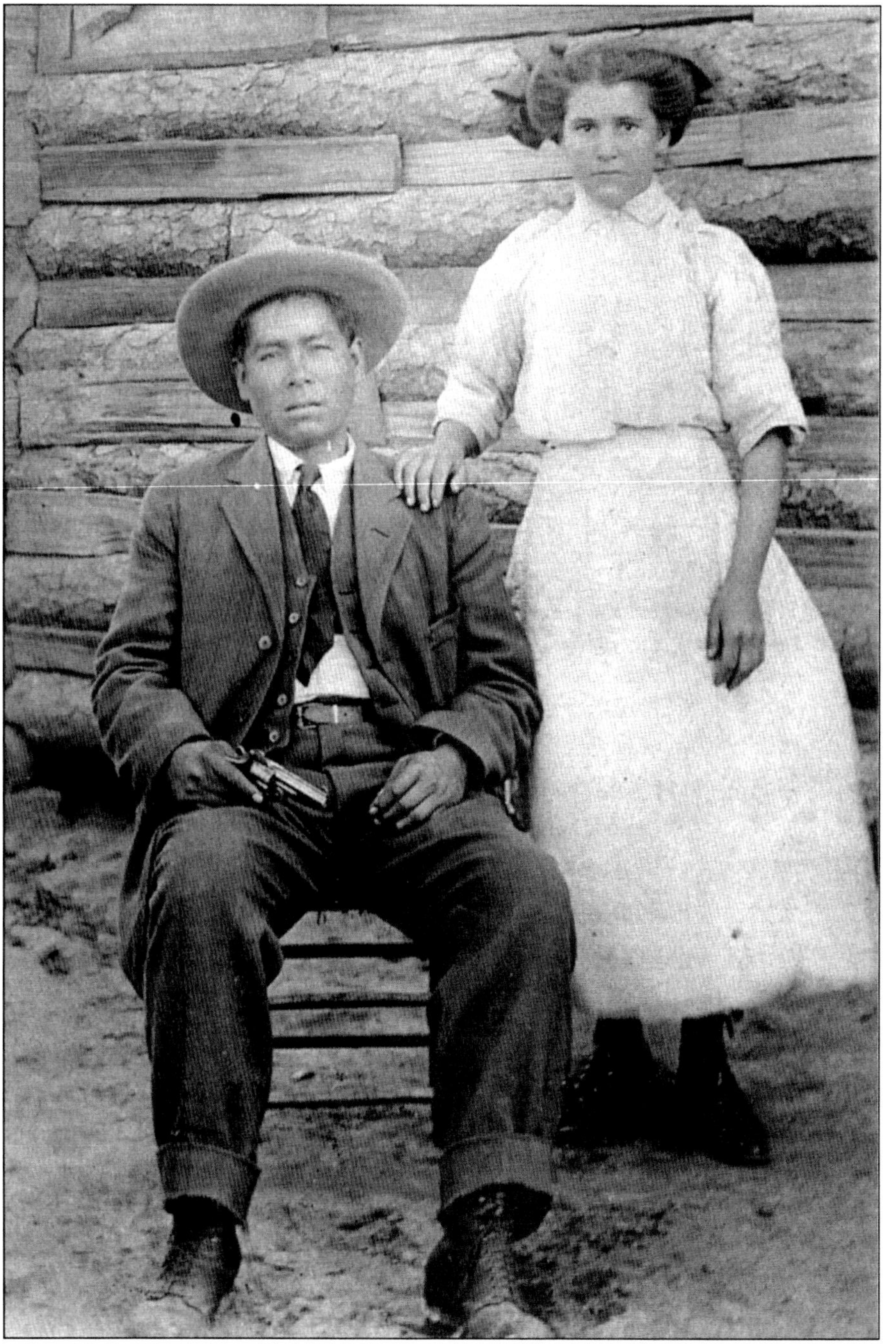

The first school system to take root in McCurtain County was the Choctaw "neighborhood schools," a school system managed by the Choctaw government. Many of these small schools were one-room log buildings, which housed about 10 to 20 students that were taught up to the eighth grade. After the coming of statehood, school districts were drawn up, and many still used the Choctaw schools until a new school building could be constructed. Shown are an unidentified man and woman posed at the Nanih Chito School and Church building in 1914. (Kenneth Sivard Jr. collection.)

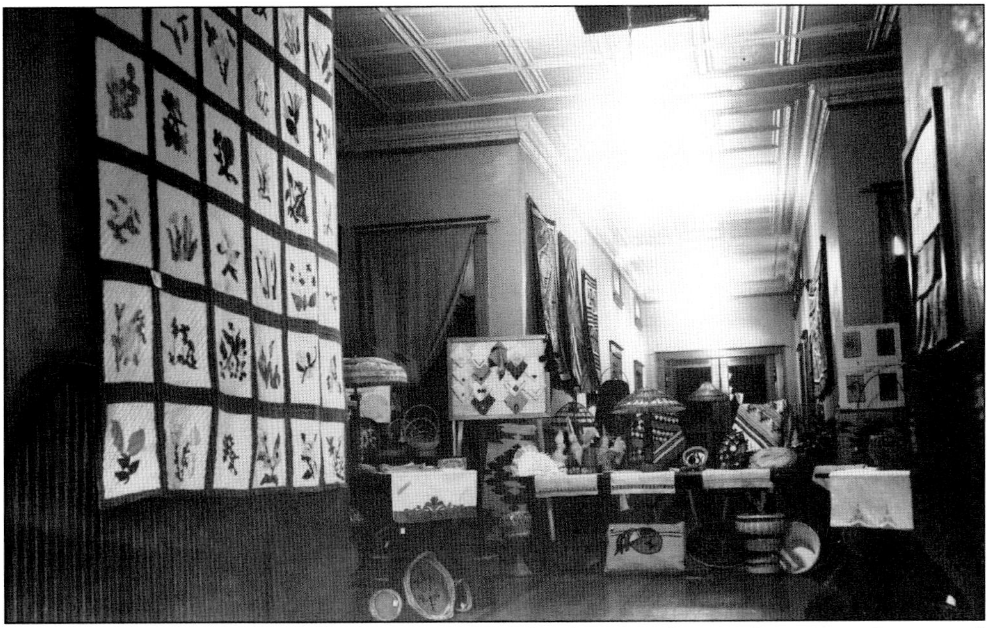

The Wheelock Academy did not just teach its pupils subjects such as arithmetic, reading, social studies, French, and Latin, it also taught its girls many vocations, such as this display of crafts made by the Wheelock girls in 1945. The image was taken in Wilson Hall, which housed the school's classrooms and gymnasium. The building is still standing today in moderate condition. (Kenneth Sivard Jr. collection.)

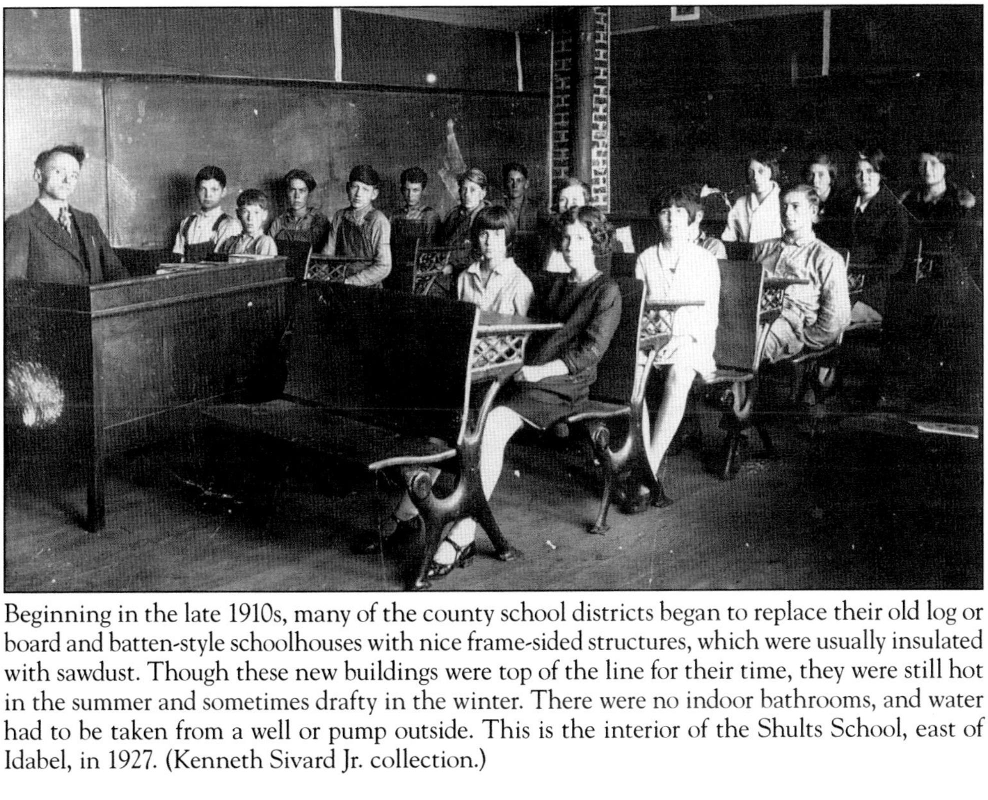

Beginning in the late 1910s, many of the county school districts began to replace their old log or board and batten-style schoolhouses with nice frame-sided structures, which were usually insulated with sawdust. Though these new buildings were top of the line for their time, they were still hot in the summer and sometimes drafty in the winter. There were no indoor bathrooms, and water had to be taken from a well or pump outside. This is the interior of the Shults School, east of Idabel, in 1927. (Kenneth Sivard Jr. collection.)

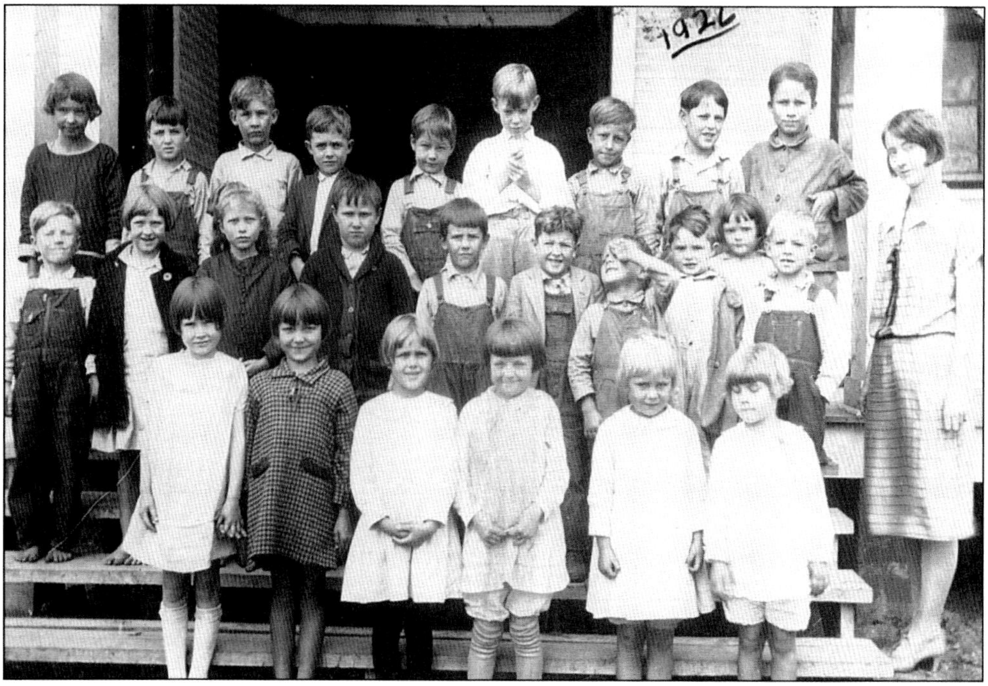

Shults School students pose for a class photograph on the steps of the school in 1926. Instead of individual pictures, most schools had a group picture taken yearly. For many county children, this was the only time of year that their picture was taken. (Kenneth Sivard Jr. collection.)

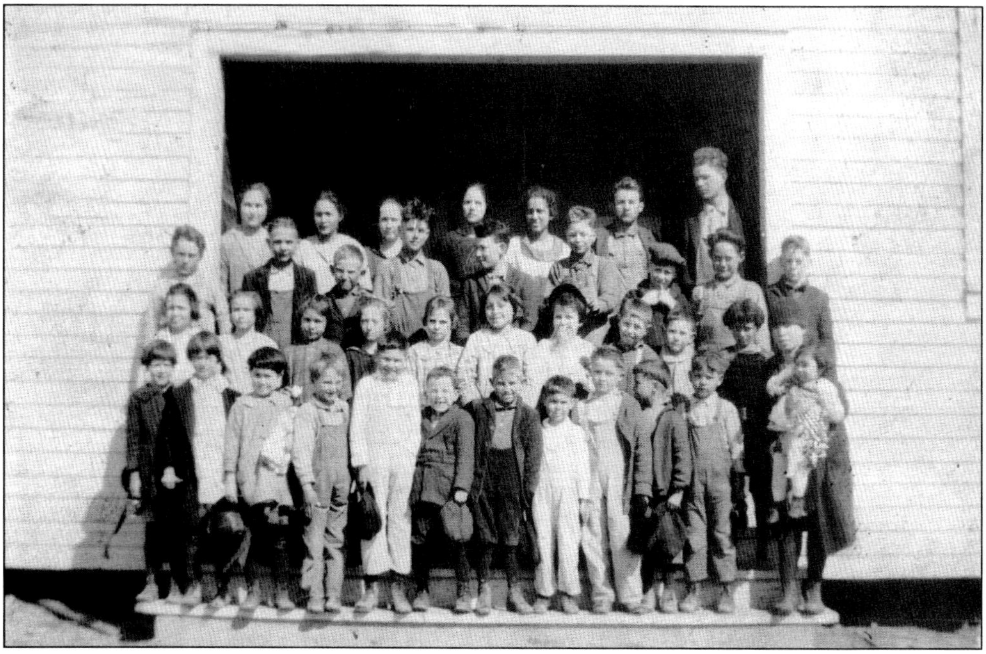

A group of students poses at the small school of Bethel in 1919. However, the area school was not just a place of education in the early days of McCurtain County, especially in the rural areas, but a community center as well. At the county schools, cakewalks, Bible studies, and even quilting parties took place. (Kenneth Sivard Jr. collection.)

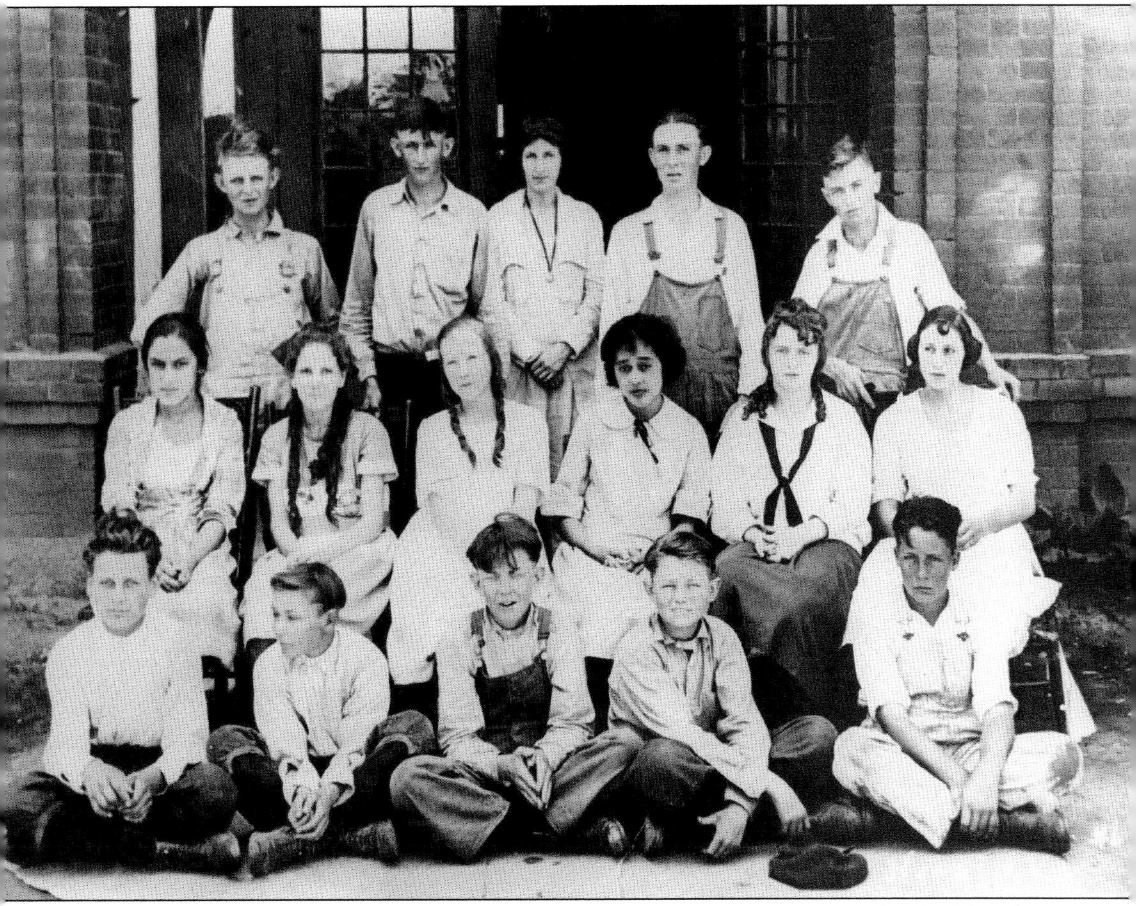

As time passed, some county schools outgrew their frame buildings and decided to build with brick. The first to have brick buildings were Broken Bow, Idabel, Garvin, Haworth, Valliant, and Forest Grove. These structures were massive two-story affairs that required much upkeep. Here is a group of students posing in front of the Garvin School in the 1920s. (Kenneth Sivard Jr. collection.)

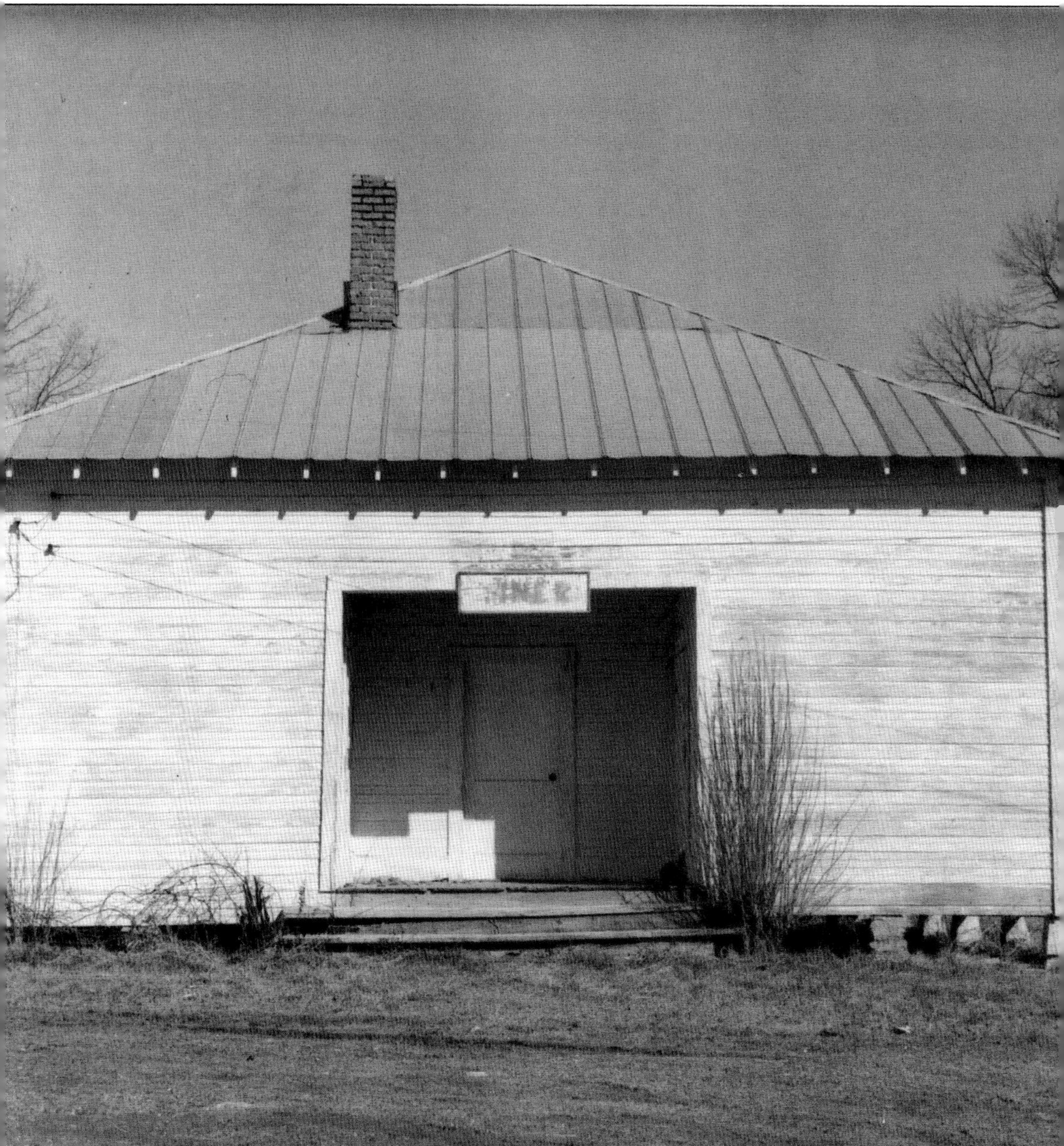

While most of the county's rural schools were one-room buildings, some did host multiple rooms as well as more than one story. Shults and Bok Homma Schools both had two stories, though this was not the norm. Most early county schools were much like the Tiner School, built in 1934 and seen here in 1978, five miles east of Broken Bow on the Military Road; it still stands today. (Kenneth Sivard Jr. collection.)

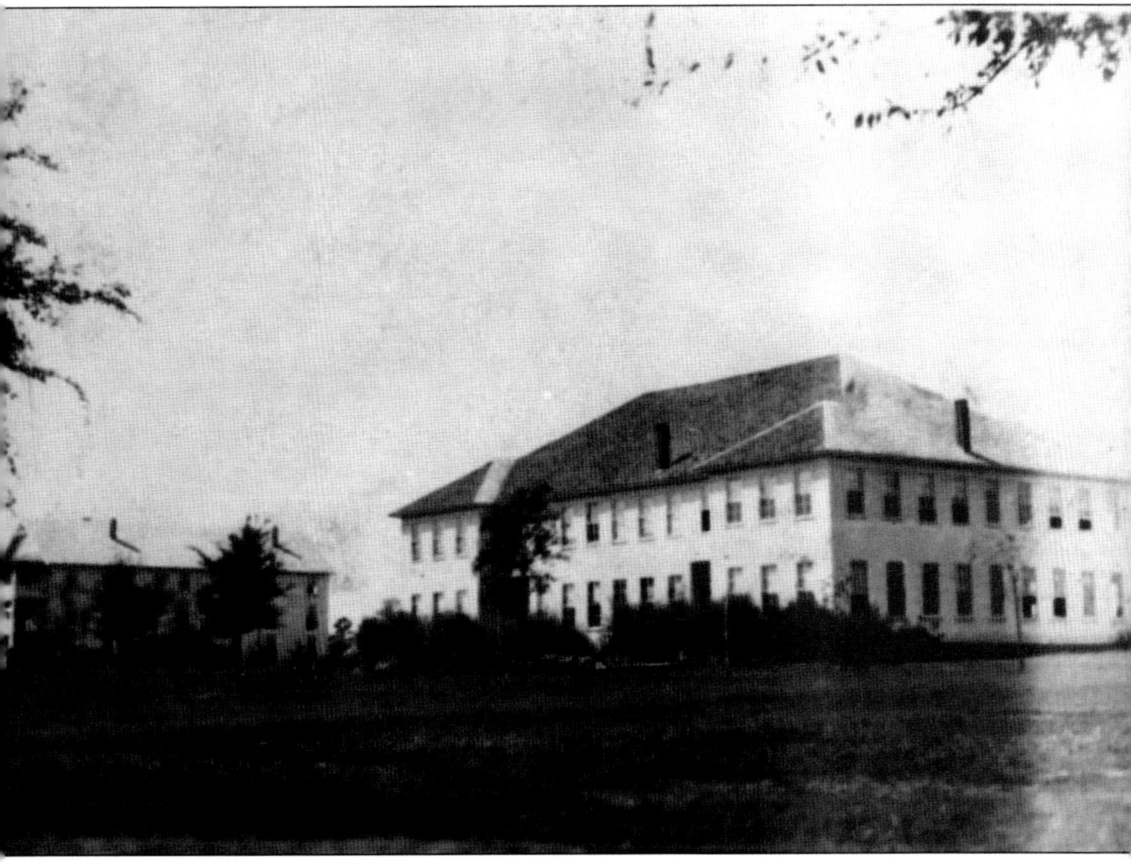

The northern portion of the county was literally cut off from the rest of the county for many years until the Williams Highway, or Old Highway 21, was constructed in the early 1920s. Because of this, the northern part of the county progressed much slower than the southern portion. There was no high school north of Broken Bow until the Methodist Church established the Folsom Training School, pictured in 1923, in Smithville in 1921. The school did not have an open enrollment, and students either had to pay their way or work to pay for their schooling. (Kenneth Sivard Jr. collection.)

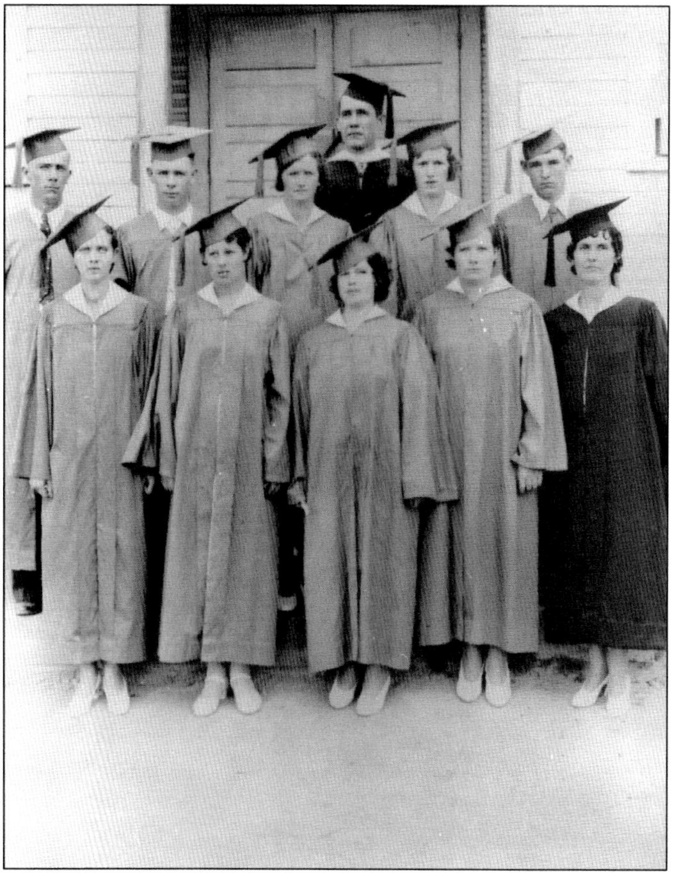

After the Folsom School's closing in 1923, some northern McCurtain County schools began offering high school classes, two of which, Smithville and Battiest, still do. Shown is the 1934 graduating class of Battiest High School. (Kenneth Sivard Jr. collection.)

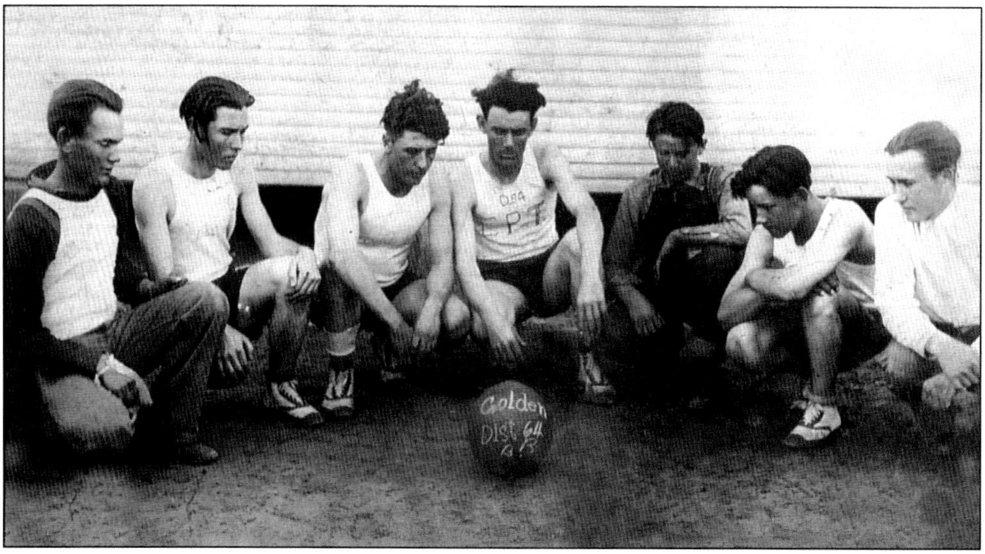

Basketball, baseball, and football have always been popular sports in the schools of McCurtain County, such as the Golden School's basketball team shown here in the 1910s. Pictured among the group are Chas Matlock, Johnia Turner, Claude Matlock, Claude Thompson, Milton Crow, and Lester Hunter. (Kenneth Sivard Jr. collection.)

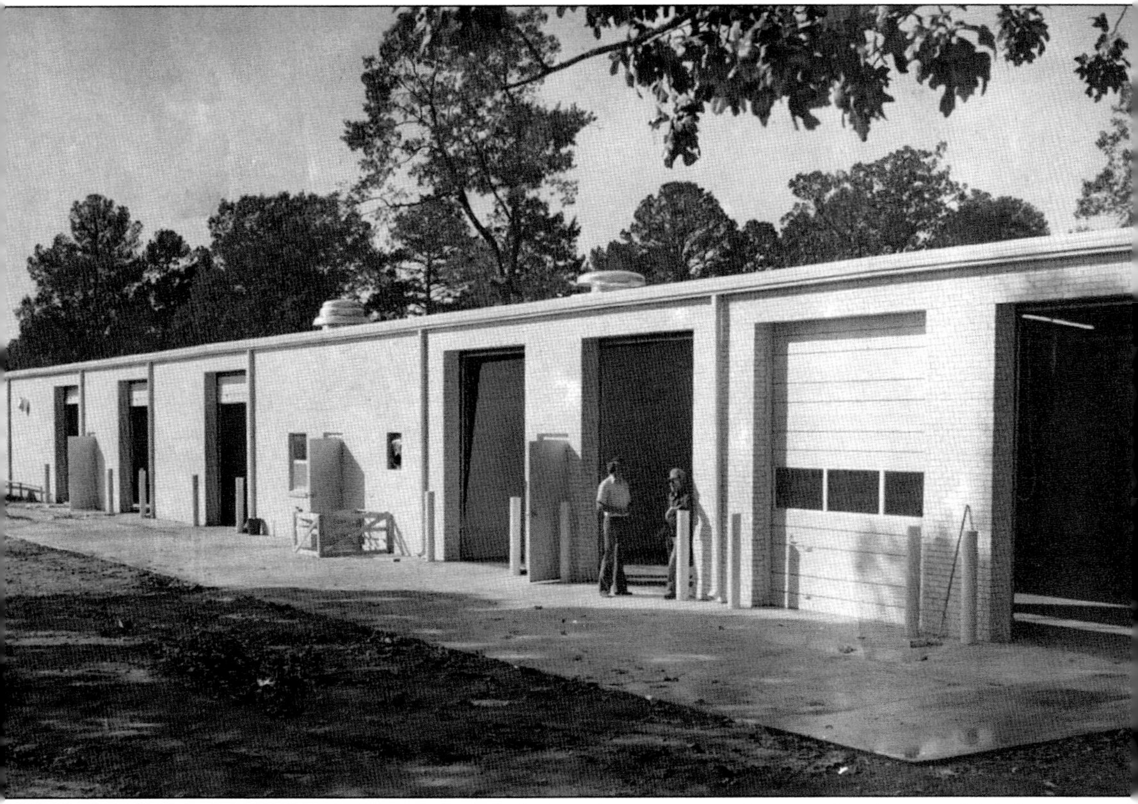

In the 1970s and 1980s, the county saw a period of modernization within its school system. Idabel, Broken Bow, Valliant, Eagletown, and Haworth all received new school facilities or improvements during this time. This is the newly built Eagletown Vocational Studies Building in the early 1980s. (Kenneth Sivard Jr. collection.)

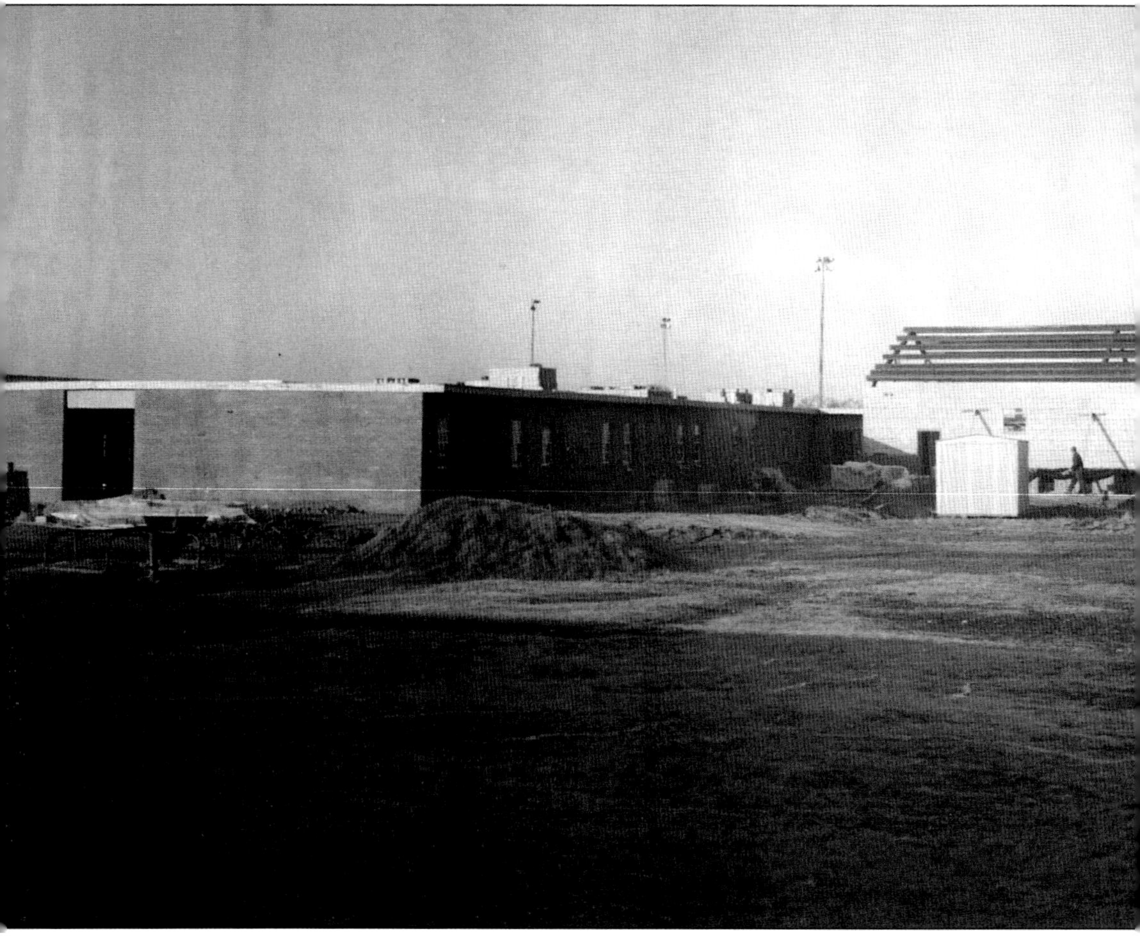

Pictured is the construction of the current Wright City School complex. The school was previously housed in a rock building constructed by the WPA in the 1930s. Today, the school uses both the rock building and the facility pictured. (Kenneth Sivard Jr. collection.)

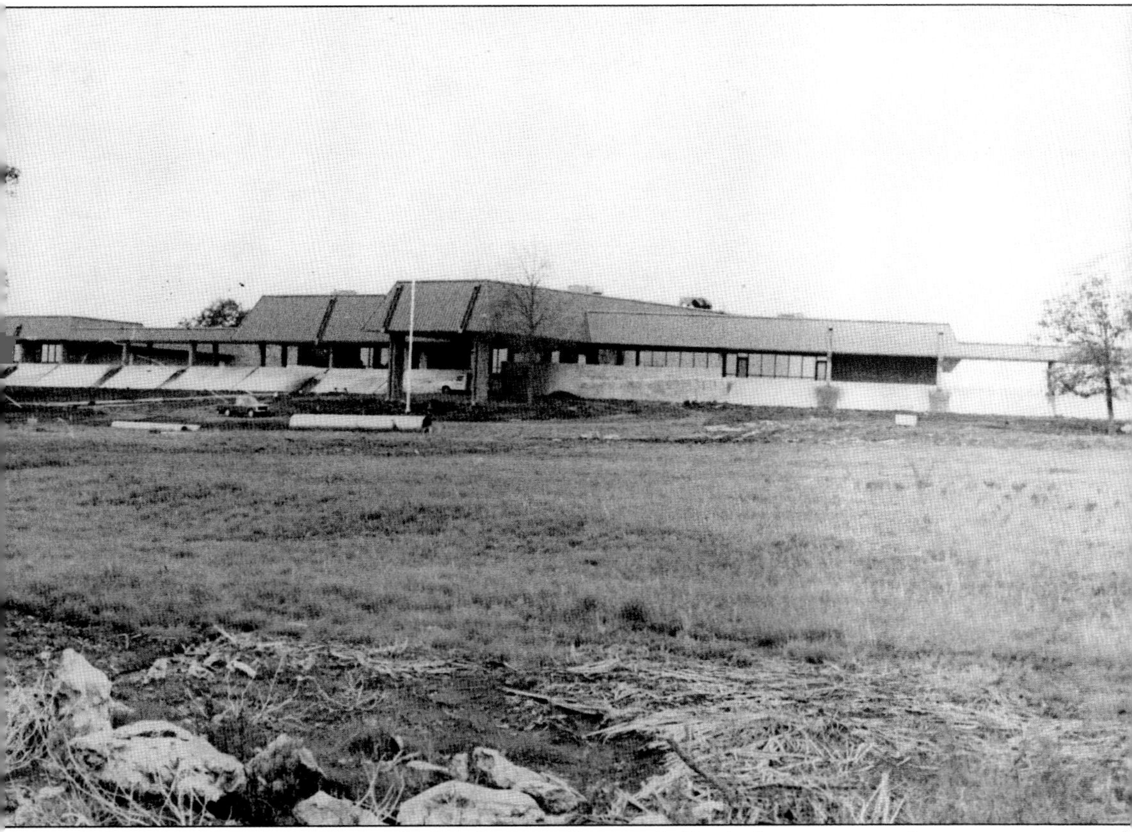

Another great advancement in the McCurtain County field of education was the opening of the Kiamichi Technology Center in 1979 northeast of Idabel. Here, many people in the county have learned vocational skills that allow them to obtain a higher standard of living. This photograph shows the campus nearly completed but still undergoing construction. (Kenneth Sivard Jr. collection.)

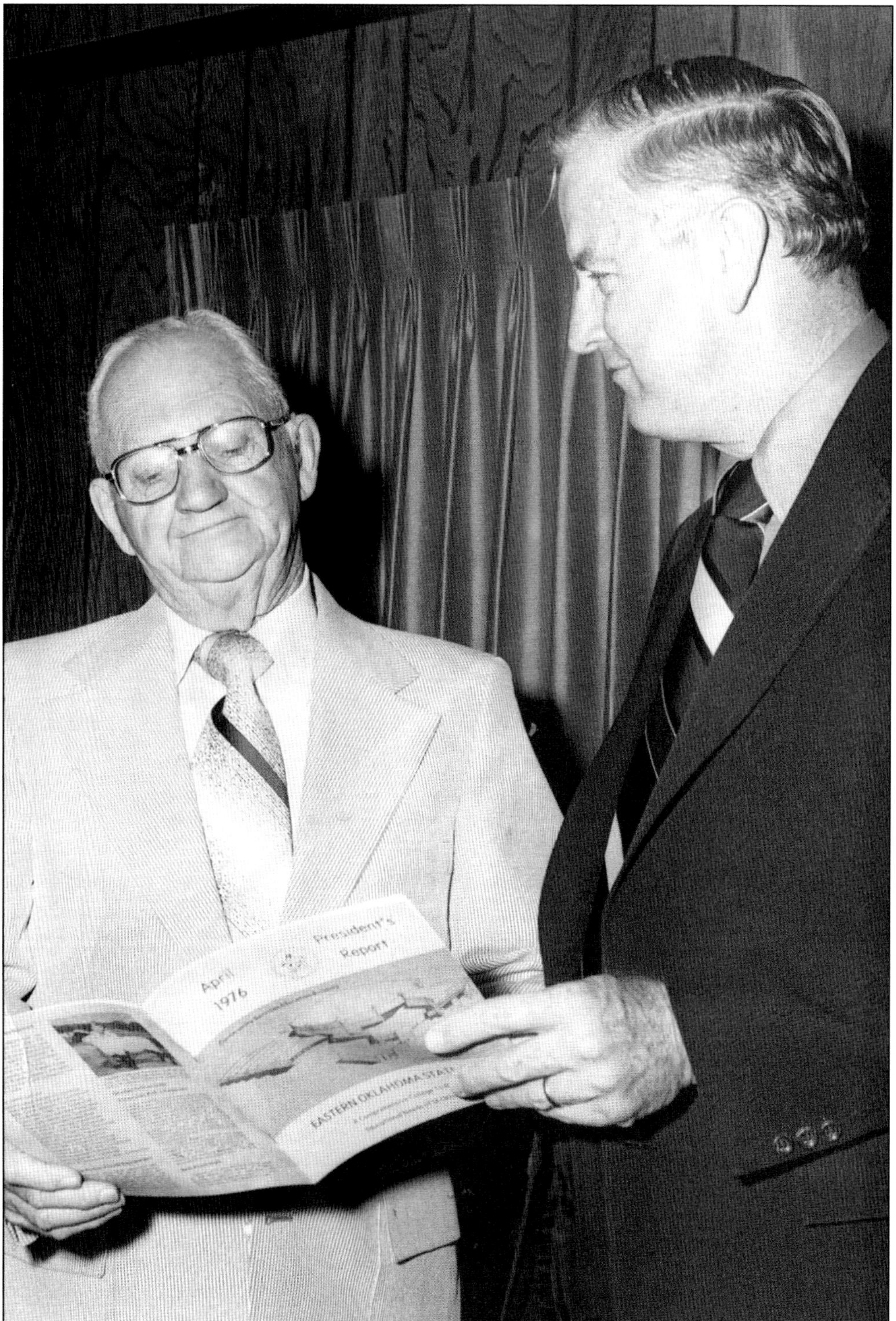

Longtime Broken Bow School superintendent Rector Johnson is pictured in 1976. He is the namesake for the Rector Johnson Middle School in Broken Bow. (Kenneth Sivard Jr. collection.)

Four

MILITARY

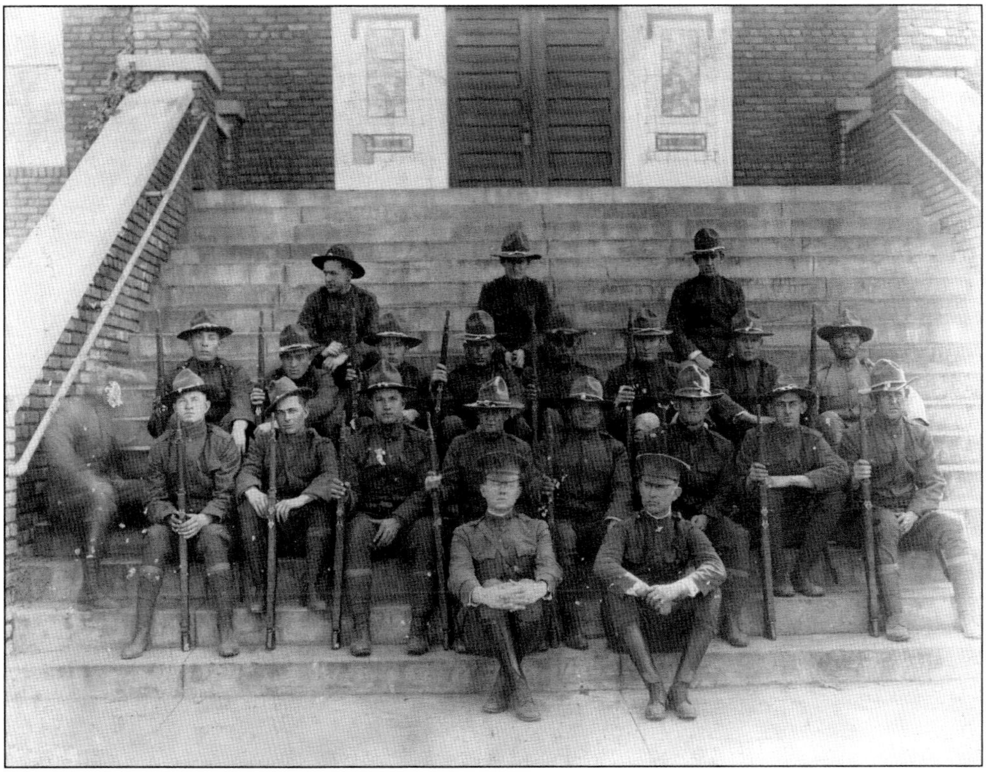

McCurtain County has had a history of lending its sons to the cause when America must defend itself. People who have made McCurtain County their home have fought in conflicts that include the Civil War, Spanish-American War, World War I, World War II, Korean War, Vietnam War, Operation Desert Storm, Operation Enduring Freedom, and Operation New Dawn. This is a group of World War I–era soldiers on the front steps of the First Methodist Church in Idabel. (Kenneth Sivard Jr. collection.)

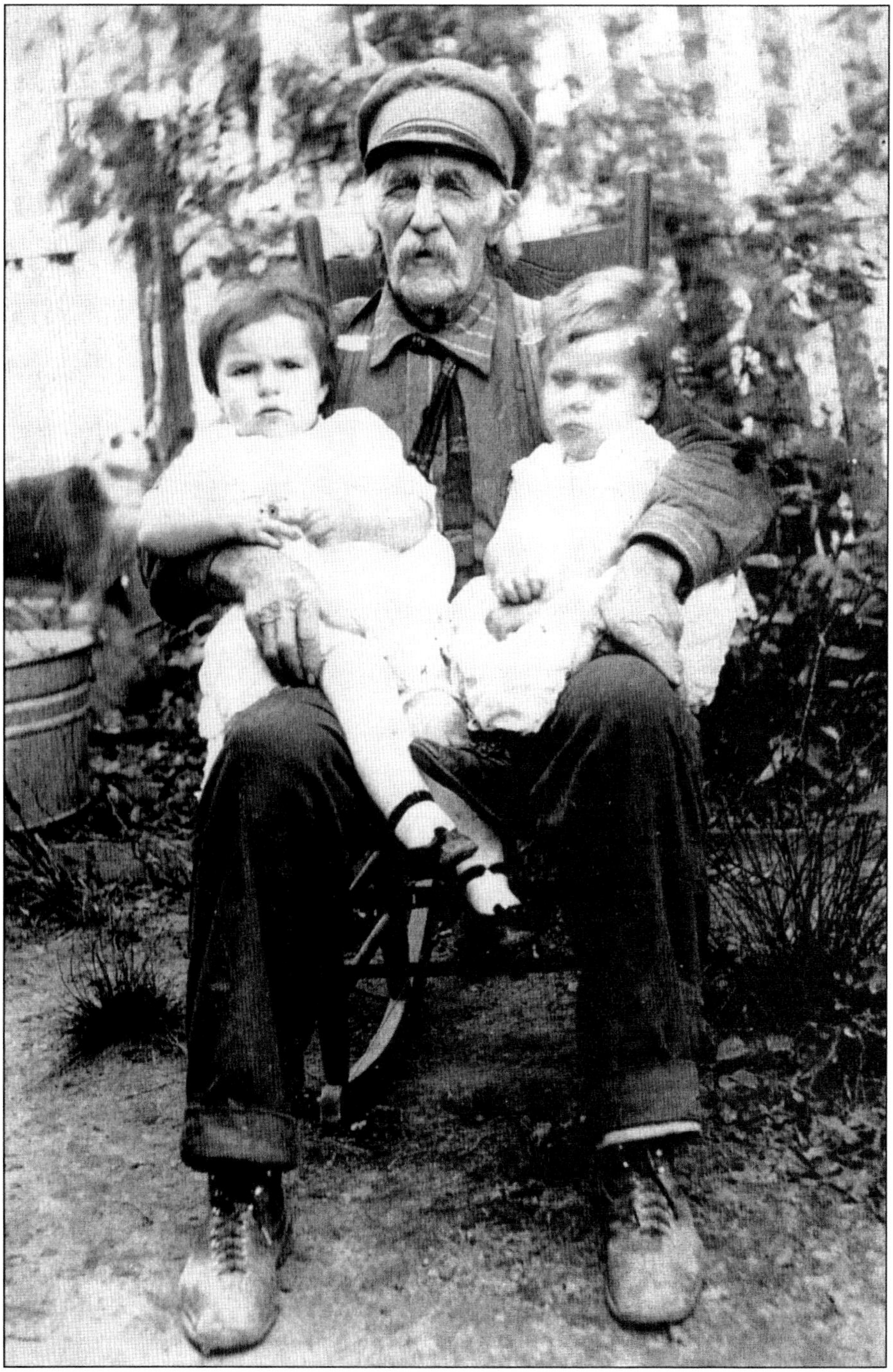

Having borders with Arkansas and Texas, McCurtain County had many Confederate Civil War veterans who made their home within its boundaries, such as Mr. Vale, a Confederate veteran from Battiest, shown here. The Choctaws also fought for the Confederacy at battles such as Back Bone Mountain, Middle Boggy Depot, and Honey Springs. Because so many Confederate veterans made their homes in southeast Oklahoma, this area became known as "Little Dixie." (Kenneth Sivard Jr. collection.)

McCurtain County sacrificed many lives in World War II. Some came back injured, such as Theodore Tohnika (pictured). Tohnika served in the 473rd Infantry regiment of the Fifth Army in Italy. He was shot three times while carrying a fellow soldier to safety. For this brave effort, he was awarded the Silver Citation Star. (Kenneth Sivard Jr. collection.)

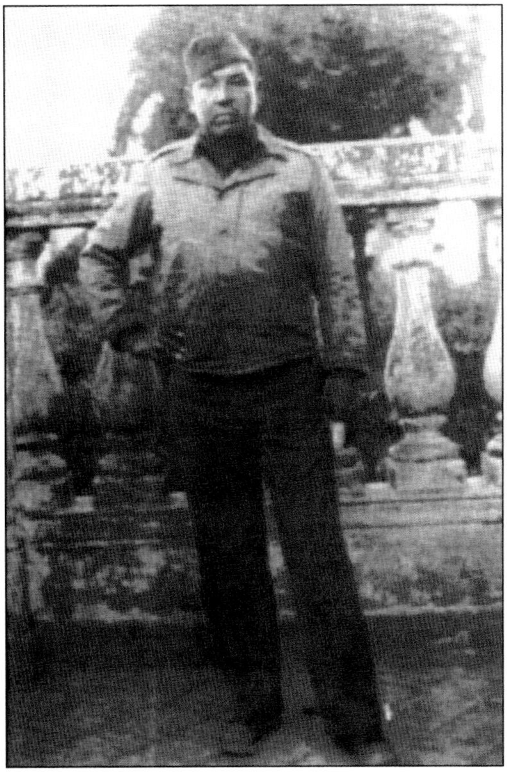

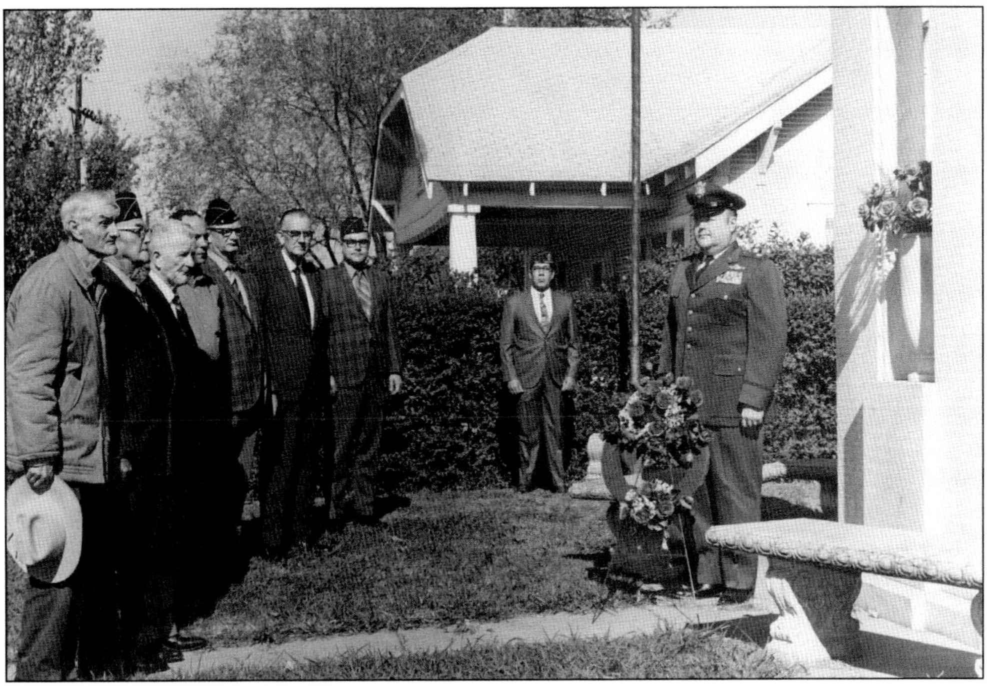

In November 1950, the county erected a memorial to all of its fallen World War I and II veterans; this monument later included the names of its Korean veterans killed in action as well. Shown is the monument's unveiling ceremony. (Kenneth Sivard Jr. collection.)

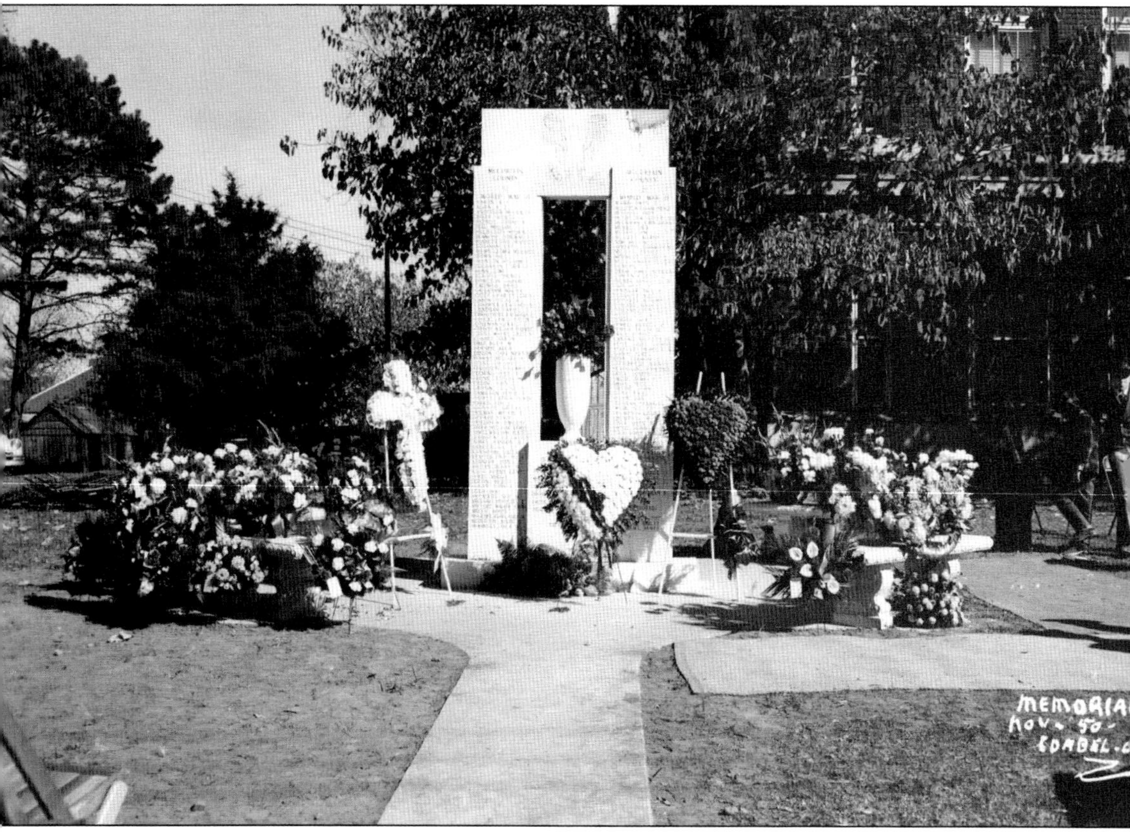

Here is another image of the McCurtain County World War monument on the day it was unveiled. The monument was originally located on the northern side of the courthouse but was moved to make room for the present McCurtain County Jail. Today, it sets on the western lawn of the county courthouse. (Kenneth Sivard Jr. collection.)

Five

ECONOMIC STRUCTURE

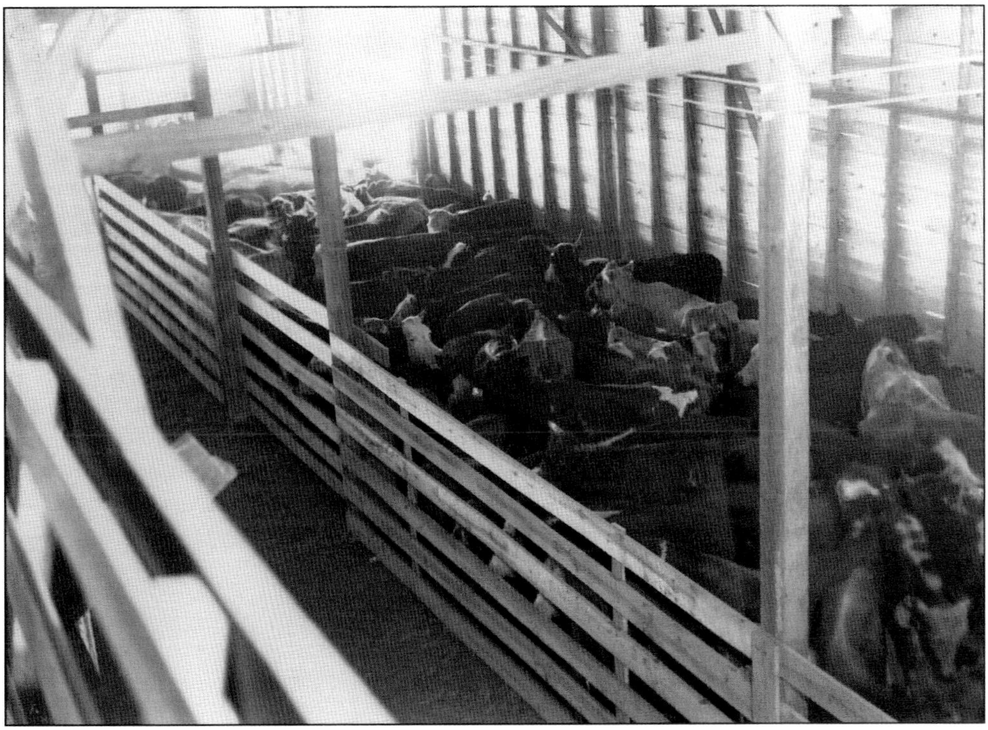

Since the county's first days of existence, the sale of livestock has always been a staple of the economy. This is a scene from the Idabel Livestock Sale in 1948. (Kenneth Sivard Jr. collection.)

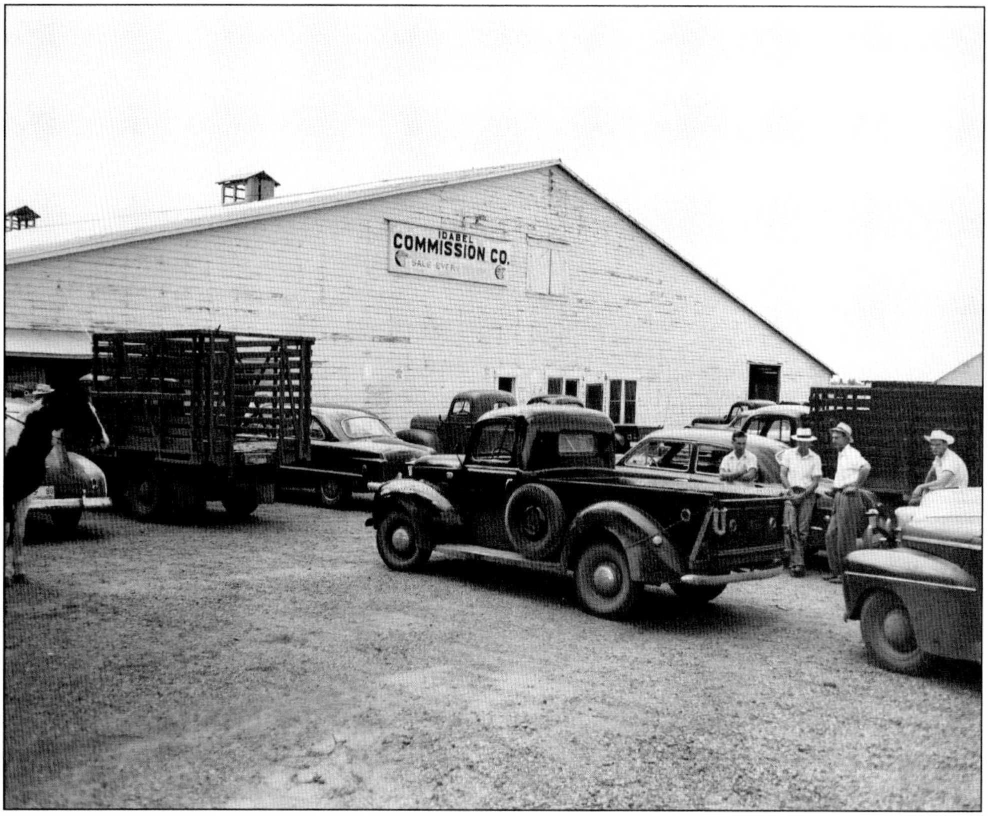

Here is a picture of the parking lot of the Idabel Commission Company Livestock Sale taken in the early 1950s. The first livestock sale in the county was held on the corner of Madison and Central Streets in Idabel in the 1910s. (Kenneth Sivard Jr. collection.)

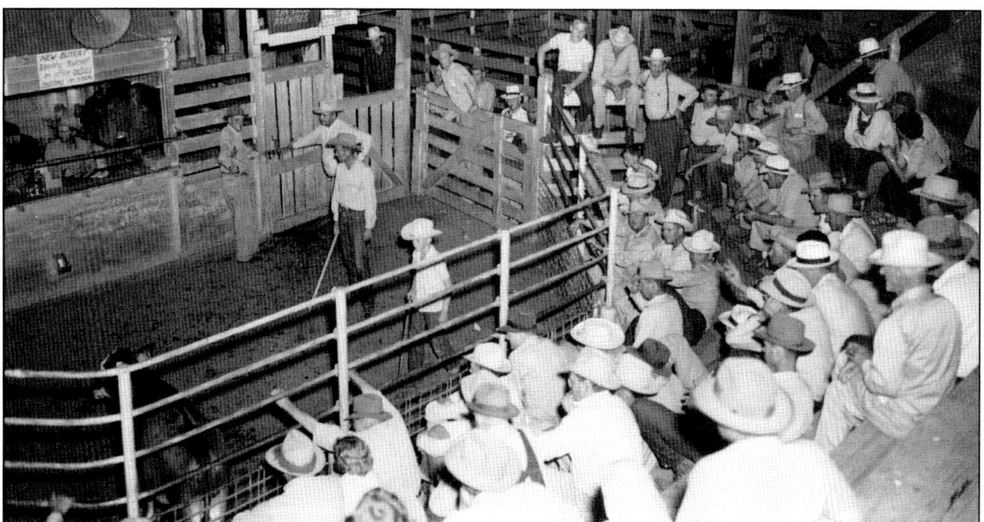

This image was taken inside the Idabel Commission Company livestock sale in the early 1950s. Note the young boy working the sale ring. (Kenneth Sivard Jr. collection.)

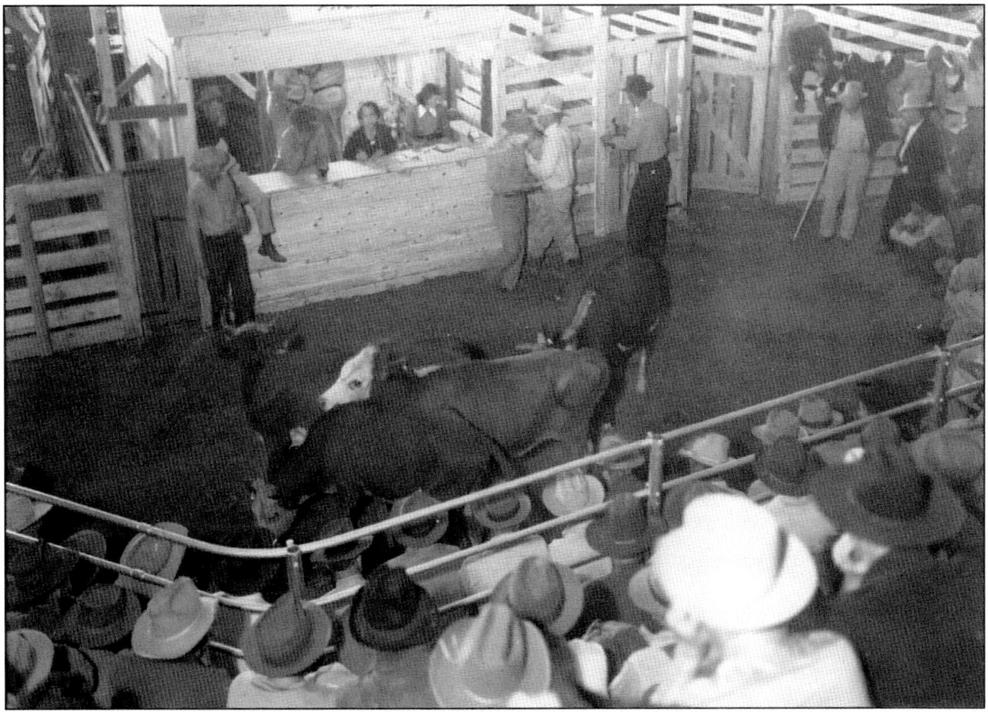

A very early picture of the Idabel Commission Company Livestock Sale is seen here. Notice the men seated inside the sale ring. (Kenneth Sivard Jr. collection.)

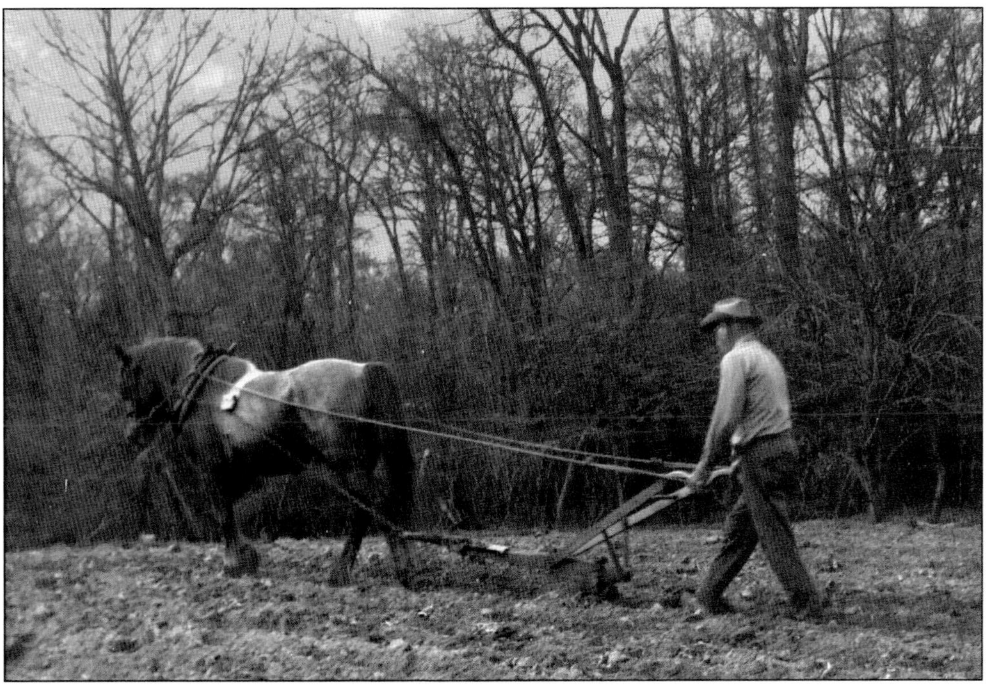

The horse was a valuable tool to the early people of McCurtain County. They were used in many capacities in the farming industry, including plowing as seen here near Harris in the 1950s. (Kenneth Sivard Jr. collection.)

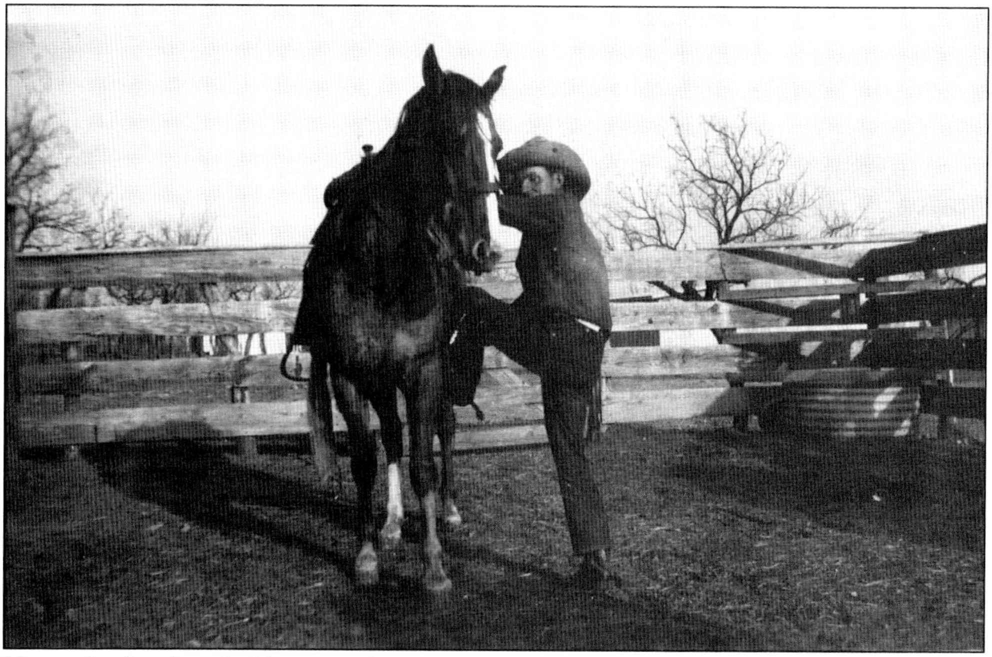

Horses also found a valuable spot in the county's ranching industry. In this picture, Milton Whitten saddles up before a day's work on the Whitten Ranch. (Kenneth Sivard Jr. collection.)

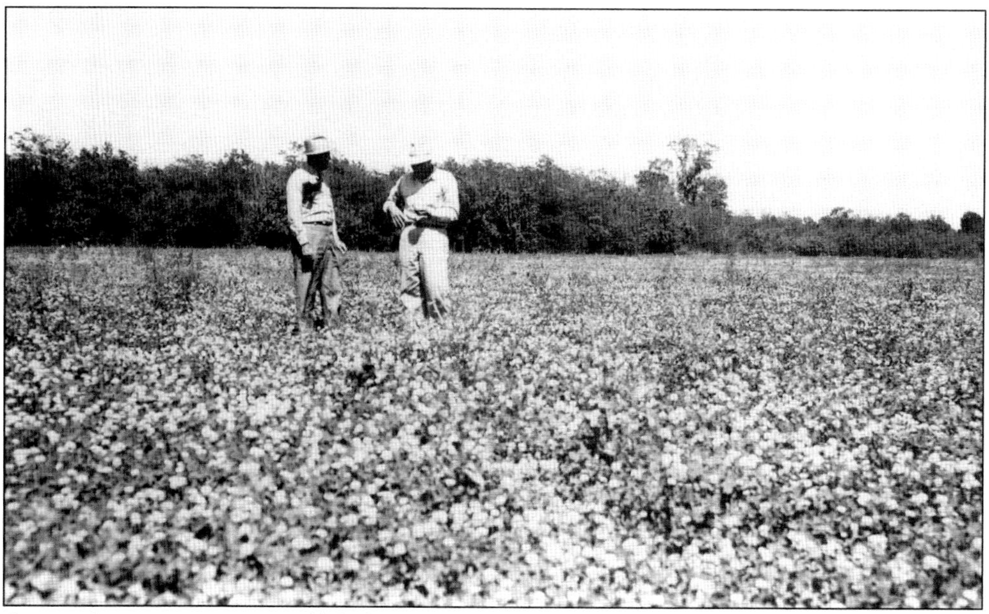

Cotton farming was a way of life for many people in McCurtain County up until the 1970s. Cotton was farmed primarily in the southern part of the county in the Haworth, Harris, Forest Grove, Valliant, Redland, and Tom areas, but it was also cultivated in the Oak Hill and Eagletown communities. Here two men are looking over the Martin farm at Iron Stobb in 1948. (Kenneth Sivard Jr. collection.)

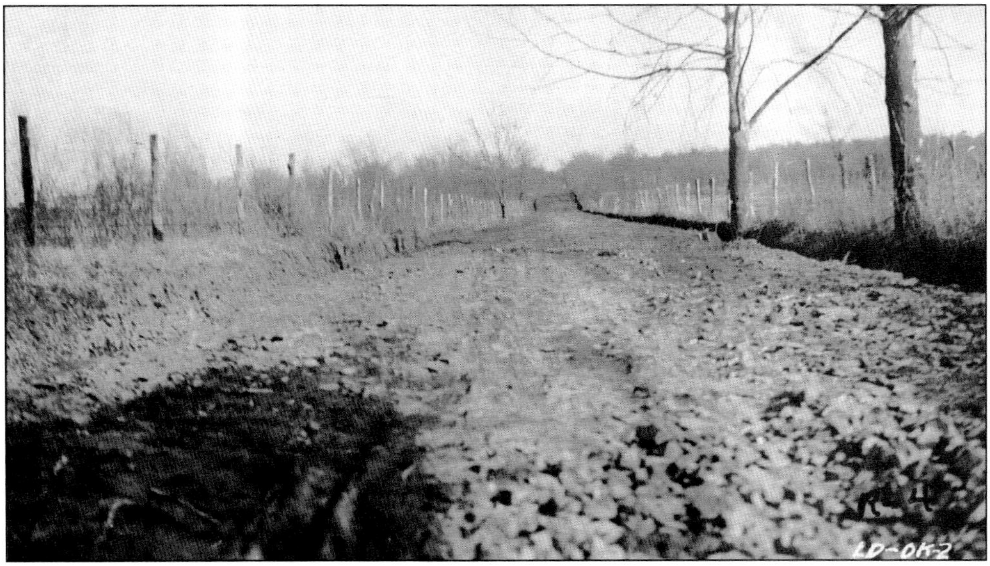

As a result of the Roosevelt government programs of the 1930s, the county began to look at things like forestry, roads, and agriculture in a new light. Here is a typical county road in the 1930s, which were nearly impassable when wet. (Kenneth Sivard Jr. collection.)

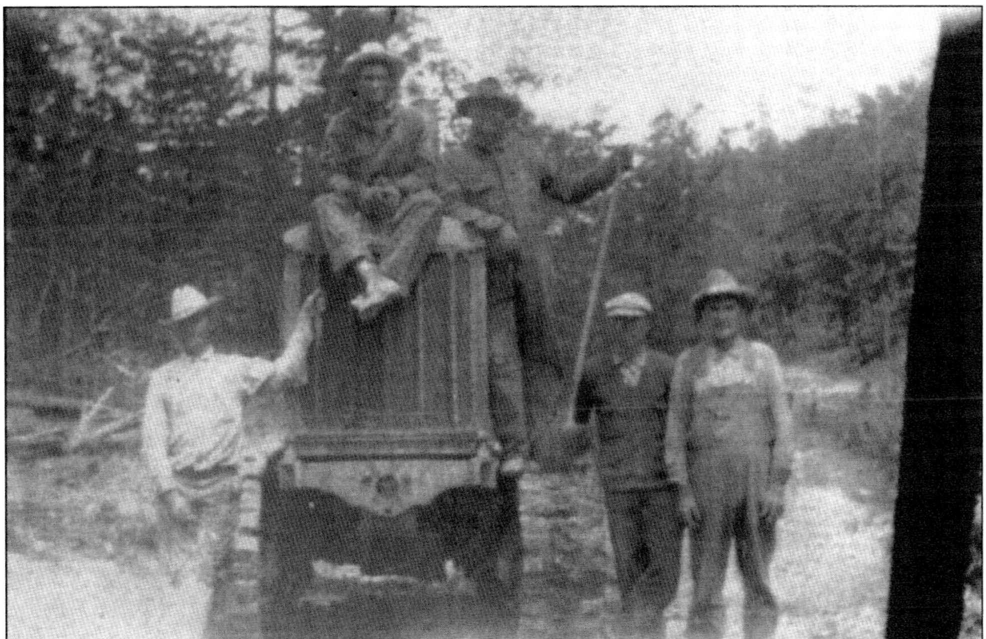

This is an early road-building team in the northern portion of the county. Road building was hard work in the early years of the county. After the 1930s, the county began to utilize heavy machinery, which made the still strenuous work a little easier. (Kenneth Sivard Jr. collection.)

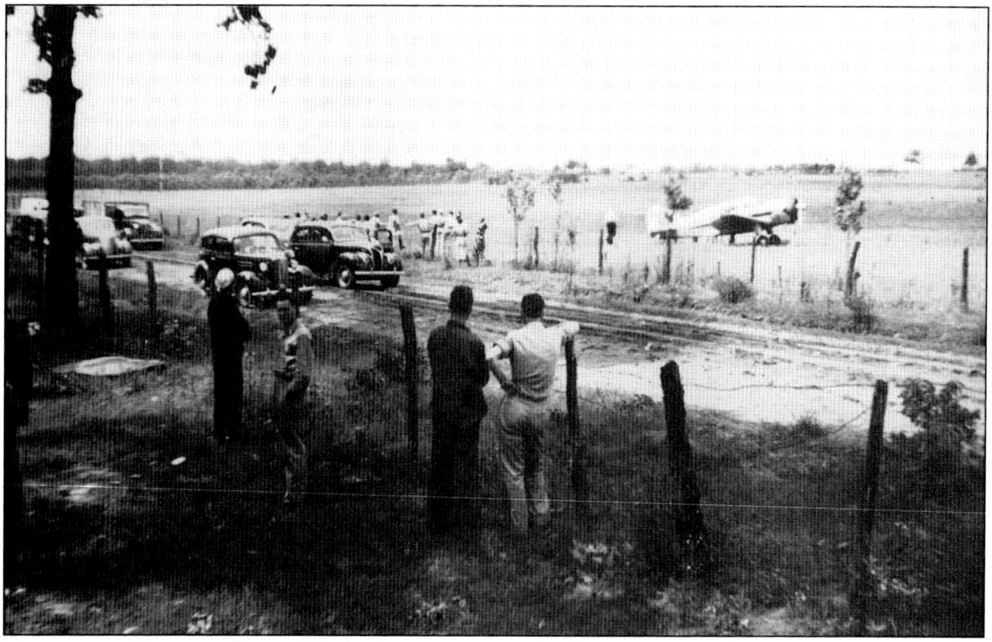

Here is a 1936 scene from Idabel's first airport, which was a field behind the Idabel Civilian Conservation Corps camp on the western side of town. (Kenneth Sivard Jr. collection.)

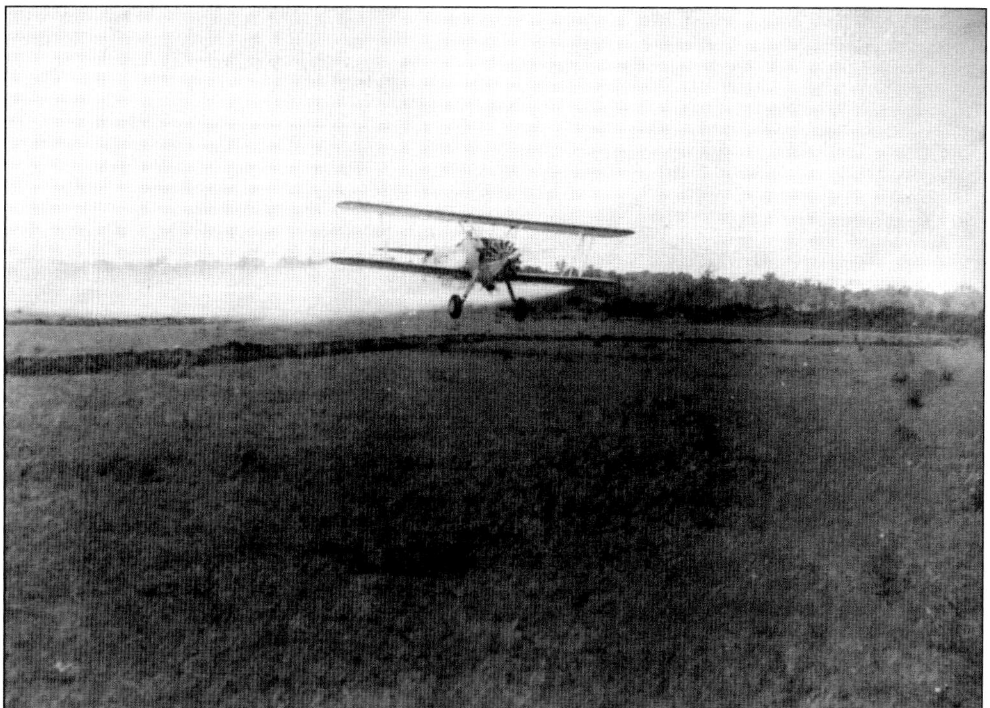

Beginning in the 1960s, farmers in McCurtain County began to use modernized farming techniques. This is an airplane fertilizing a rice field three miles west of Tom in June 1964. (Kenneth Sivard Jr. collection.)

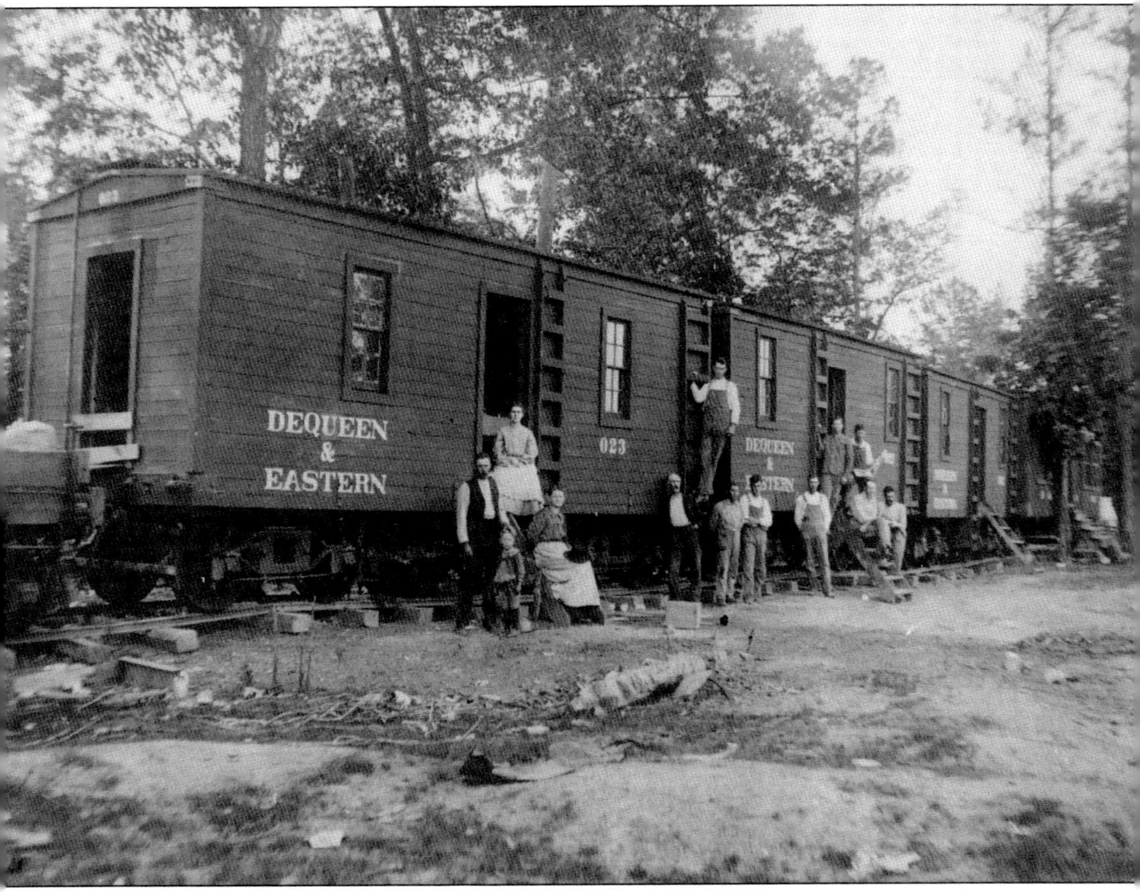

When the Choctaw Lumber Company first started its business interests in McCurtain County, it needed a way to transport goods to and from logging sites as well as mill towns in Bismark and Broken Bow. It would soon build a railroad system through the county, which helped connect it with the rest of the world. Here is a 1920 camp of railroad workers for the DeQueen and Eastern Railroad in the county. (Courtesy of the McCurtain County Historical Society.)

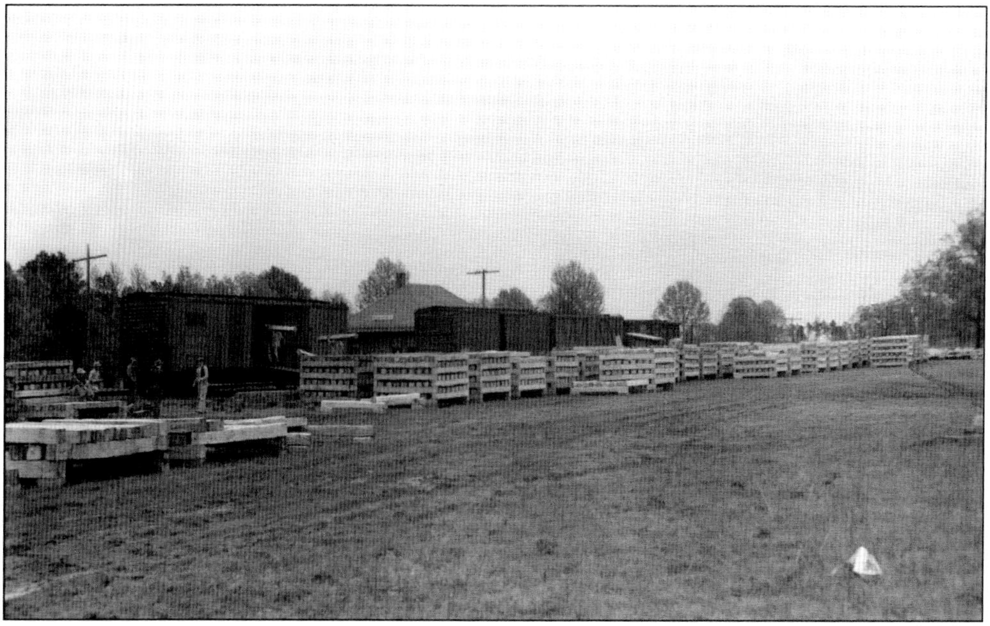

The Frisco Railroad built a line through the southern portion of the county in 1902, establishing the towns of Bok Homma, Idabel, Garvin, and Valliant as they are known today. This railroad line allowed for the export of goods, such as lumber and crops, to destinations in Arkansas and beyond. Men are seen here loading green railroad ties onto a train car at the Bok Homma train station in 1941. (Kenneth Sivard Jr. collection.)

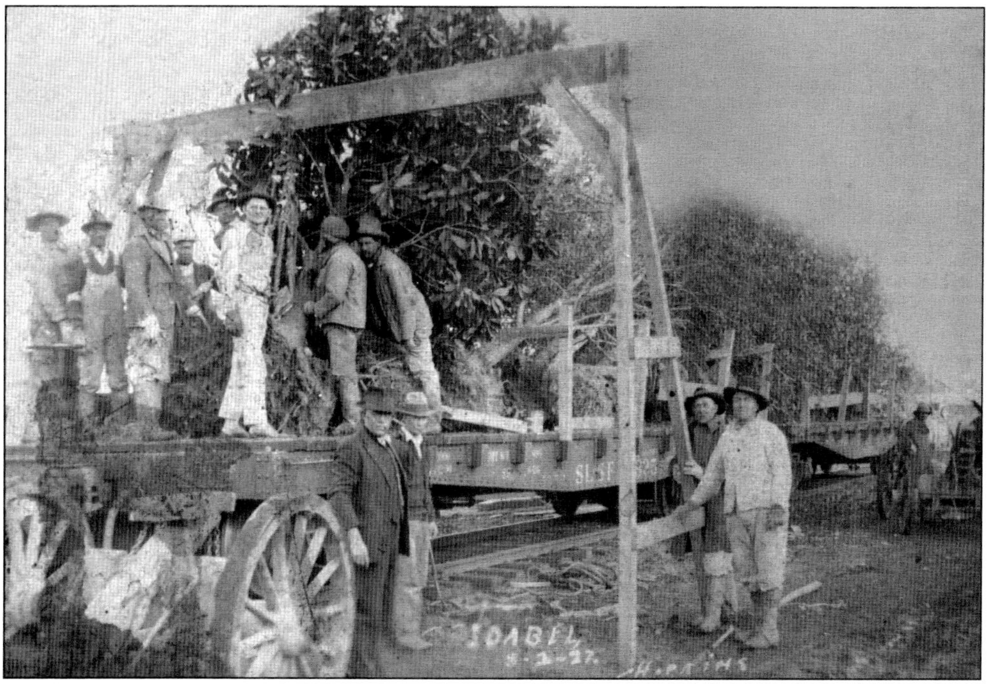

A group of men loads decorative trees onto rail cars at the Idabel Train Depot. These trees were grown in and around Idabel and exported by train to Arkansas and Texas. (Kenneth Sivard Jr. collection.)

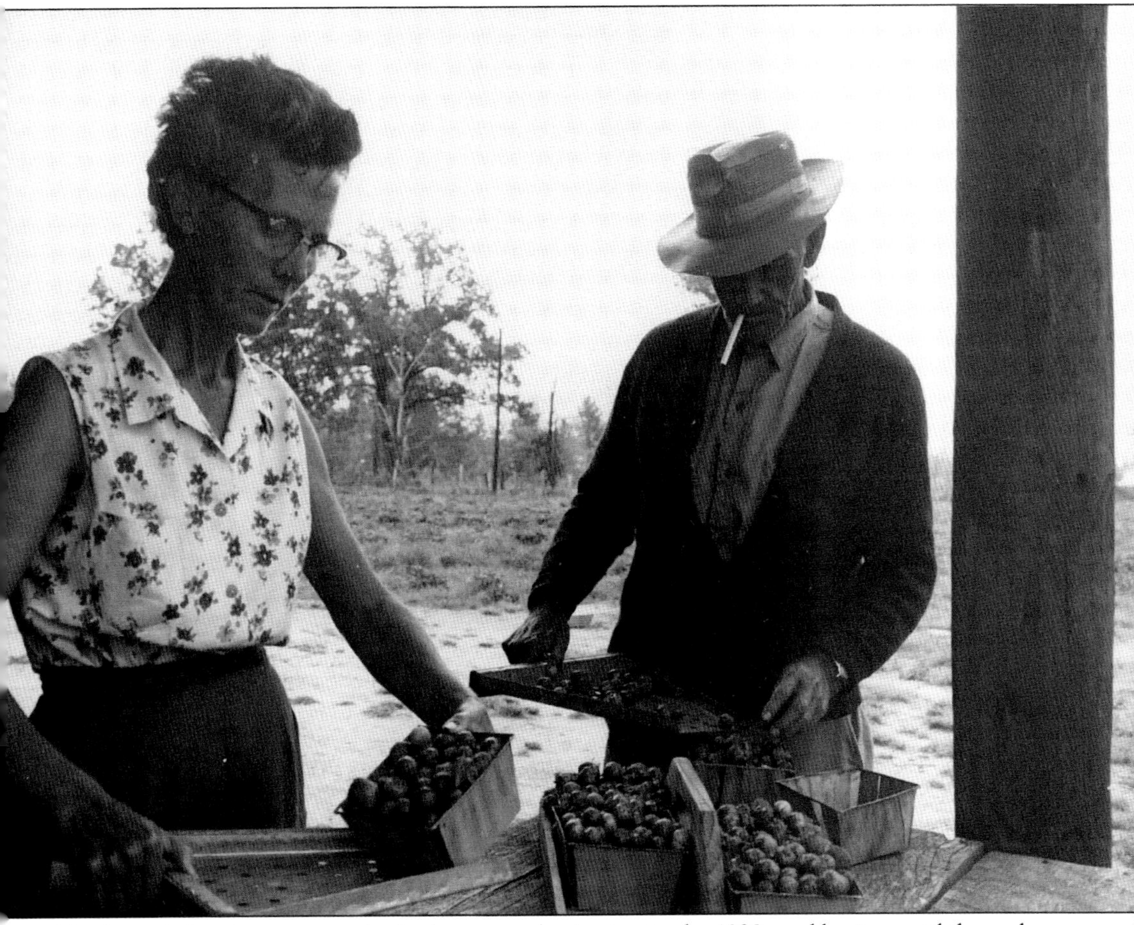

Truck patch farming was popular in the county beginning in the 1930s and lasting until the early 1970s. These small farming operations provided a good source of extra income to area families. Truck patch farmer Wilson DeGroot is shown with strawberries he harvested off of his operation in Haworth. It is recorded that when this picture was taken in 1961, DeGroot had added an additional $1,600 to his annual income with his truck patch. Strawberries were commonly grown in the Holly Creek, Sweet Home, Oak Hill, Haworth, and Pleasant Hill areas. The berries were often shipped from the Idabel and Broken Bow train stations. (Kenneth Sivard Jr. collection.)

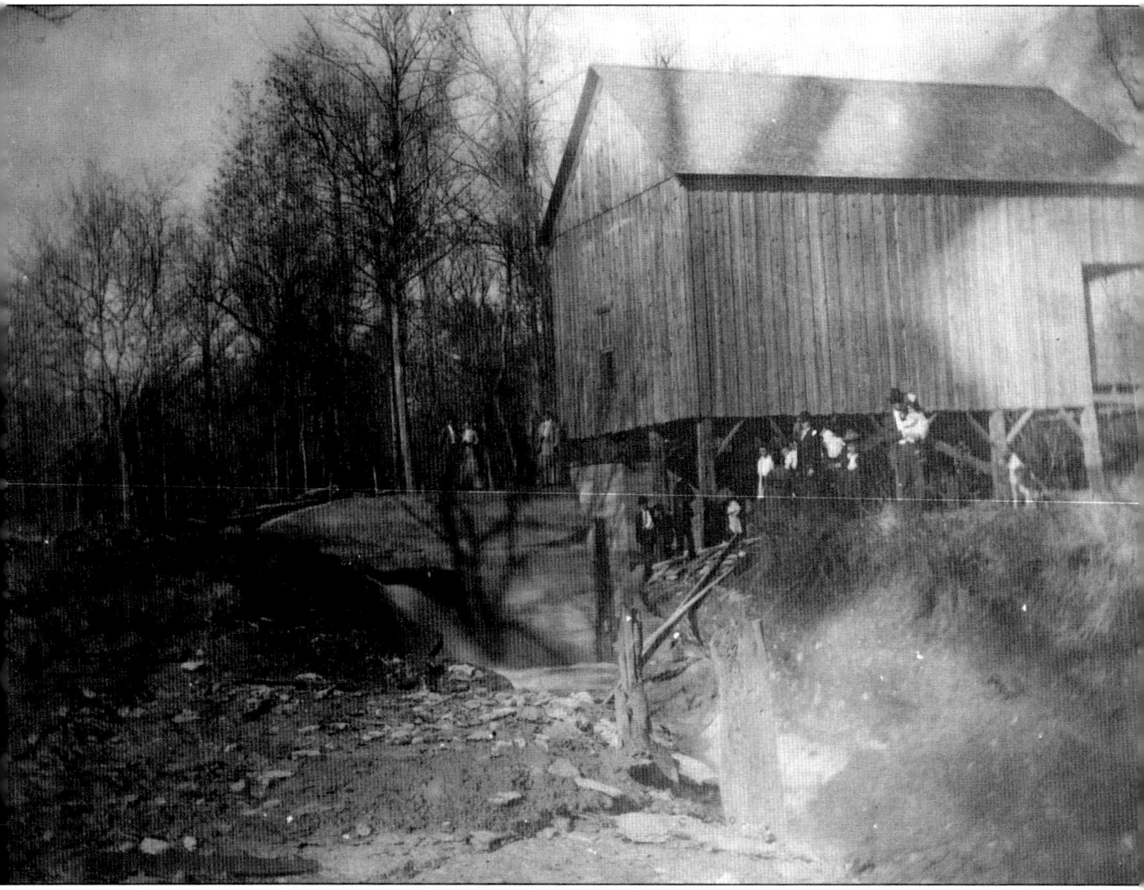

One of the first economic endeavors in the county was the Clear Creek Water Mill. First built in 1819 when this land was part of Miller County, Arkansas, the mill was rebuilt in 1909 by the Prince family, who also built a large home near the mill that still stands today. It was used to grind cornmeal as well as flour. The water mill had been closed for many years when it was destroyed by high waters in 2008. This is the Prince mill shortly after it was built, with the Prince family standing in front. (Kenneth Sivard Jr. collection.)

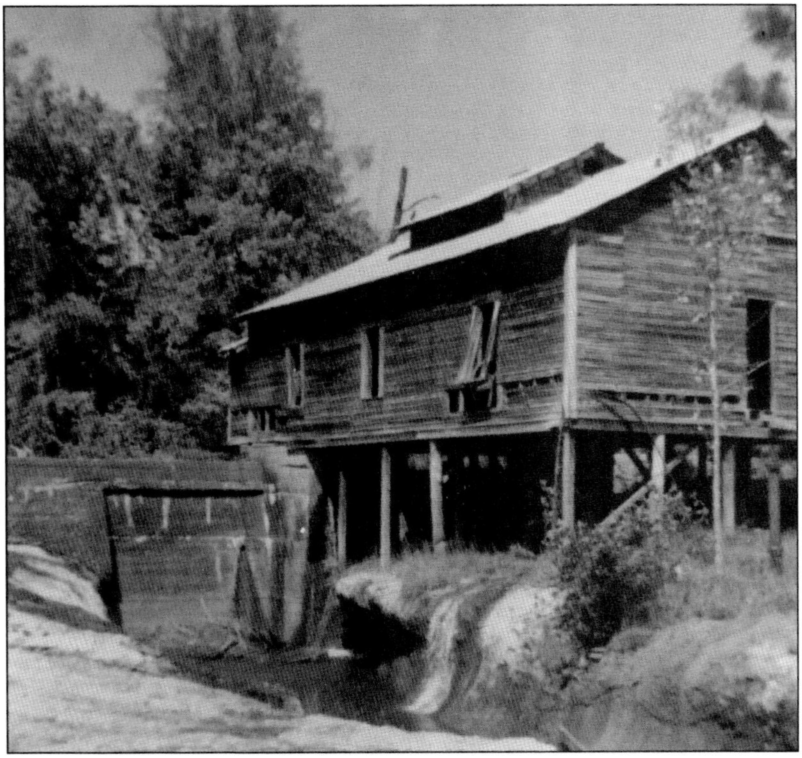

The Clear Creek Water Mill was rebuilt in 1937. This was to be the last building to house the mill; it is shown here in 1978 after many years of being unused. (Courtesy of the MCHS.)

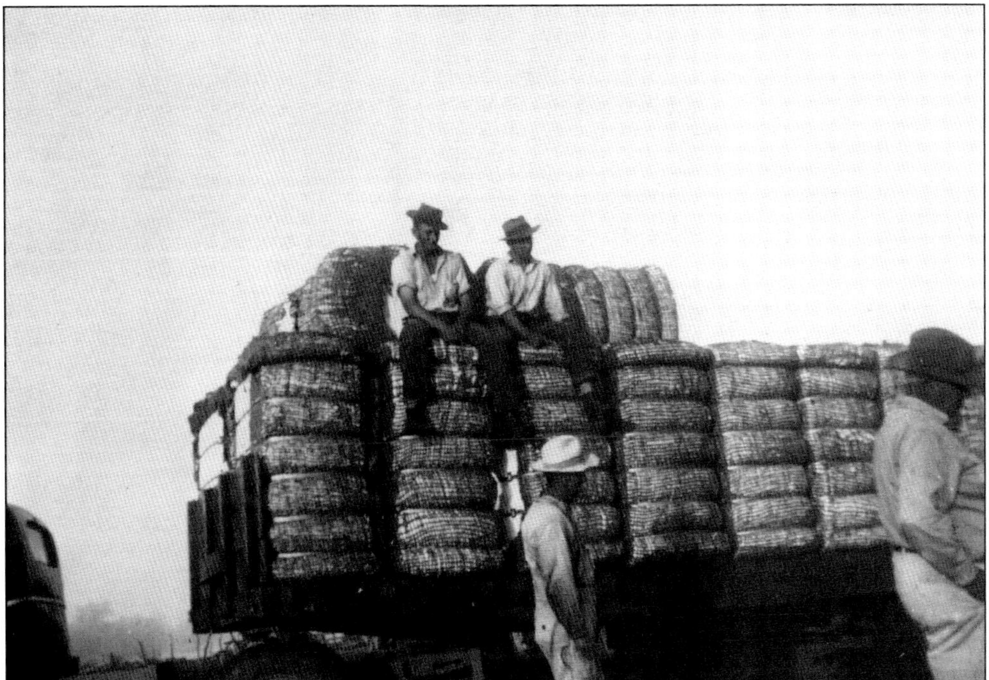

Pictured are some men and their product at the Idabel Cotton Market in the late 1950s. Cotton was an important cash crop to the people of McCurtain County for more than 140 years. (Kenneth Sivard Jr. collection.)

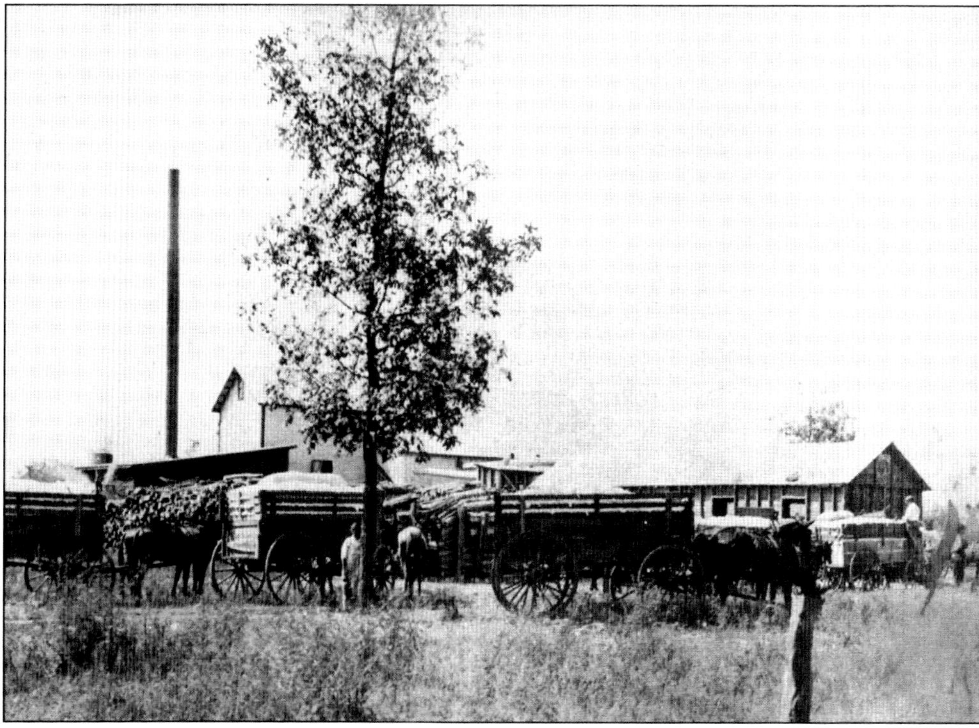

After the cotton crop was picked for the year, it had to be hauled to town to be ginned. Many cotton gins have existed in McCurtain County through the years at places that include Idabel, Eagletown, Rufe, Valliant, Goodwater, Haworth, Beachton, and Kulli Tuklo. Here is a cotton gin in Idabel in the late 1920s. Note the stacks of wood, which fueled the gin. (Kenneth Sivard Jr. collection.)

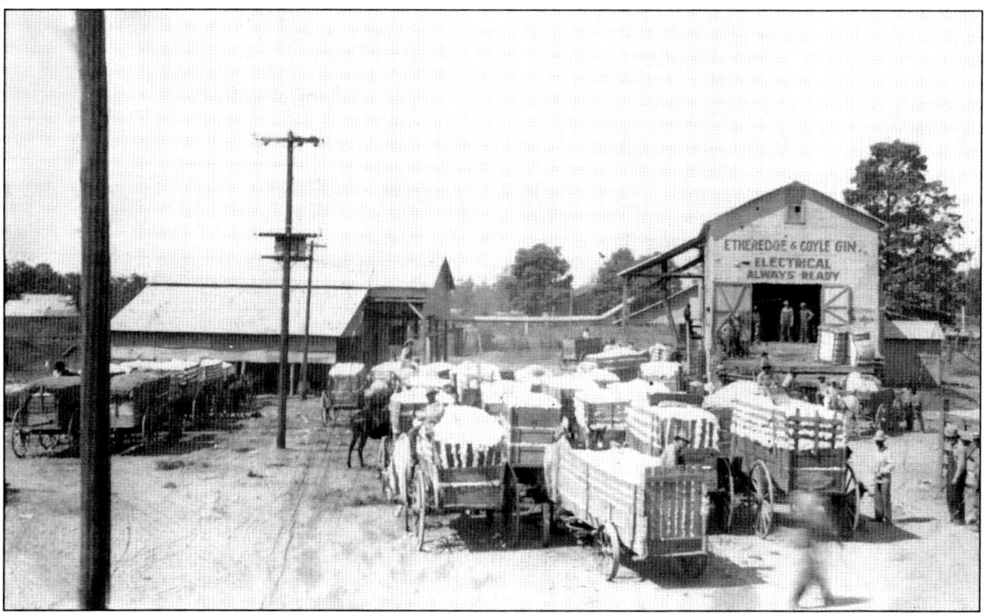

One of the first electric cotton gins in the area, the Etheredge and Coyle Cotton Gin, was important because it could be used at any time without great expense. (Kenneth Sivard Jr. collection.)

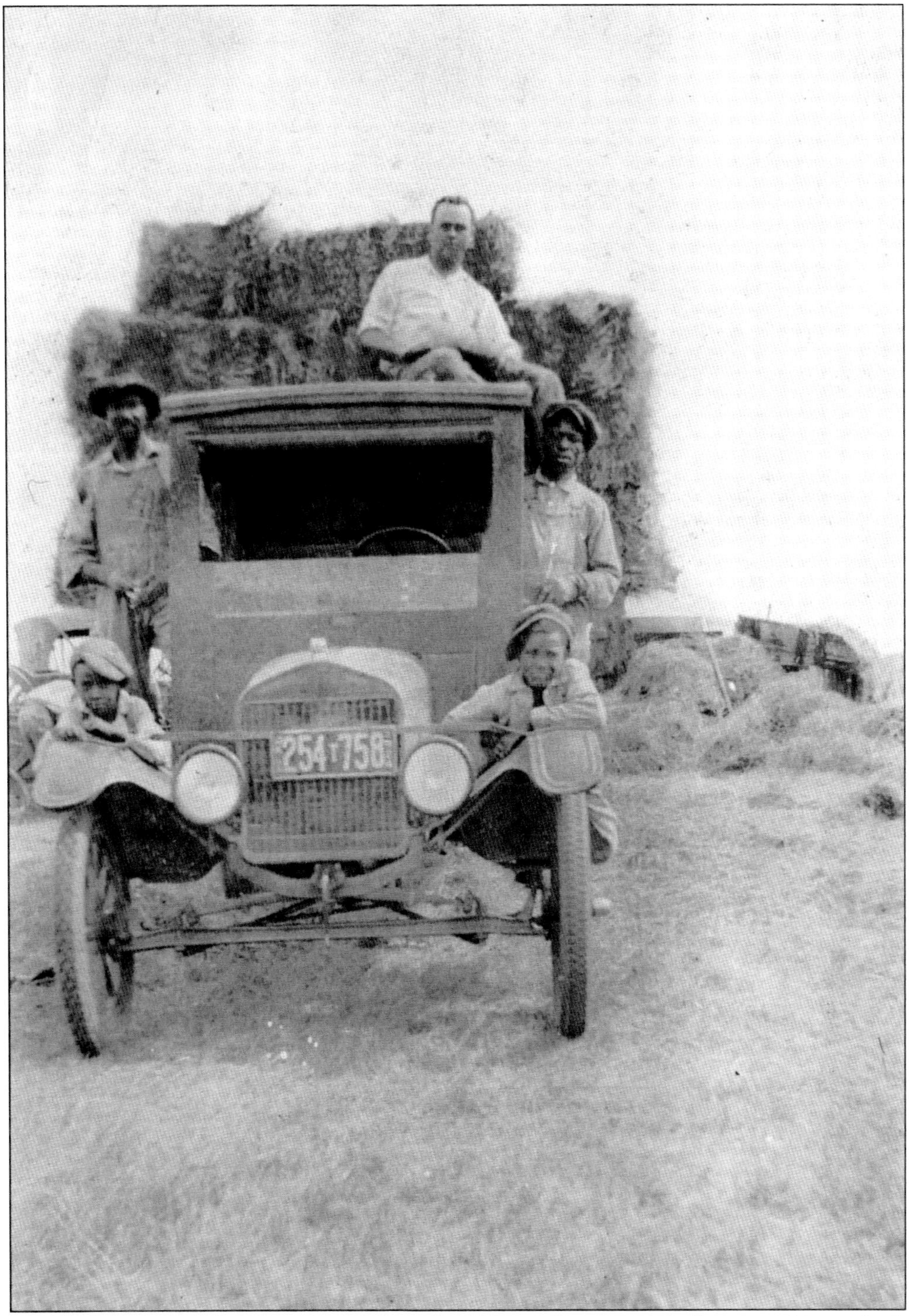

An important part of McCurtain County's livestock operations is the harvest of hay, which provides valuable fiber and nutrients during the winter. This is a truck loaded with hay grown and baled on the Barnes hay farm south of Idabel in the early 1920s, with Barnes seen atop of the truck. Note the two little boys riding on the front fenders. (Courtesy MCHS.)

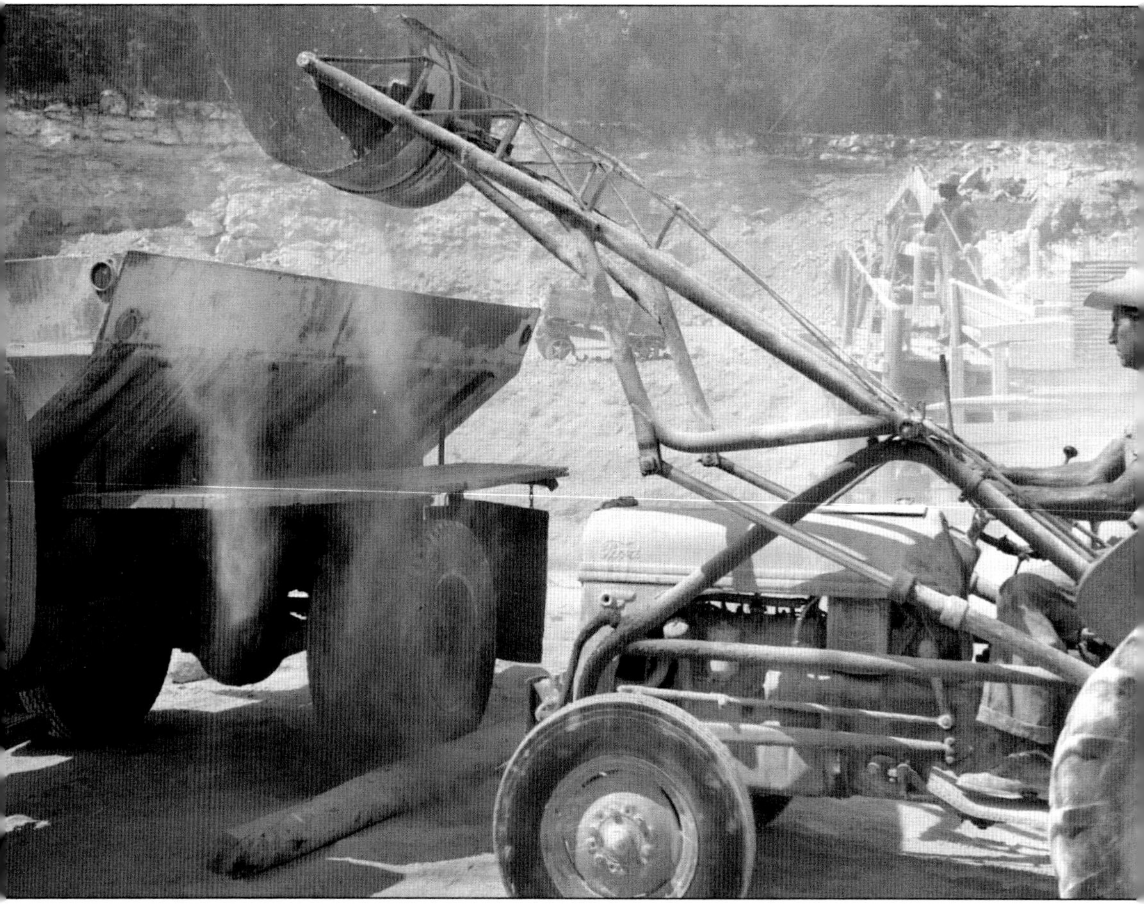

This picture, taken in 1957, shows another interesting McCurtain County economic venture—harvesting limestone. There is a limestone ridge that runs east to west across the county, where it is harvested and shipped out to several places in Oklahoma as well as Arkansas and Texas. The limestone resource was instrumental in building many county roads in the early days, as it still is. In the photograph, a truck is loaded with limestone to be shipped to Texas from a quarry near Idabel that was owned by the Little River Soil Conservation District. (Kenneth Sivard Jr. collection.)

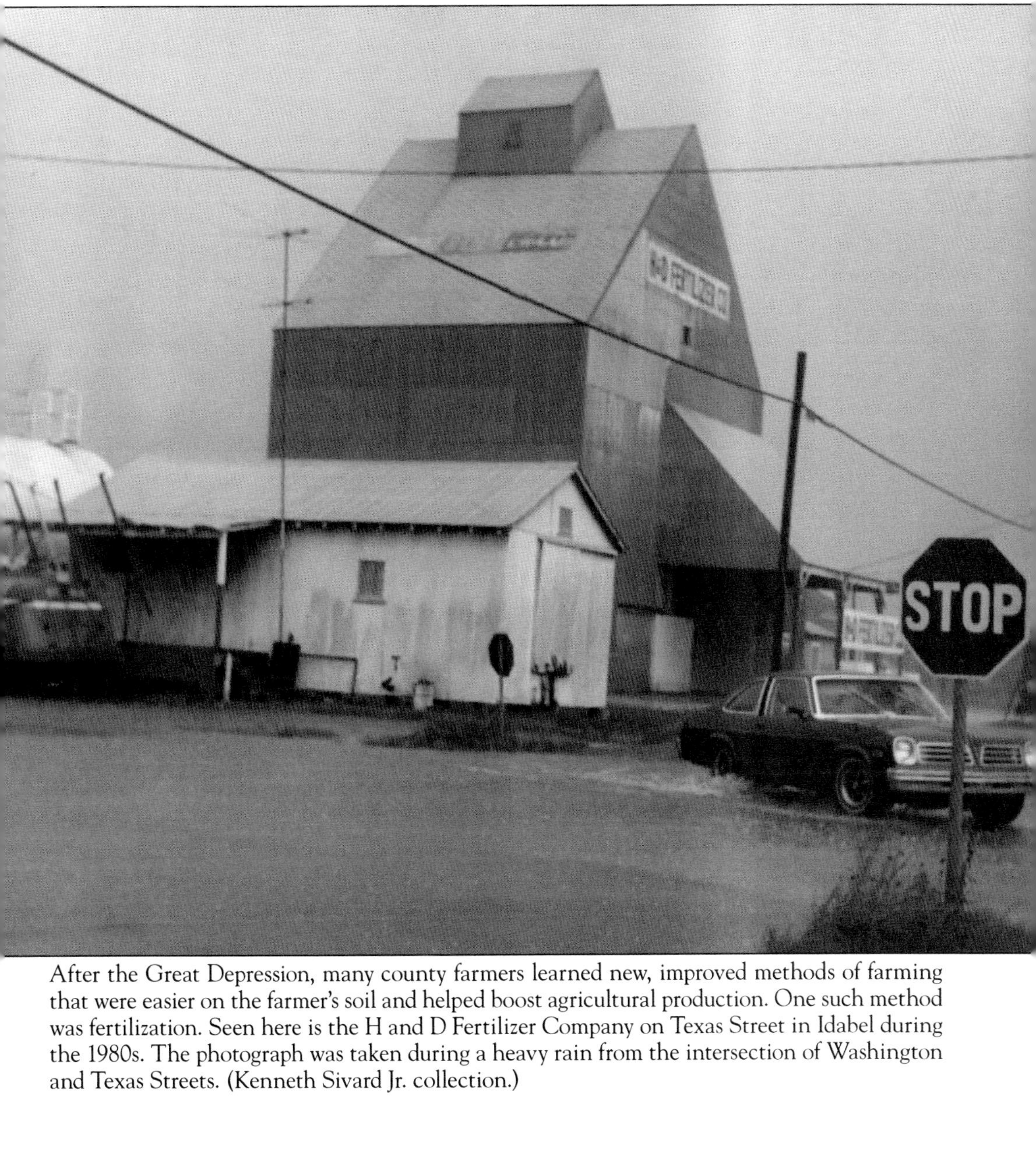

After the Great Depression, many county farmers learned new, improved methods of farming that were easier on the farmer's soil and helped boost agricultural production. One such method was fertilization. Seen here is the H and D Fertilizer Company on Texas Street in Idabel during the 1980s. The photograph was taken during a heavy rain from the intersection of Washington and Texas Streets. (Kenneth Sivard Jr. collection.)

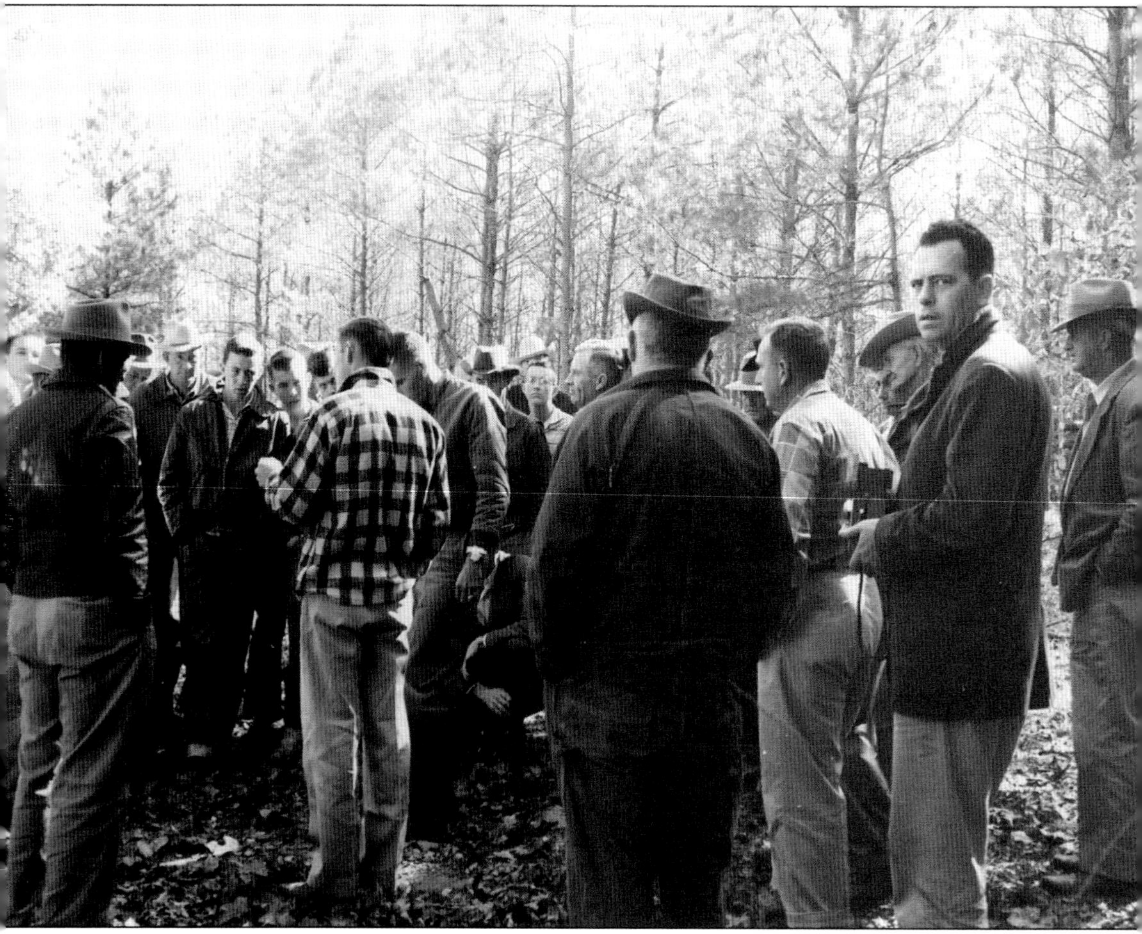

After the hardships of the 1930s, many farmers were open to new ideas about farming. Some even turned their farming interests to forestry production. Seen here is a 1956 Little River Soil Conservation District field day in which a conservationist gives a pine harvesting and management demonstration to a new group of county foresters. The pine plantation where this demonstration took place was formerly a peanut farm in 1929. (Kenneth Sivard Jr. collection.)

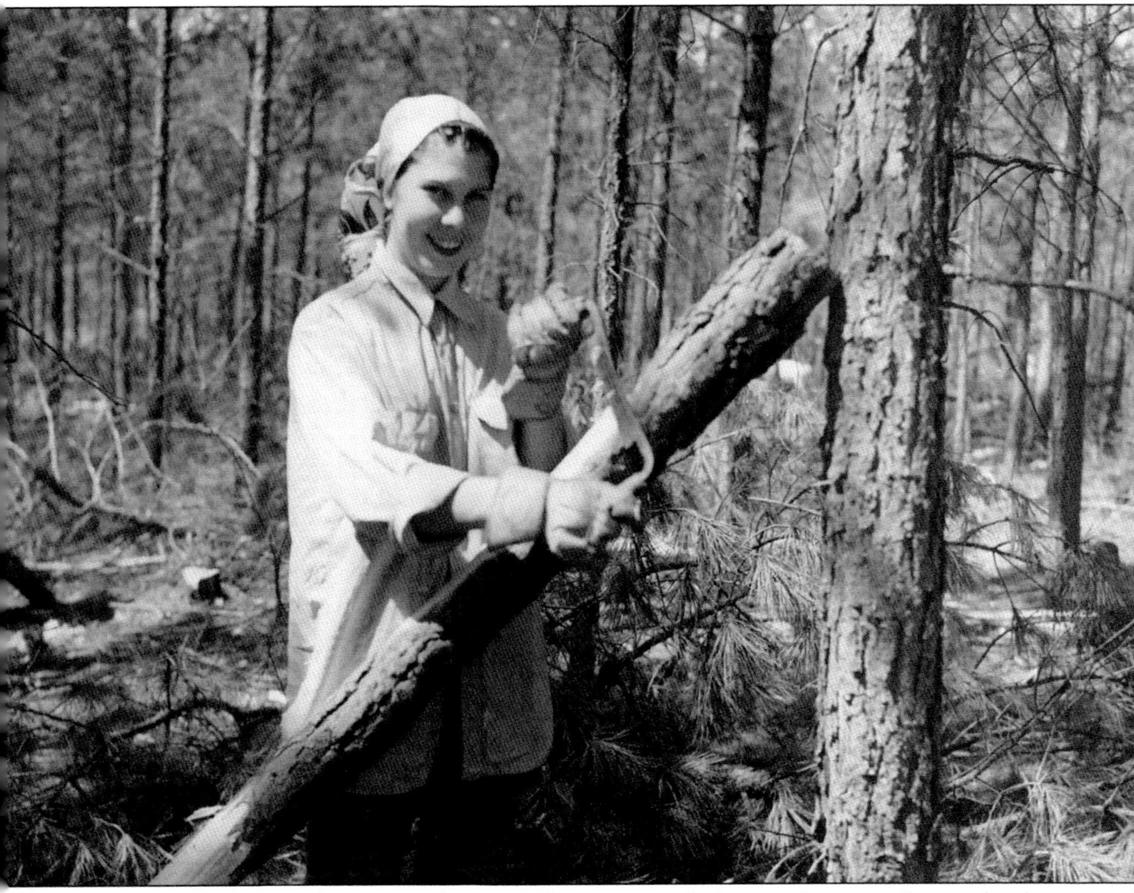

In the 1950s, the private forestry production industry received a boom of interest. Some schools even had school forests so that students could learn about forestry while also making extra money for their school. These schools would often have workdays in which students and parents alike would come to help work the forests; this included thinning some trees out. Here Betty Fairless is seen peeling a post thinned from the Beach Brushy Ridge school forest in 1956. (Kenneth Sivard Jr. collection.)

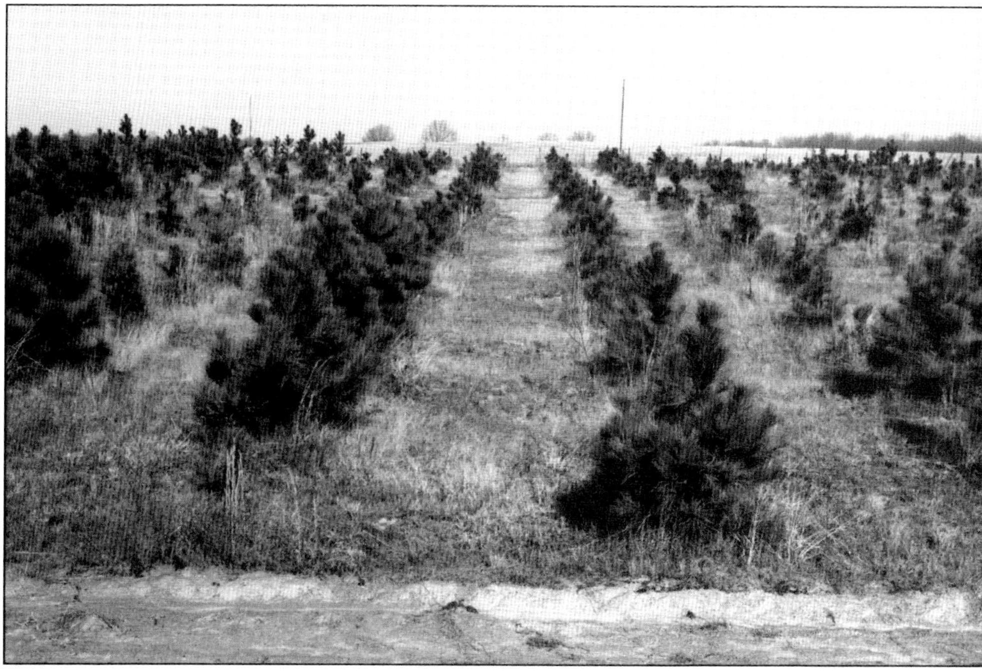

A young pine plantation near the Kulli Tuklo area is pictured in 1971. Today, there is still much timber produced in this area. (Kenneth Sivard Jr. collection.)

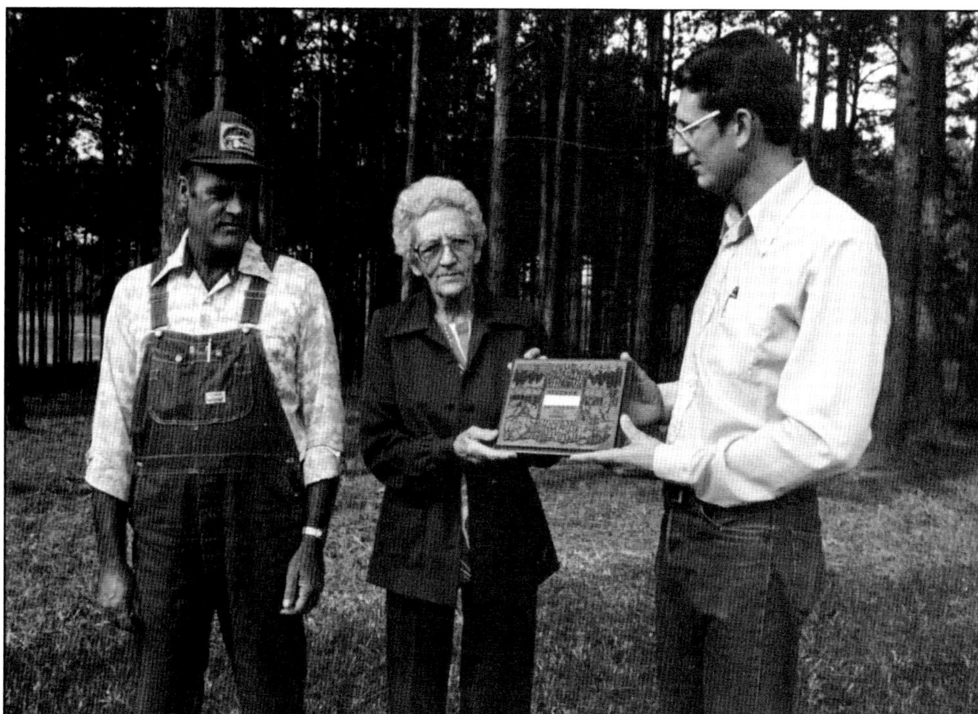

McCurtain County has led the way in the forestry industry in Oklahoma. Here, Ed Hurliman awards Mrs. R.V. Coffman the 1981 Oklahoma Tree Farmer of the Year Award as Von Coffman looks on. (Kenneth Sivard Jr. collection.)

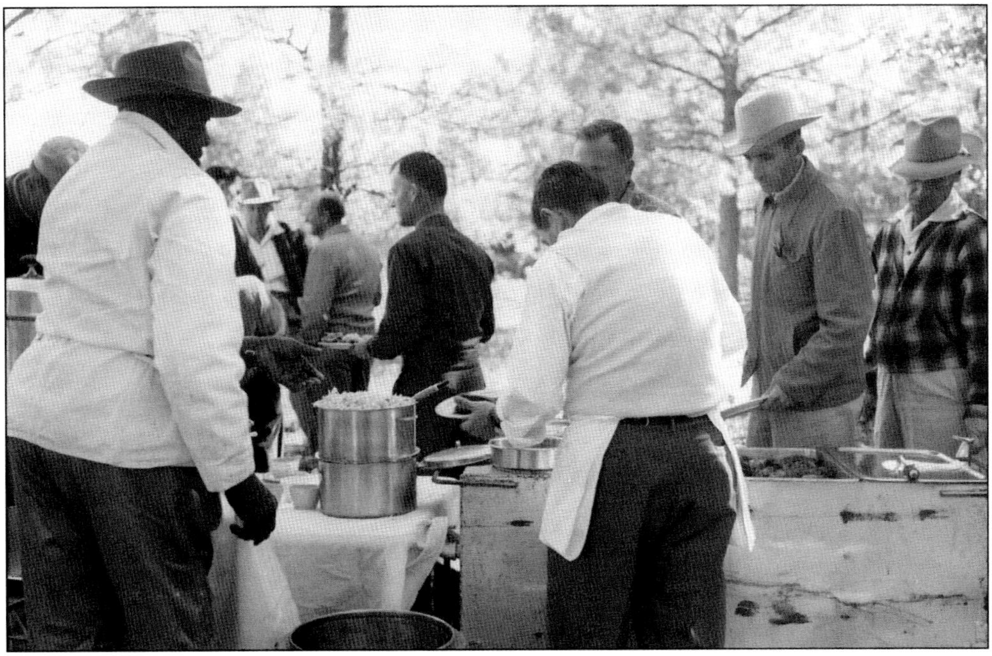

This is a forest field day hosted by International Paper Company in November 1956, where attendees enjoyed a lunch of steak, chick, and pie. These field days helped to nurture the valuable timber industry of McCurtain County that has employed countless people over the years. (Kenneth Sivard Jr. collection.)

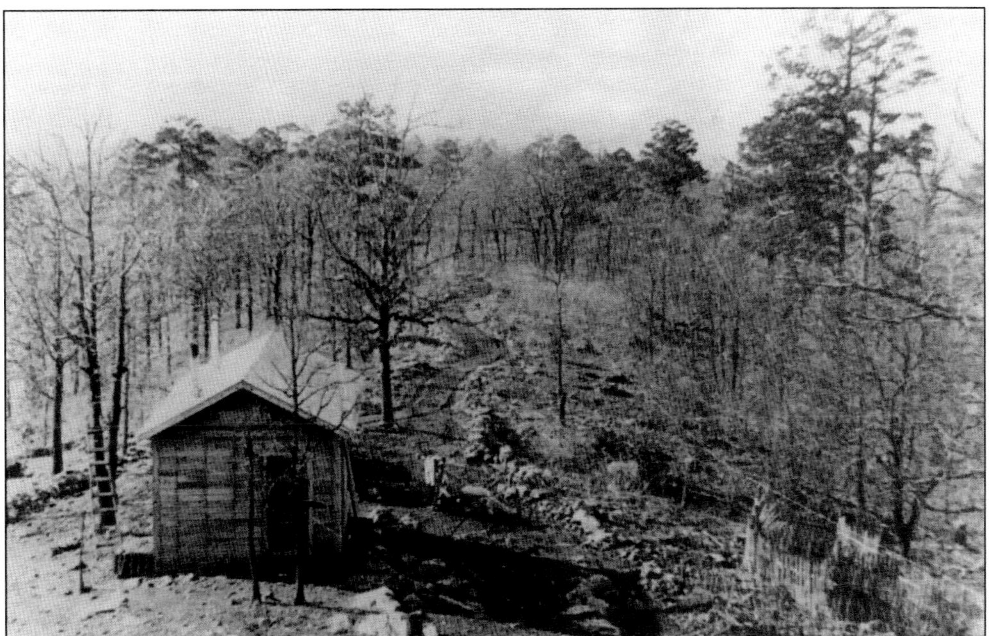

Fire watchtowers are valuable assets to the McCurtain County timber industry. Over the years, these watchtowers have saved an unimaginable amount of forestry materials and lands from destruction. Here is an 1940s bird's-eye view of the caretaker's cabin at the Carter Mountain watchtower. (Kenneth Sivard Jr. collection.)

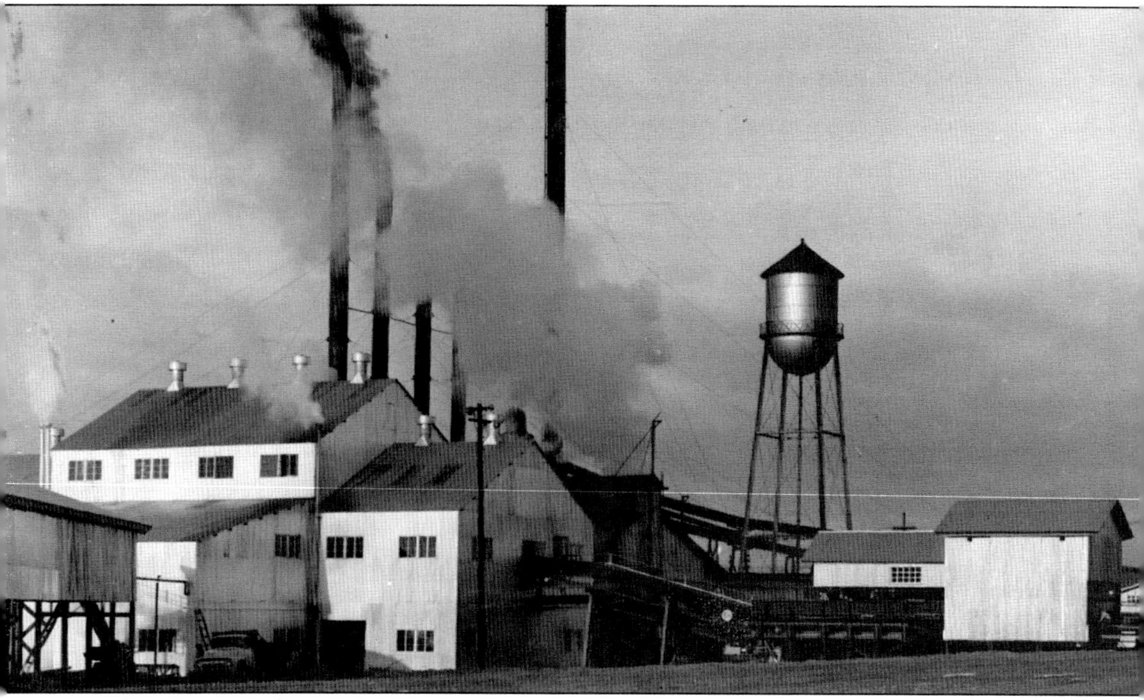

There has never been a shortage of outlets for timber in McCurtain County. The Dierks brothers established mills in Broken Bow and Wright City in 1910. Later they opened one in Garvin, which also had a privately owned sawmill. There have also been large-scale milling operations at Eagletown, Bok Homma, Millerton, America, and Kulli Tuklo. Pictured is the Wright City Mill, which ran for 99 years before closing in 2009. (Kenneth Sivard Jr. collection.)

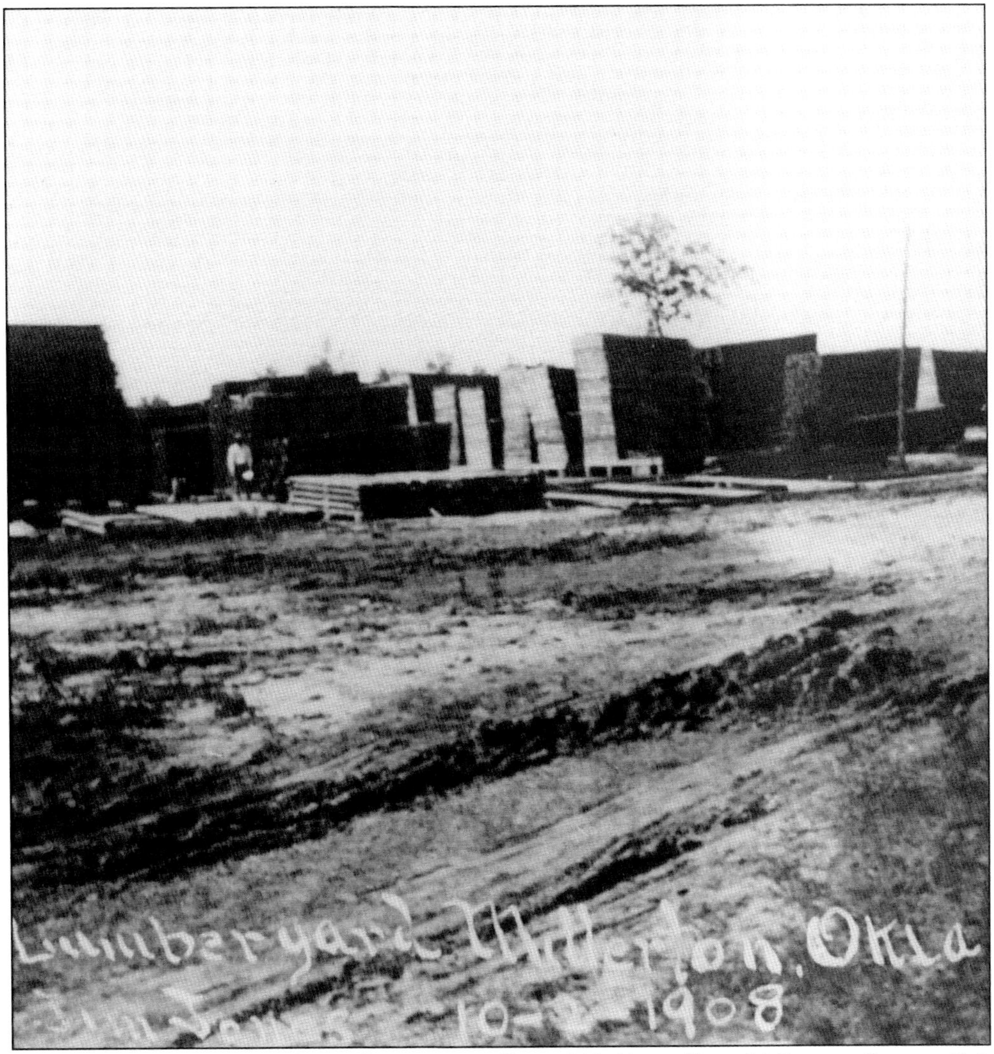

Here is the lumberyard at the Millerton sawmill in 1908. Sawmills at Millerton, Garvin, Bok Homma, America, and Kulli Tuklo shut down in the 1930s due partially to the financial strains of the Great Depression and also to the fact that once the virgin forests of the county were harvested they were not often replanted, which led to a shortage of raw materials. (Kenneth Sivard Jr. collection.)

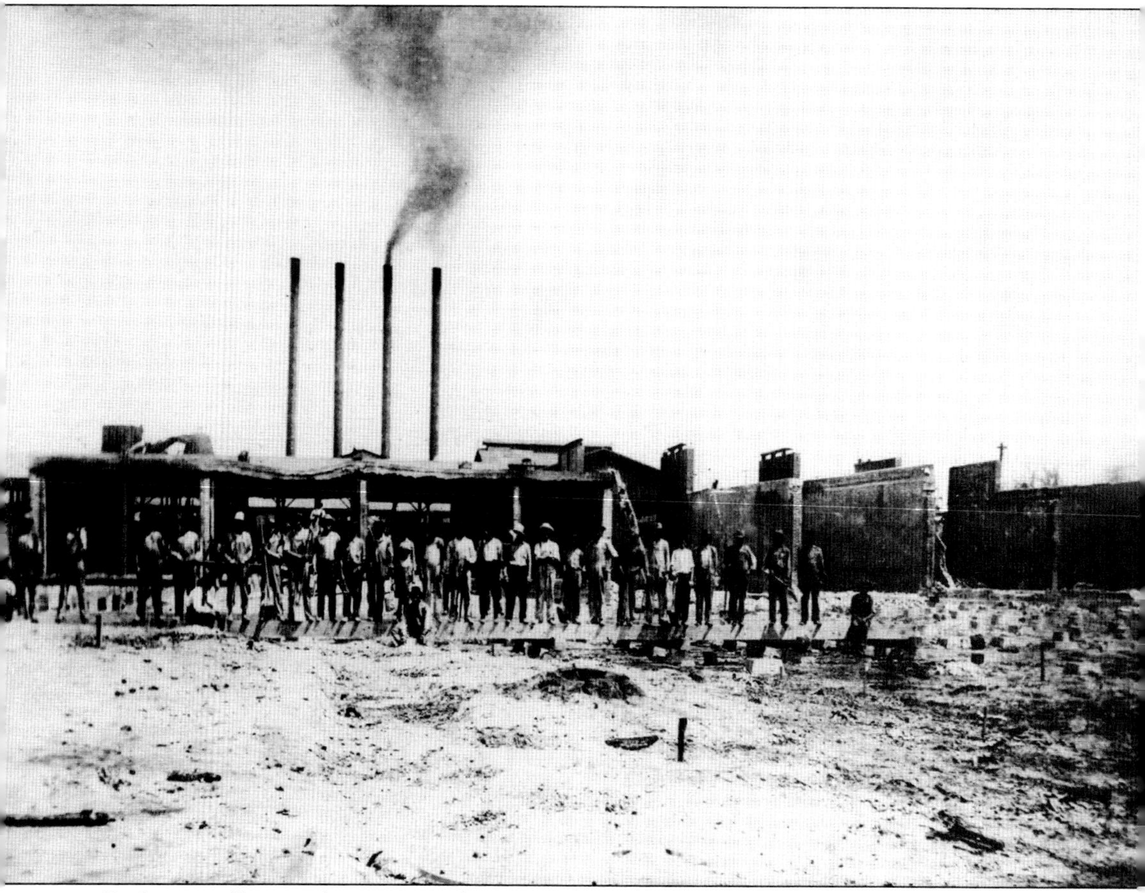

Early sawmills were dangerous and unsafe. It was not uncommon to have at least one death a year, and employee injuries were a weekly occurrence. There were no safety guards on machines or safety officers to enforce mill safety. The county's early sawmills were mostly made from wood, which made them susceptible to fire. Here is a group of men rebuilding the Wright City planer mill after a fire destroyed it in 1916. (Kenneth Sivard Jr. collection.)

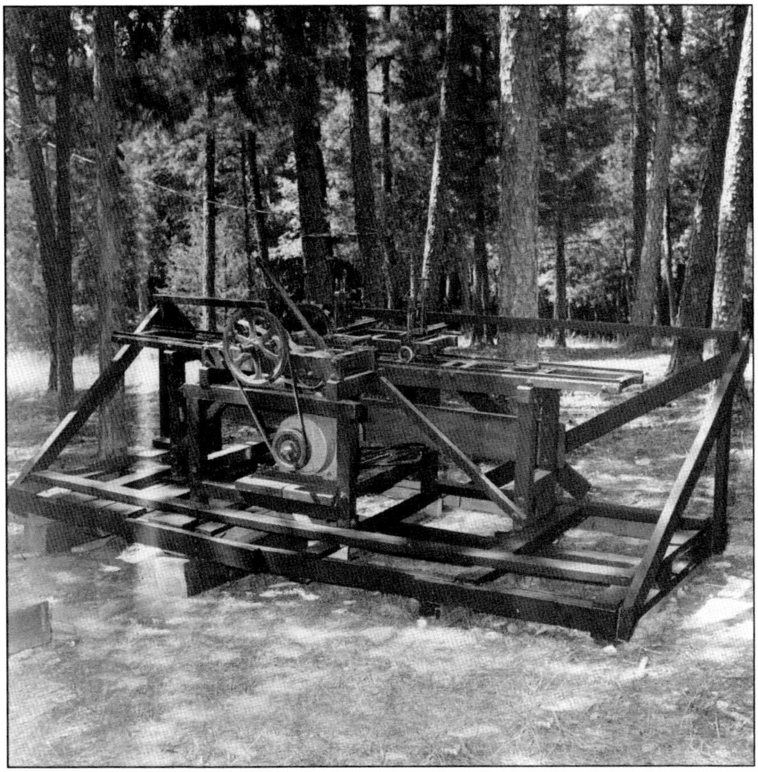

Along with the big industrial sawmills in McCurtain County, there were also many privately owned sawmills where the owner and family might saw small logs for sale or personal use. Here is one such mill in the 1970s. (Kenneth Sivard Jr. collection.)

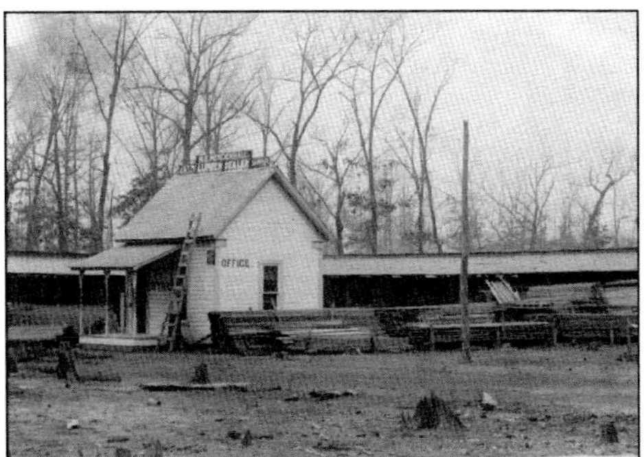

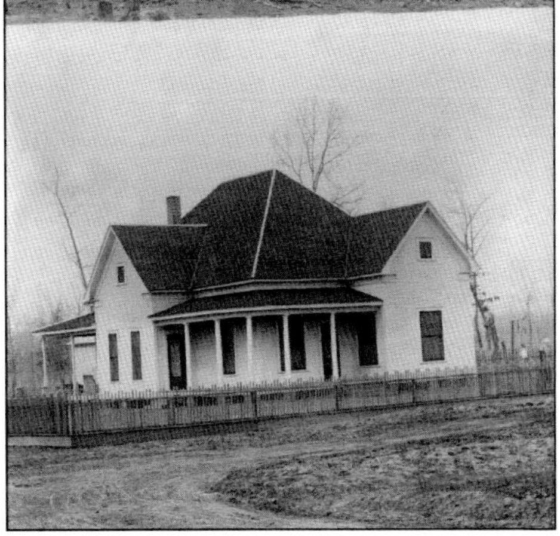

With the early-day growth of the county after statehood, along with the abundance of lumber, lumberyards and homes began to pop up; the Mendenhall family home in Idabel is seen on this 1910 postcard. (Kenneth Sivard Jr. collection.)

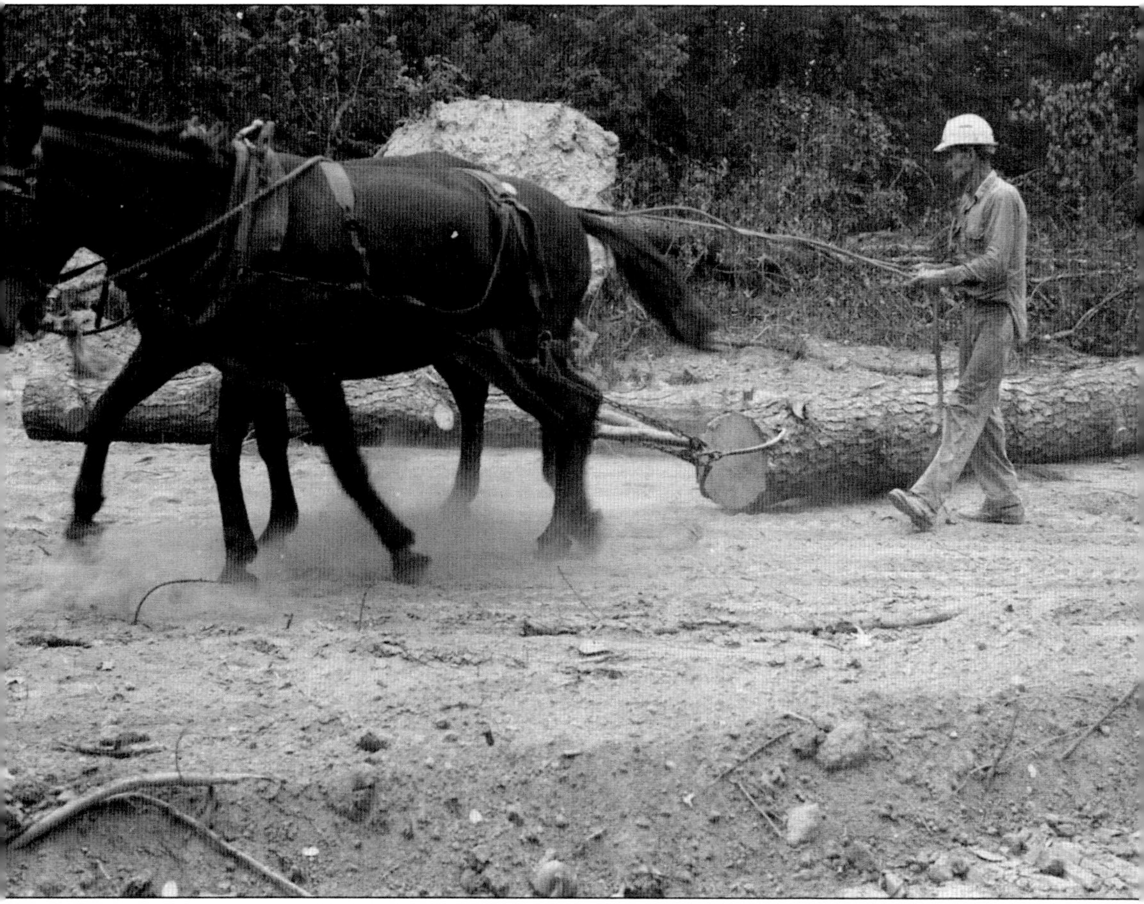

An important part of the timber industry is transporting raw materials to the mills to be processed. In the early days, mules and horses were used to skid logs from the fall site to the loading site where a team of mules, horses, or oxen would then make the long haul over the rough terrain to the mills. Nickey Lambeth is seen using a team of mules to skid a log near Eagletown in the late 1970s. (Kenneth Sivard Jr. collection.)

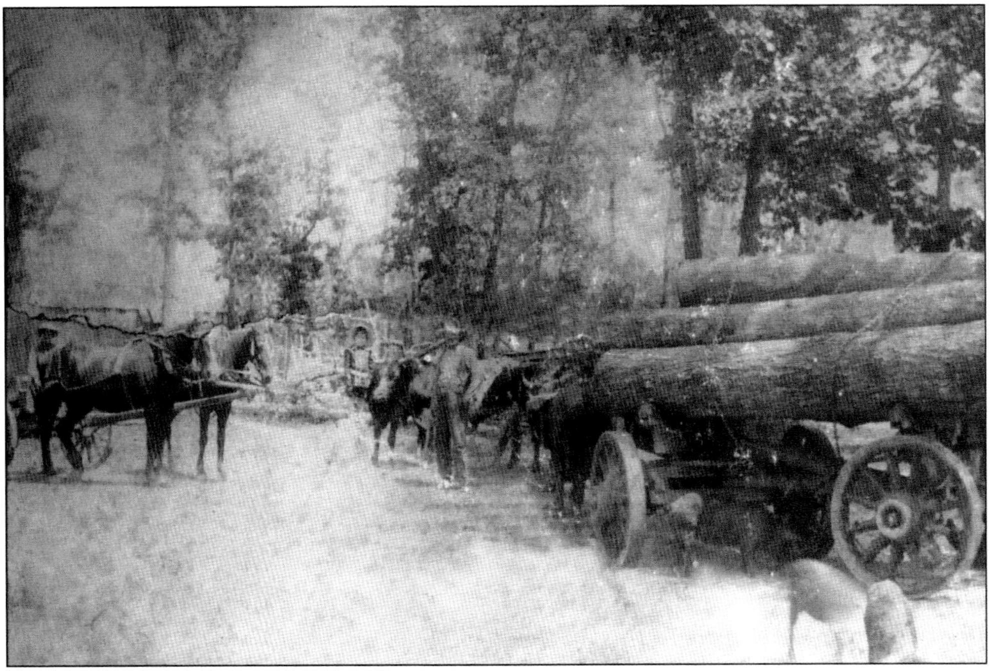

Here a team of oxen hauls a load of logs to the Wright City Mill. Note the pigs in the right foreground. (Kenneth Sivard Jr. collection.)

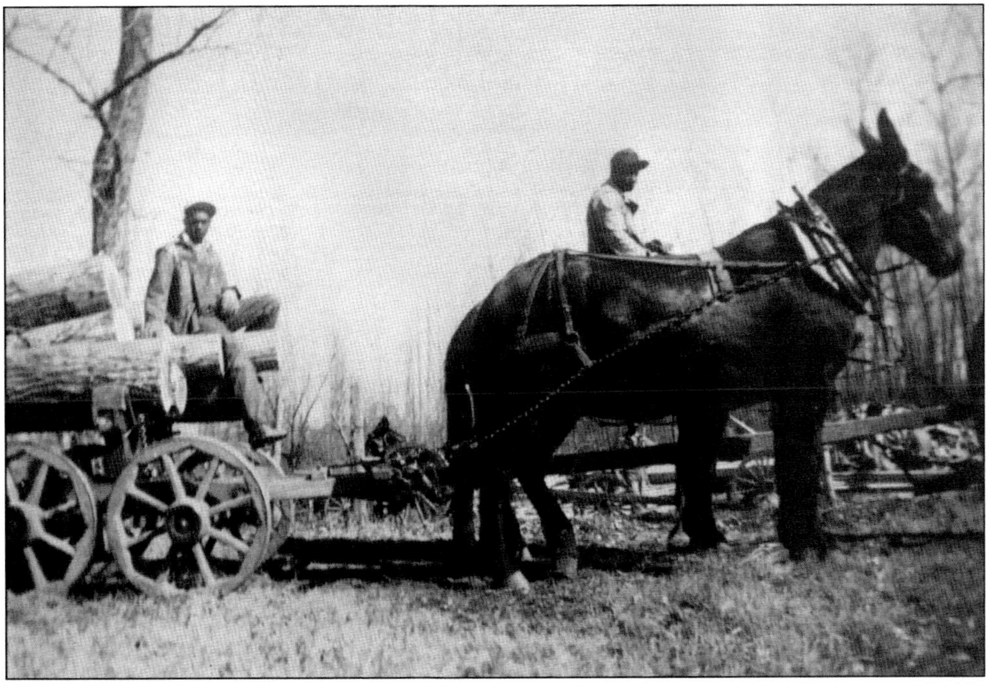

Two men make a log haul using mules in the southern portion of the county. Mules were a valuable part of the workforce in the early timber industry. (Kenneth Sivard Jr. collection.)

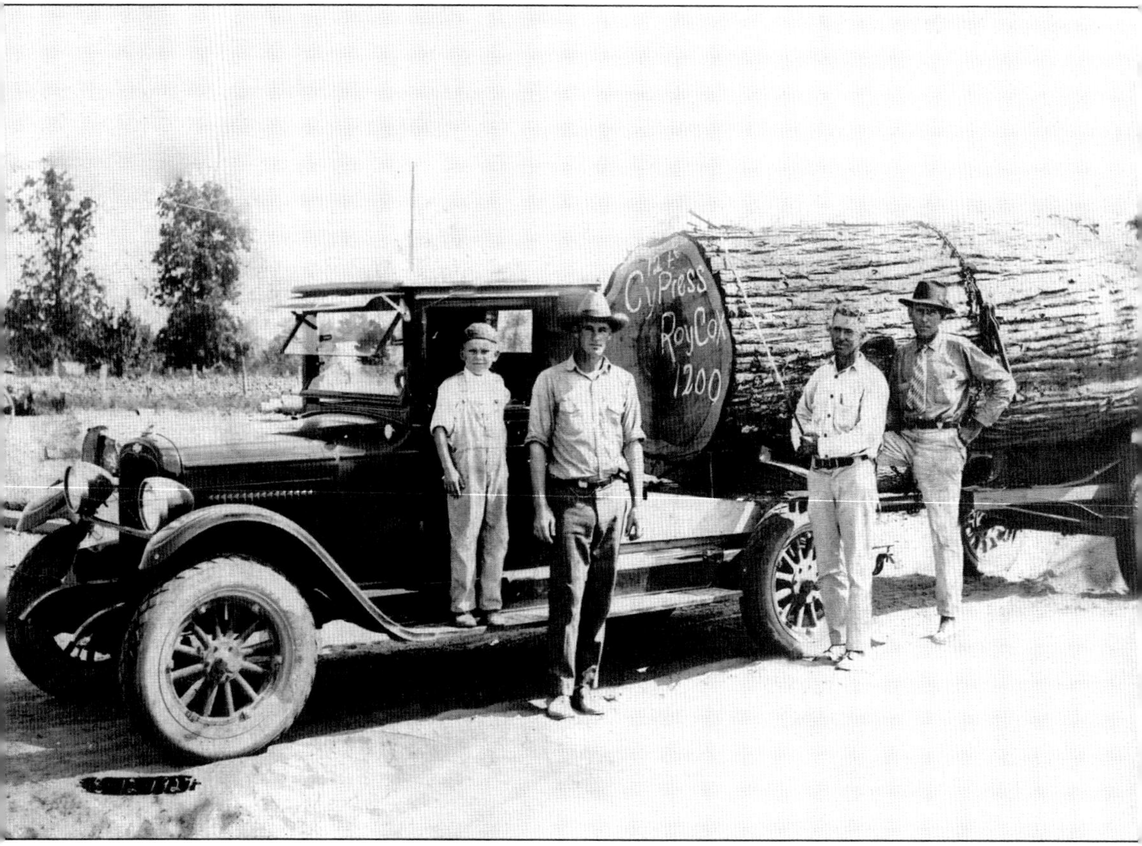

In the 1920s, log trucks helped the evolution of the county's timber industry. Even though roads were long and rough—sometimes even impassable—they still made the job of getting timber to the mills much easier. Here is a fallen 12-foot cypress log in August 1927 being hauled by a Chevrolet truck. (Kenneth Sivard Jr. collection.)

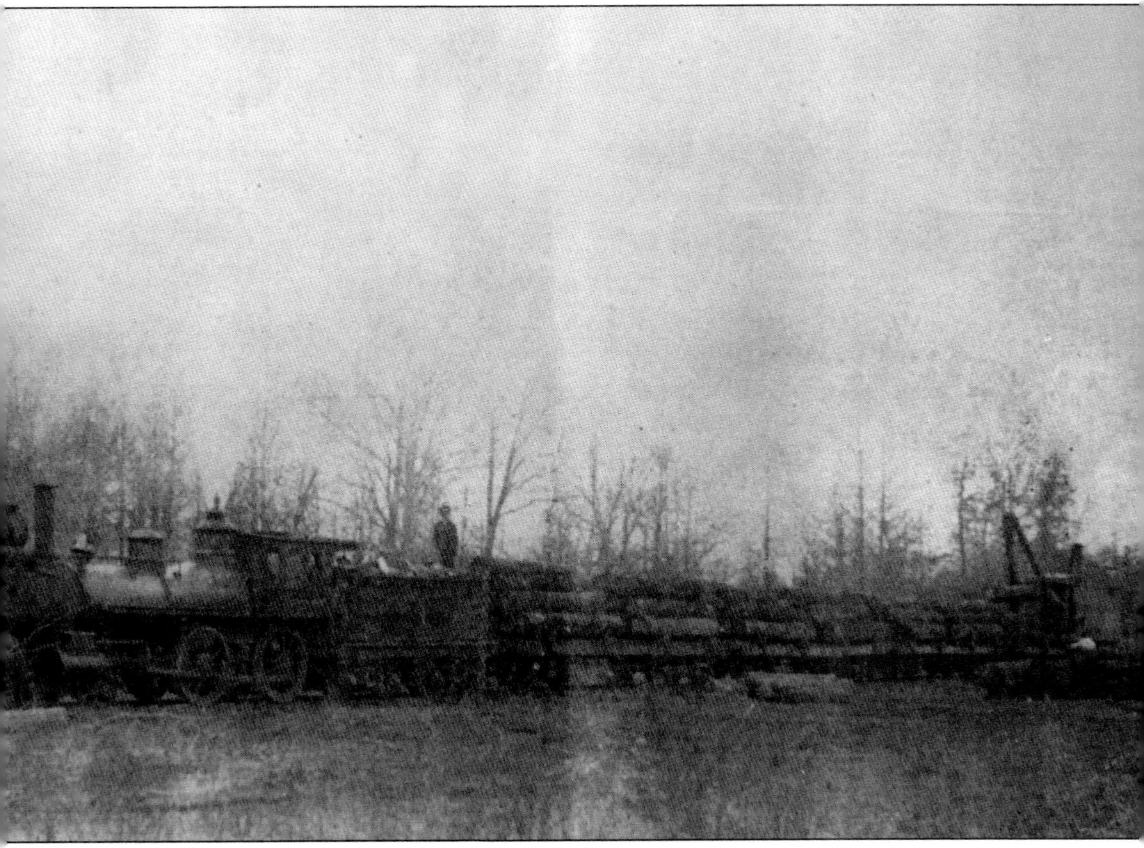

Ever since the Frisco Railroad was completed in 1902, logs were hauled using train power. The Dierks Brothers made the most use out of this form of transportation, building railroad spurs to its logging sites beginning in 1910. This is a Choctaw Lumber Company (which was owned by the Dierks Brothers) log train hauling timber to the company's sawmill in Garvin. (Kenneth Sivard Jr. collection.)

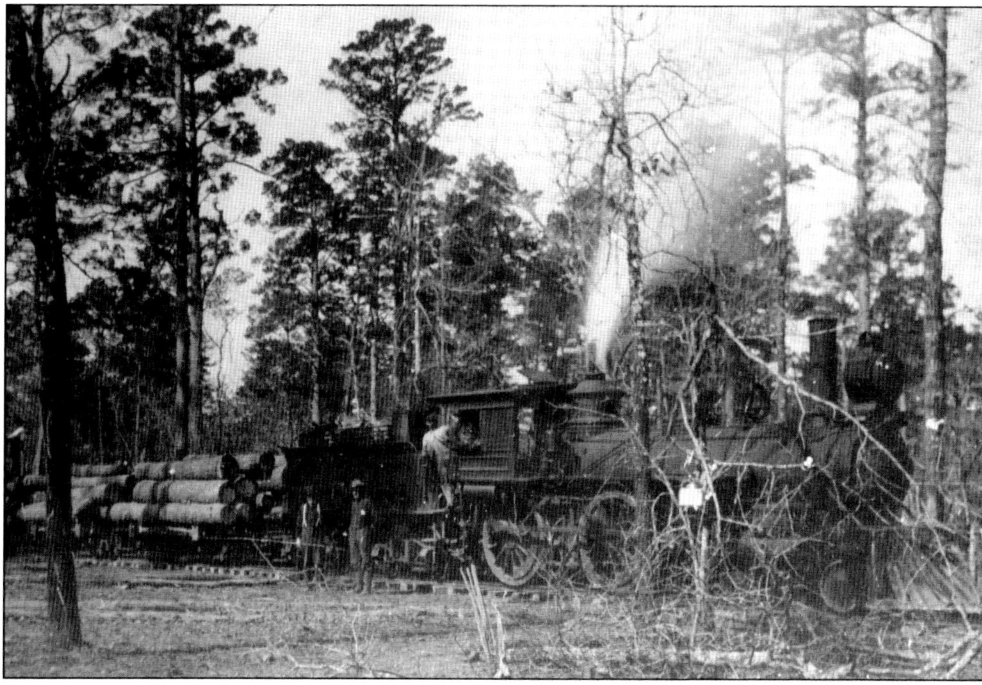

Here is a train loaded with logs making a delivery from the logging site to a mill in Bok Homma in 1906. Trains made it possible to deliver more materials much faster than by ox, horse, or mule. (Kenneth Sivard Jr. collection.)

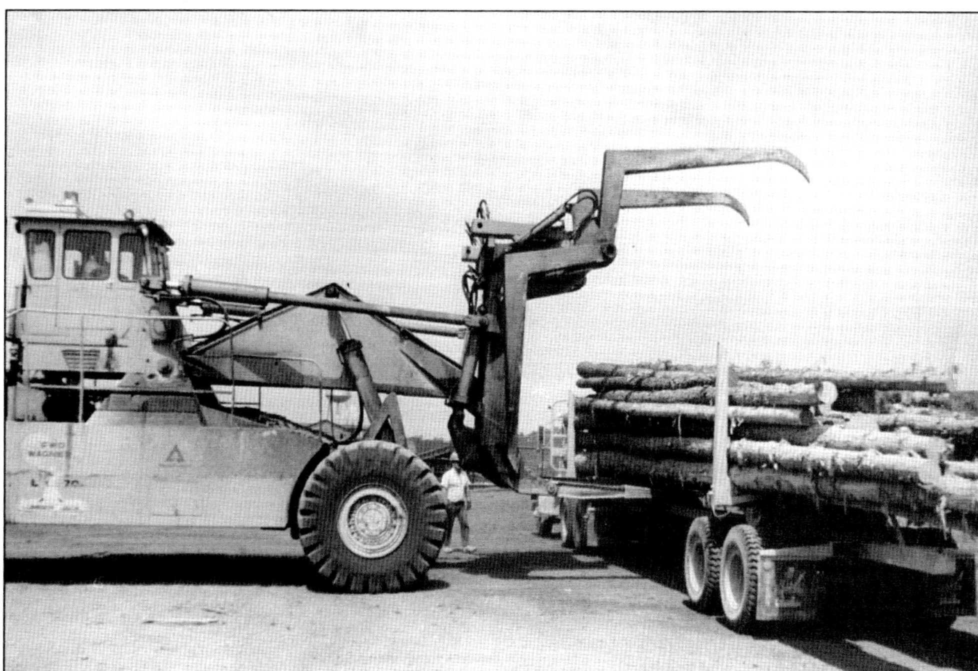

Another aspect getting the raw materials to the mills was the issue of unloading. Seen here is a log unloader moving in to take a load of timber off of a truck in the Wright City Mill in the 1970s. (Kenneth Sivard Jr. collection.)

Beginning in the late 1930s, the bulldozer became a valuable piece of equipment at logging sites. The dozers were used for many tasks, including making roads and skidder trails. Pictured is a dozer at work clearing a road near Bethel in the late 1960s. (Kenneth Sivard Jr. collection.)

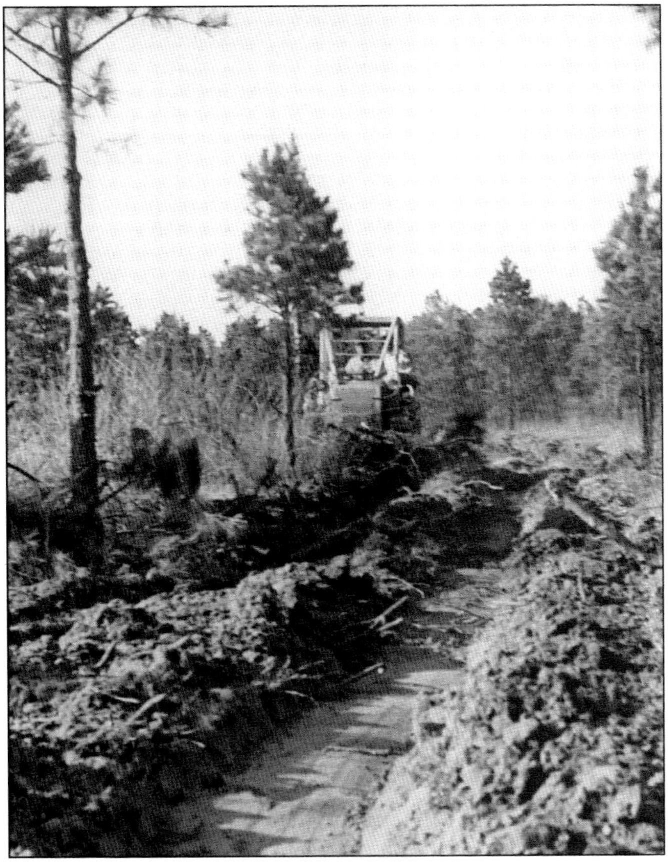

Reforestation became a common conservation practice at most logging sites after the Weyerhaeuser Corporation purchased all of the Dierks Brothers forestry land and mills within the county in 1969. (Kenneth Sivard Jr. collection.)

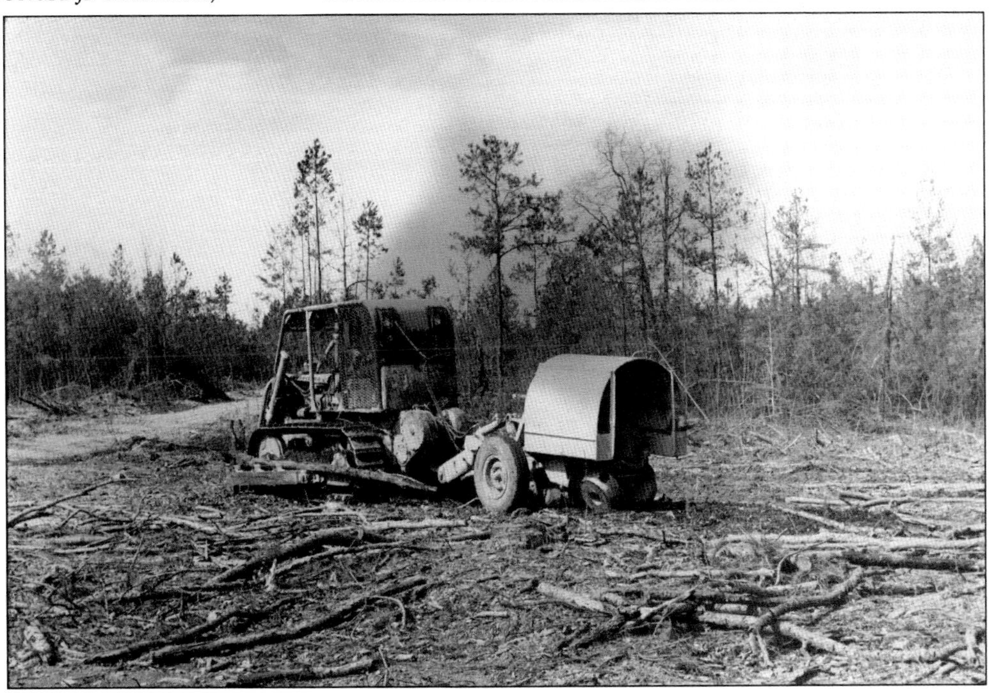

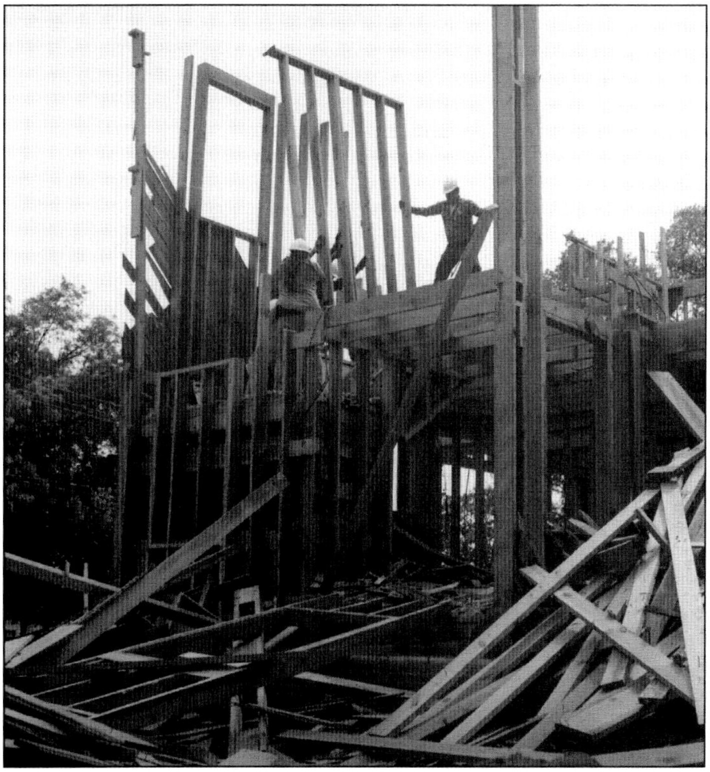

After the Weyerhaeuser Company purchased the Dierks Brothers' holdings in 1969, it began an effort to modernize the mill at Wright City while closing the one at Broken Bow. Here is a scene from the Broken Bow mill's demolition. (Kenneth Sivard Jr. collection.)

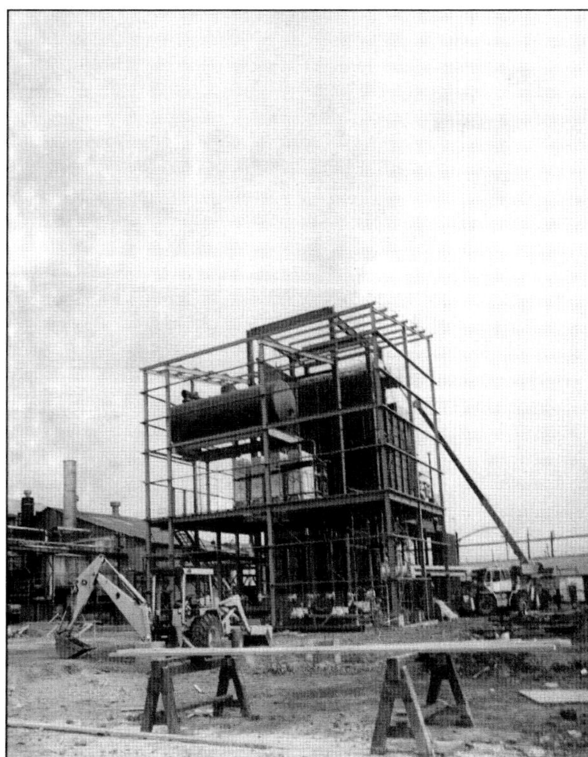

As the modernization of the Wright City mill began, metal structures began to replace wooden ones, some of which were nearly 50 years old. This is a construction project at the mill in the 1970s. (Kenneth Sivard Jr. collection.)

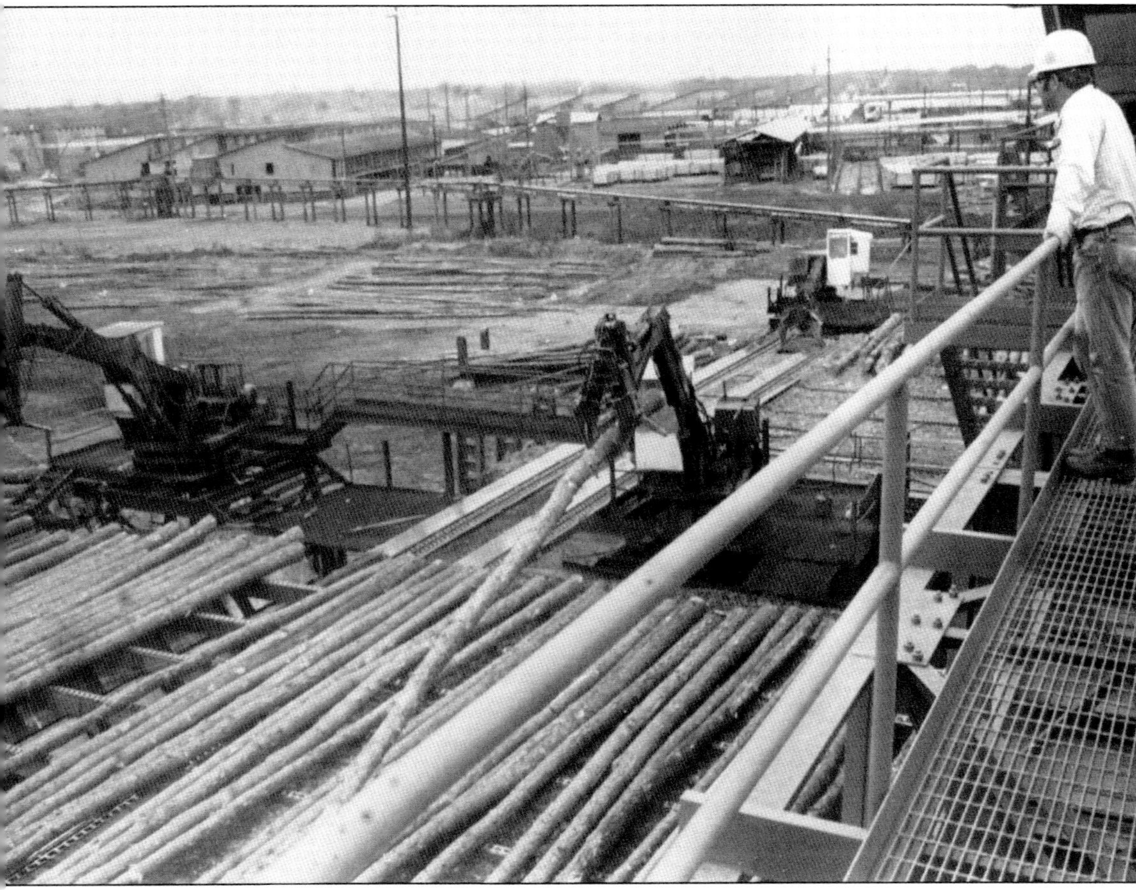

Modern machinery meant that the employees at the Wright City mill were now safer than ever. Jobs that once took manpower and physical force could be completed using machines, which took people out of harm's way. Here are logs being fed into the mill as two knuckle booms straighten cross-ups, or crooked logs. (Kenneth Sivard Jr. collection.)

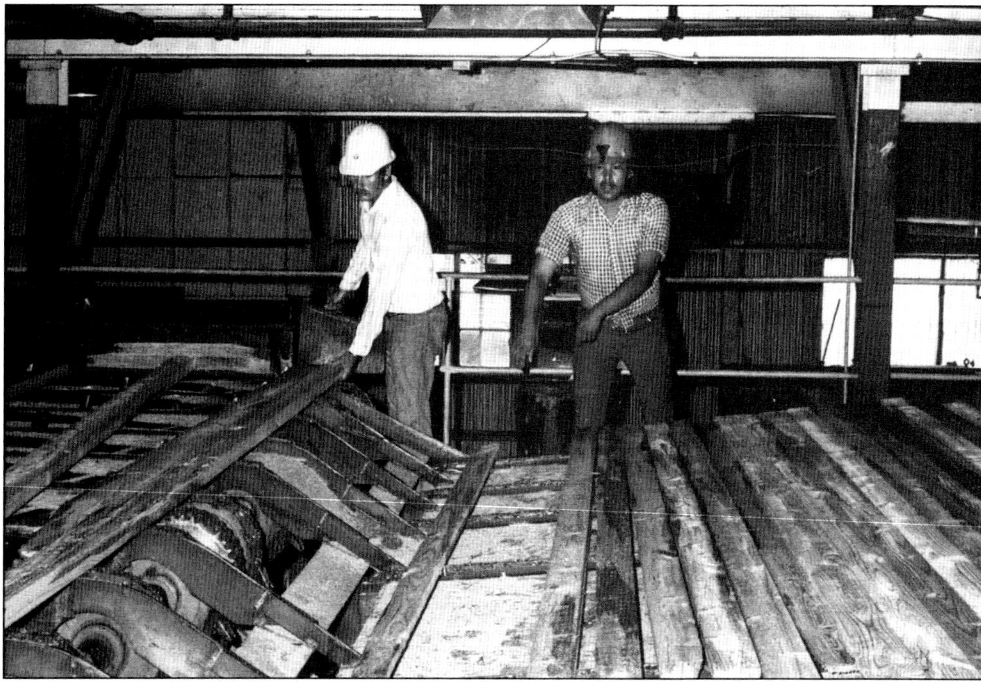

The Wright City mill employed a variety of people to perform a variety of tasks, such as the two men shown here at work at an unscrambler in the mill during the 1970s. (Kenneth Sivard Jr. collection.)

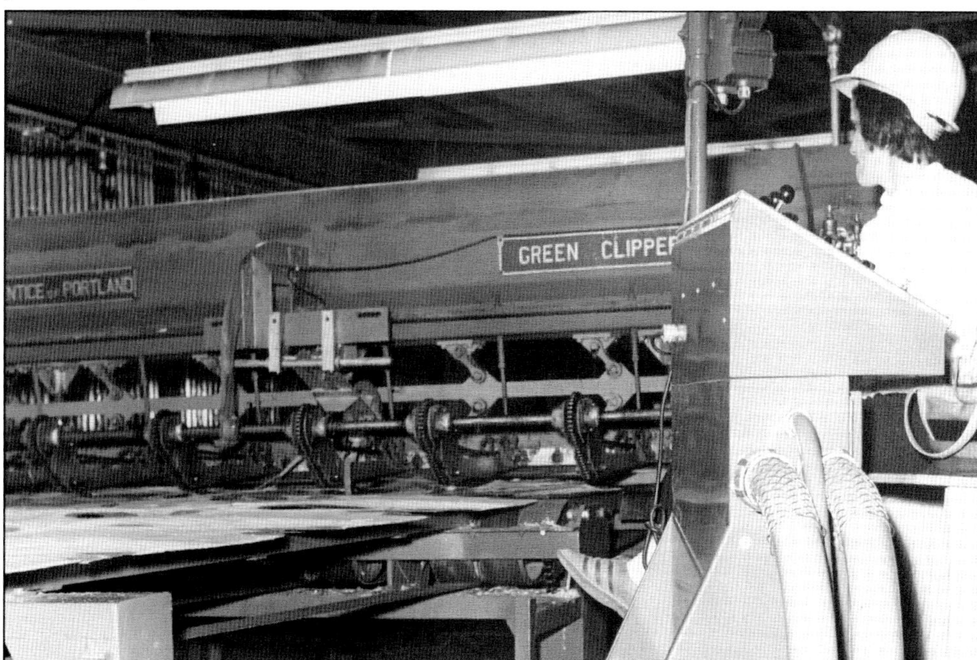

One addition that Weyerhaeuser brought to the Wright City mill was the plywood mill. A woman is seen at work in the mill operating a piece of equipment safely at a control panel. (Kenneth Sivard Jr. collection.)

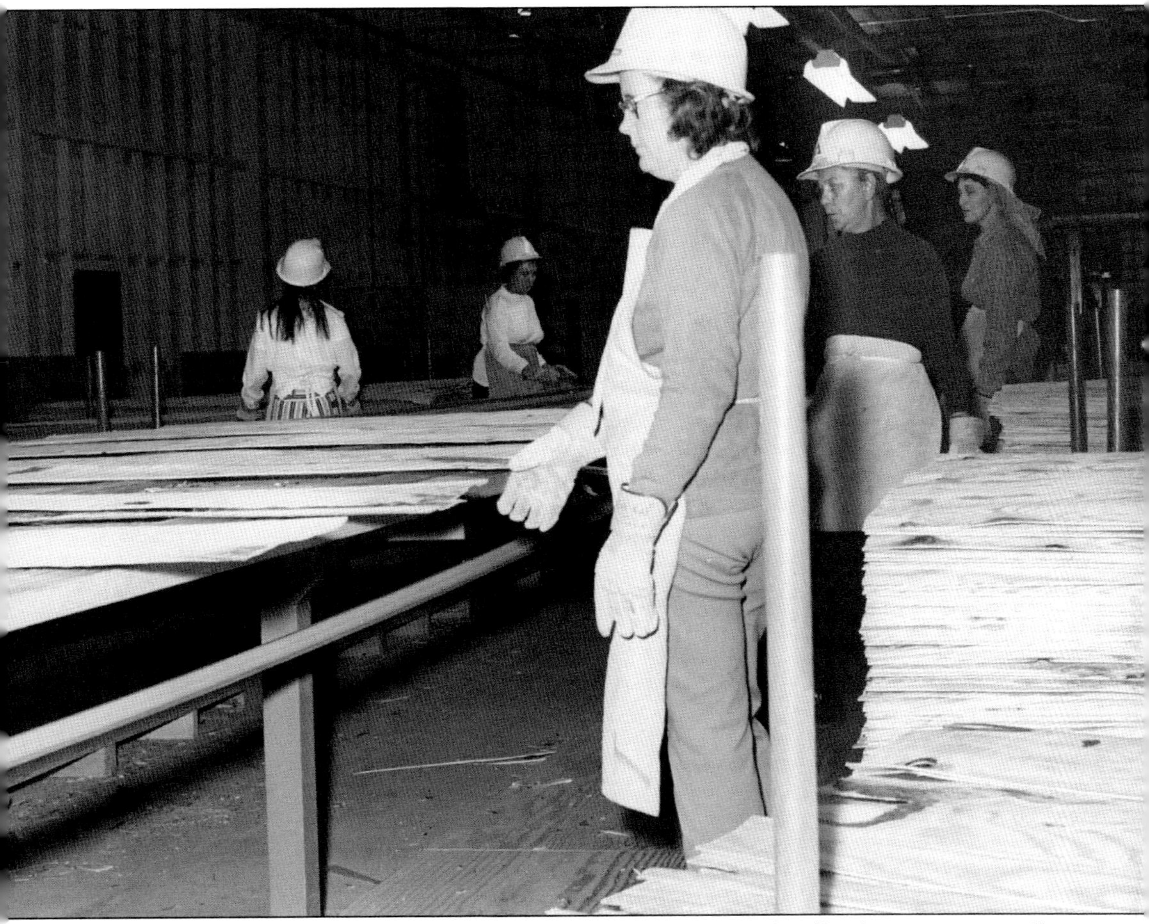

Here a group of women stacks veneer in the Wright City plywood mill. The women are all wearing personal protective equipment, such as leather aprons and leather gloves, to defend against splinters. Safety practices like these cut the job injury rates in the county drastically. (Kenneth Sivard Jr. collection.)

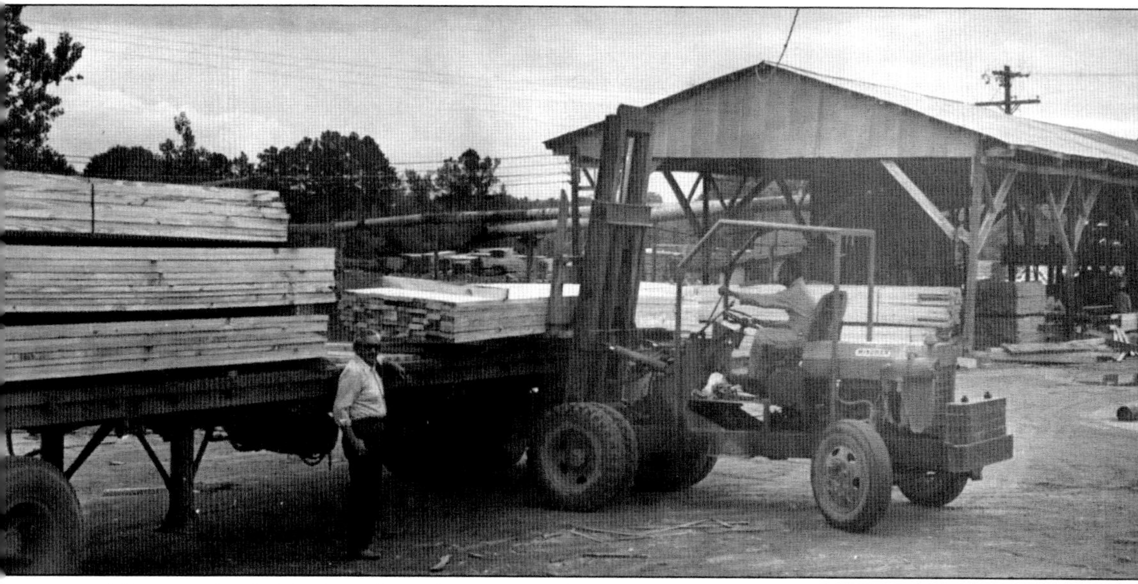

Shipping the finished products from the mill was also an important task that employed people at the mill as well as truck drivers who delivered the lumber all over the nation. Some of the lumber was also shipped out by train. Here an employee loads a flatbed truck full of lumber at the Wright City mill in 1972. (Kenneth Sivard Jr. collection.)

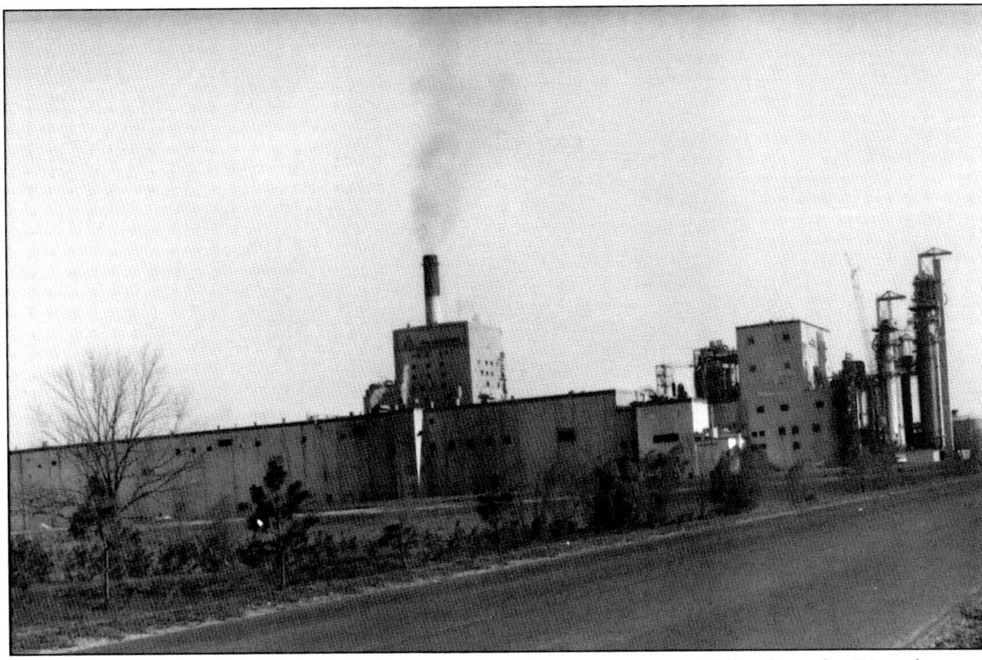

A major development in the economy of McCurtain County came in 1970, when the Weyerhaeuser Company built the Valliant Paper Mill. At the time of its construction, it was the largest paper mill in the world. Here is the mill as it looked the year it began operation. (Kenneth Sivard Jr. collection.)

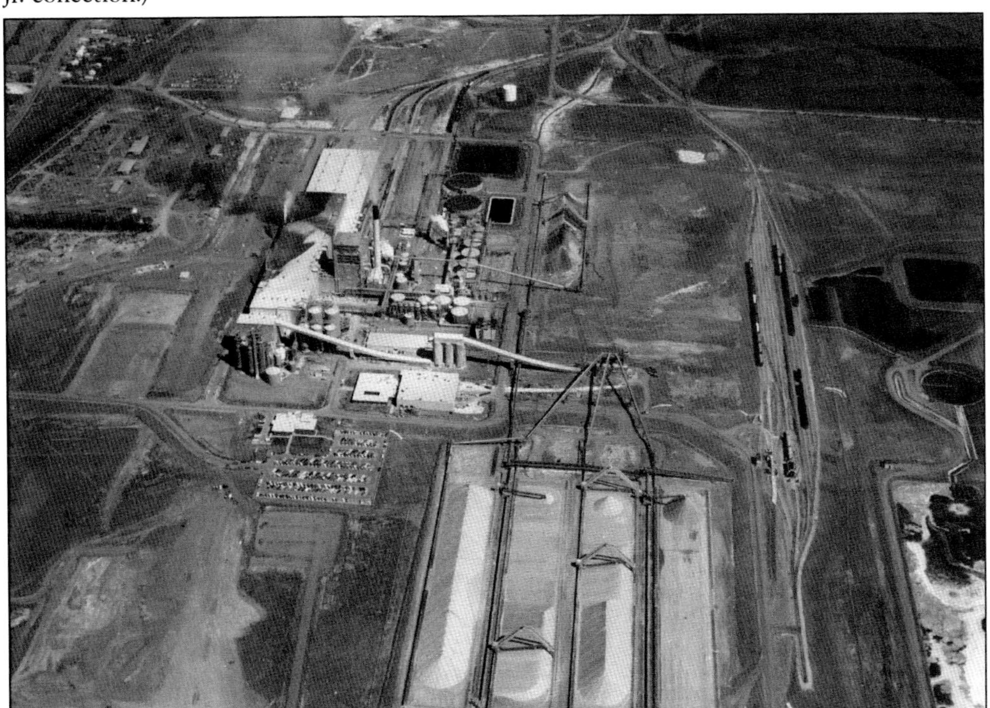

An aerial view of the Valliant Paper Mill is pictured. The mill provided a local outlet for pulp and waste wood materials. (Kenneth Sivard Jr. collection.)

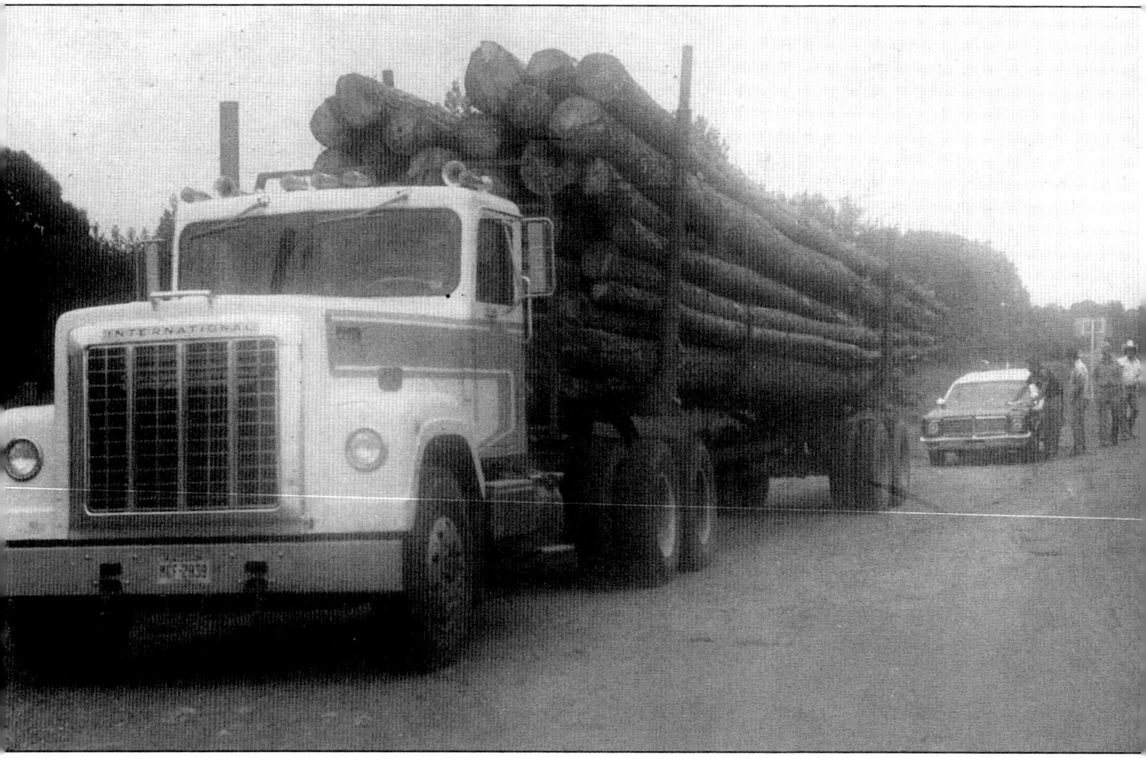

As the forestry industry and roads to the mills improved, new laws began to take effect, such as weight limits and yearly truck inspections. These laws were to make the roads and trucks safer and also reduce the wear and tear on the highways leading to and from the mills. A log truck driver is seen after being pulled over by an Oklahoma Highway patrolman for a weight check in the late 1970s. (Kenneth Sivard Jr. collection.)

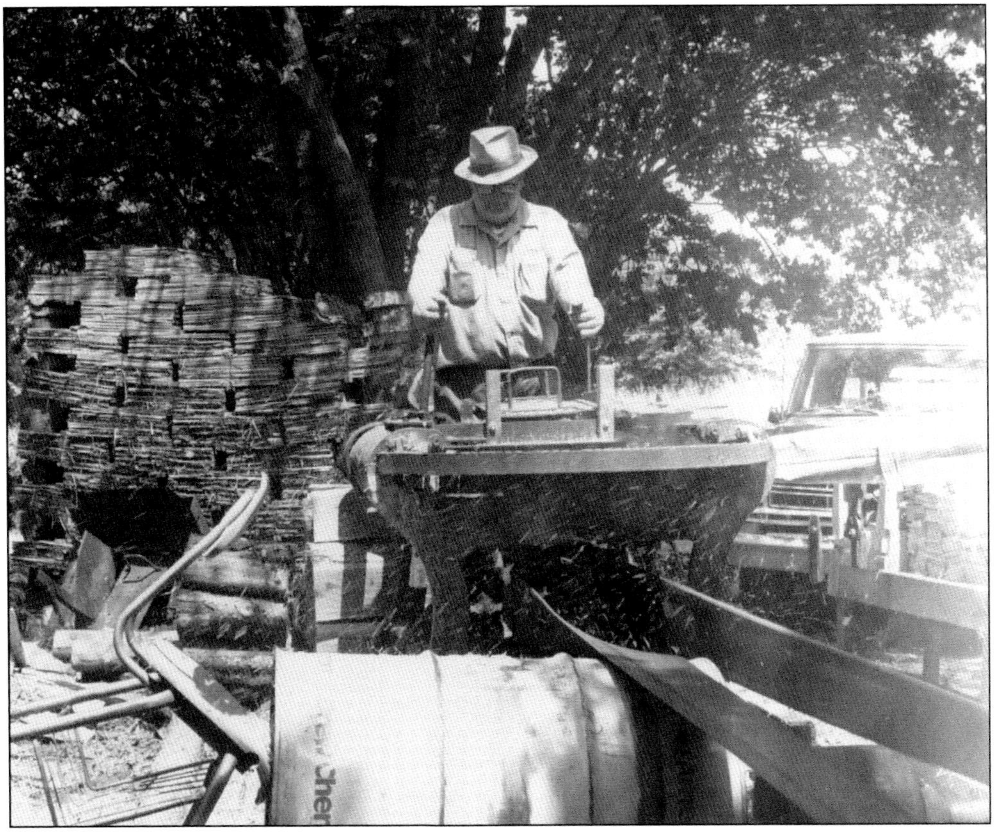

The lumber industry in McCurtain County has been very diverse; everything from plywood to paper has been made here. This is a shingle mill, which was run six miles east of Broken Bow near the Tiner community. (Kenneth Sivard Jr. collection.)

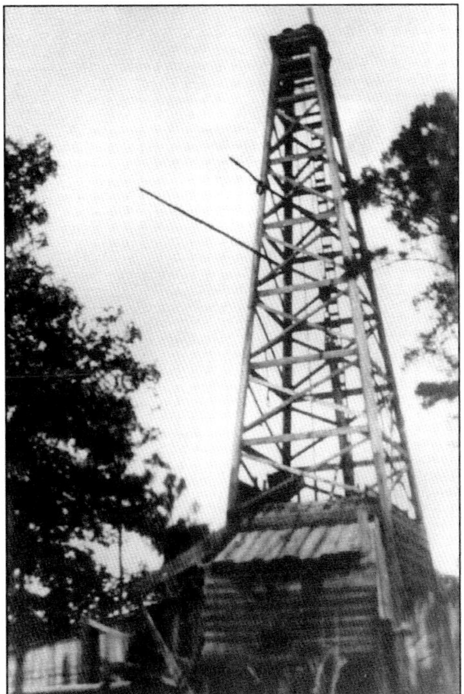

An often overlooked economic venture that has operated in McCurtain County is the oil wells, which were in use at Cisco, Jadie, and Redland in the 1920s. Here is the derrick at Redland in 1927. (Kenneth Sivard Jr. collection.)

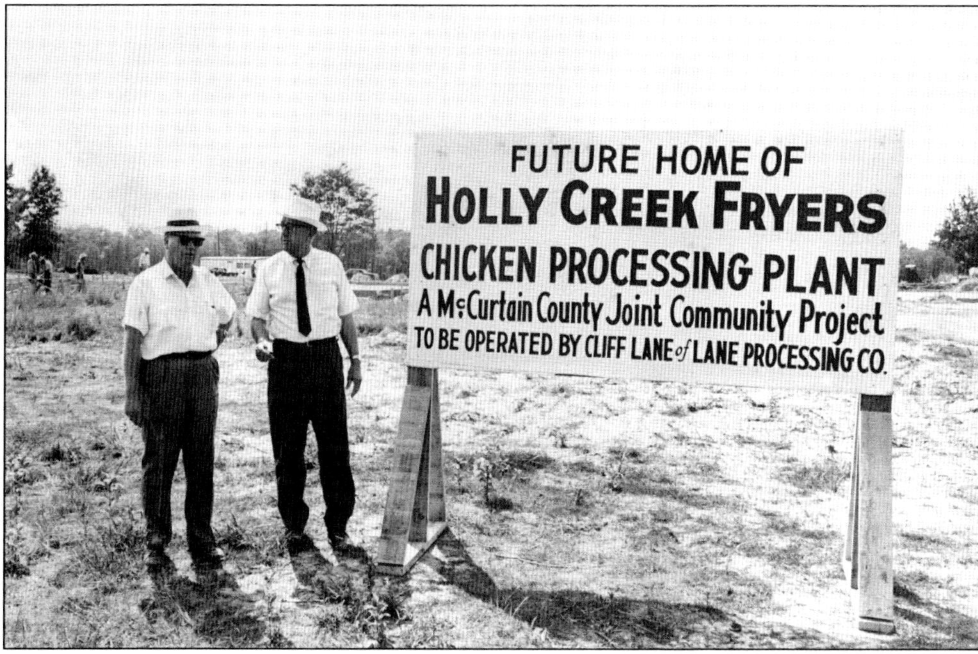

The chicken-processing plant between Broken Bow and Idabel has been a large employer of people in McCurtain County since the 1970s. The mill began as Lane Processing Company before being bought by Tyson Foods. A sign marks the construction site as the plant is being built by construction workers who labor in the background. (Kenneth Sivard Jr. collection.)

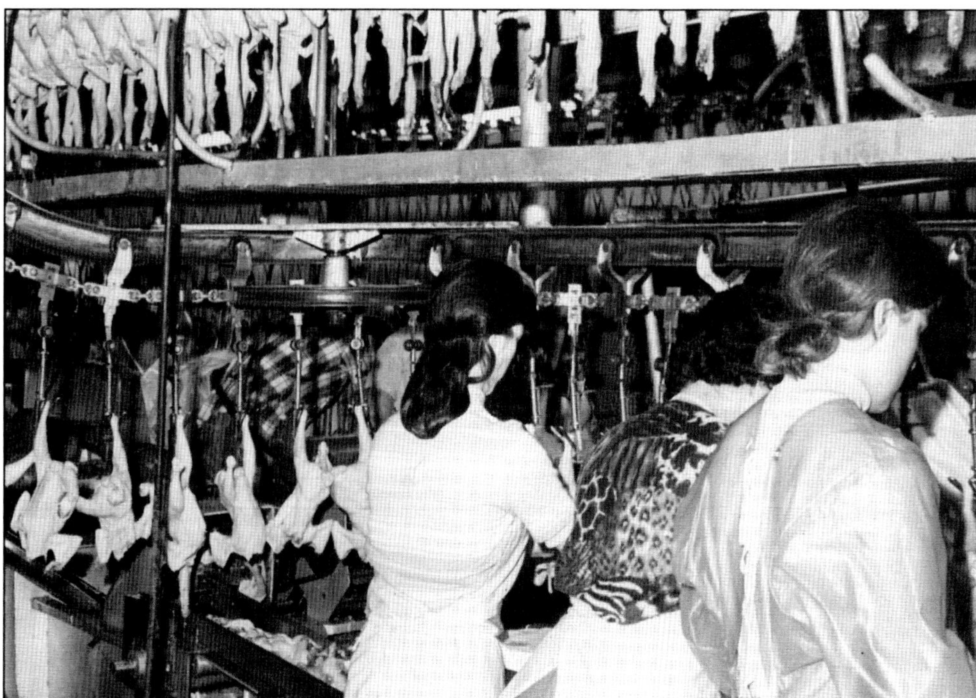

Here is a picture of one of the lines inside of the Lane Processing Plant shortly after it began operation. (Kenneth Sivard Jr. collection.)

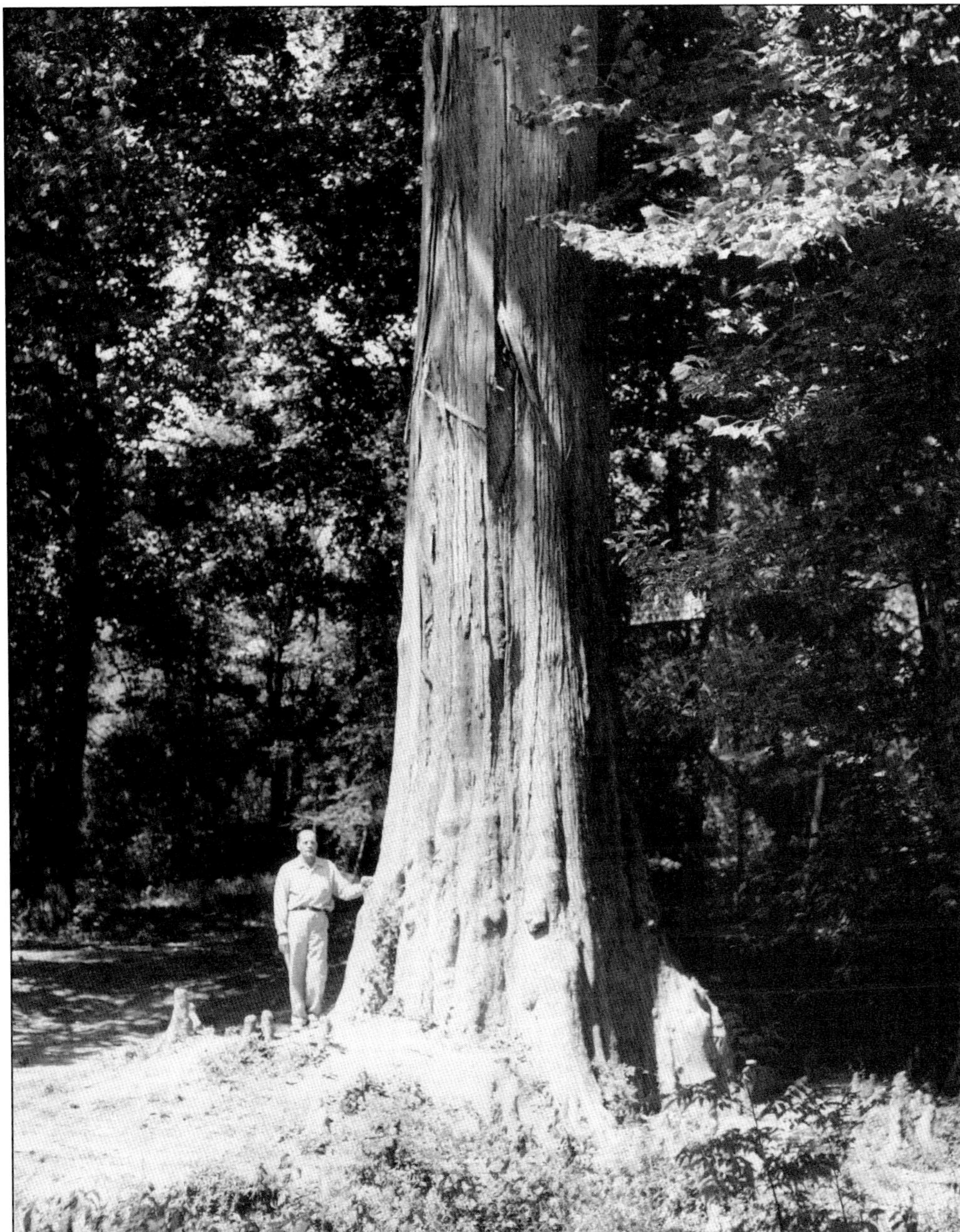

The tourism industry has brought millions of dollars to McCurtain County's economy over the years. Even before statehood, people would travel to the county from Texas to go on guided hunting trips and to camp. This is the "Big Cypress" tree near the original site of Eagletown on the Stiles ranch, six miles east of Broken Bow. This tree was the stopping point for the Choctaws traveling the Trail of Tears in 1831. Coined as the "largest tree east of the Rockies," it was a popular meeting place for family outings, picnics, and photo opportunities. Robert Stiles stands beside the massive tree that was more than 2,000 years old in 1954. It was killed by lightning in the 1980s and fell to the ground in 2007. (Kenneth Sivard Jr. collection.)

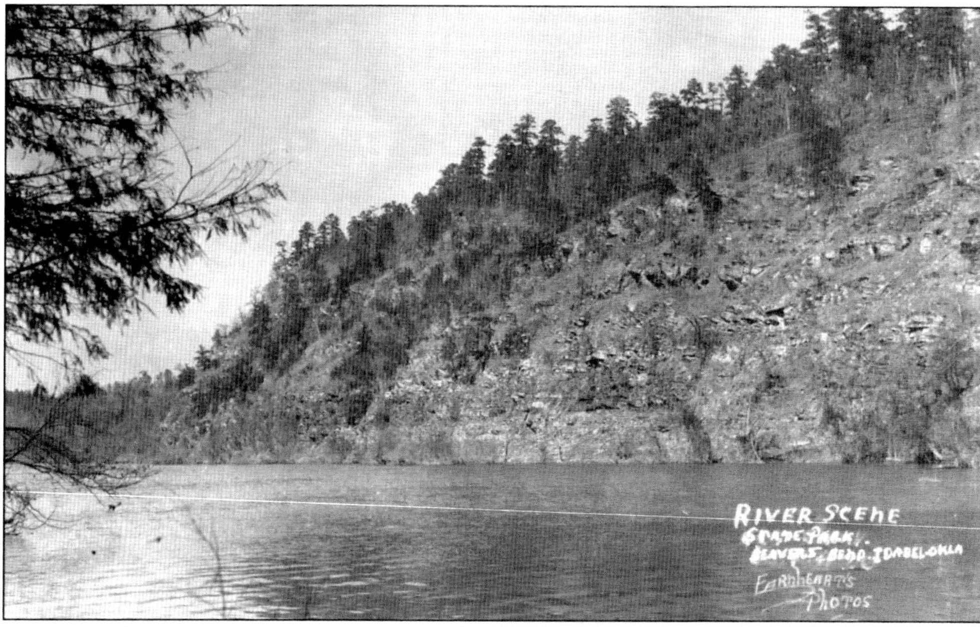

After the Great Depression, Beavers Bend State Park was created near the original site of Hochatown, when Johnny Beavers sold his farm to the state. The park has been a great attraction for countless people who have camped or rented one of the many beautiful cabins offered privately or by the park. This is a scene from the Mountain Fork River where it runs through the park. (Kenneth Sivard Jr. collection.)

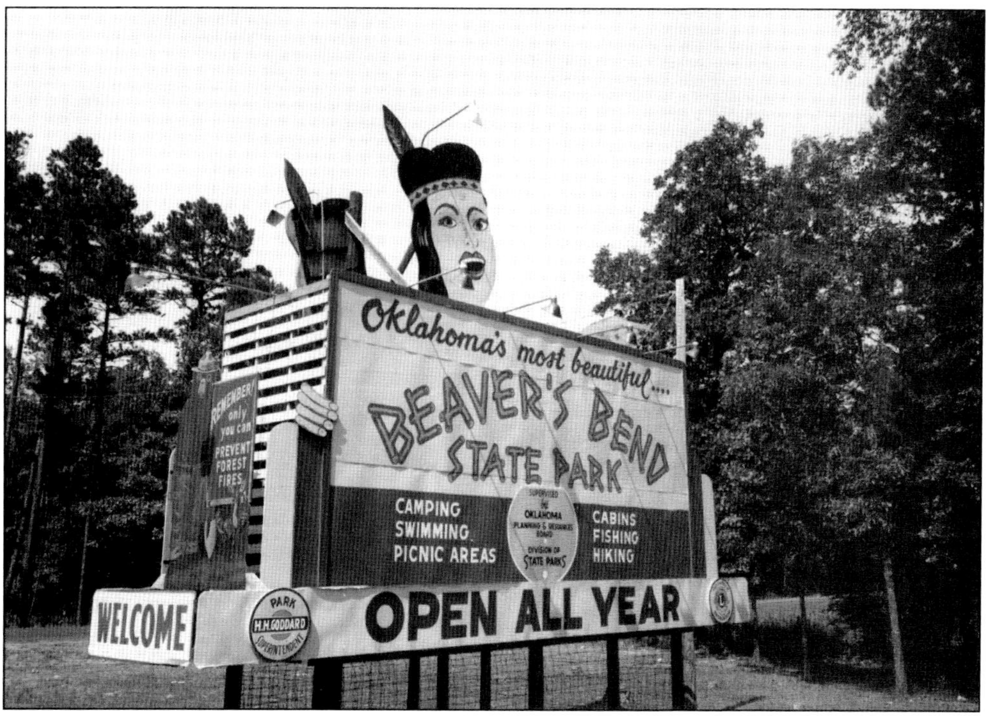

This sign greeted thousands of tourists to Beavers Bend State Park as they turned off of US Highway 259 to enter the park. (Kenneth Sivard Jr. collection.)

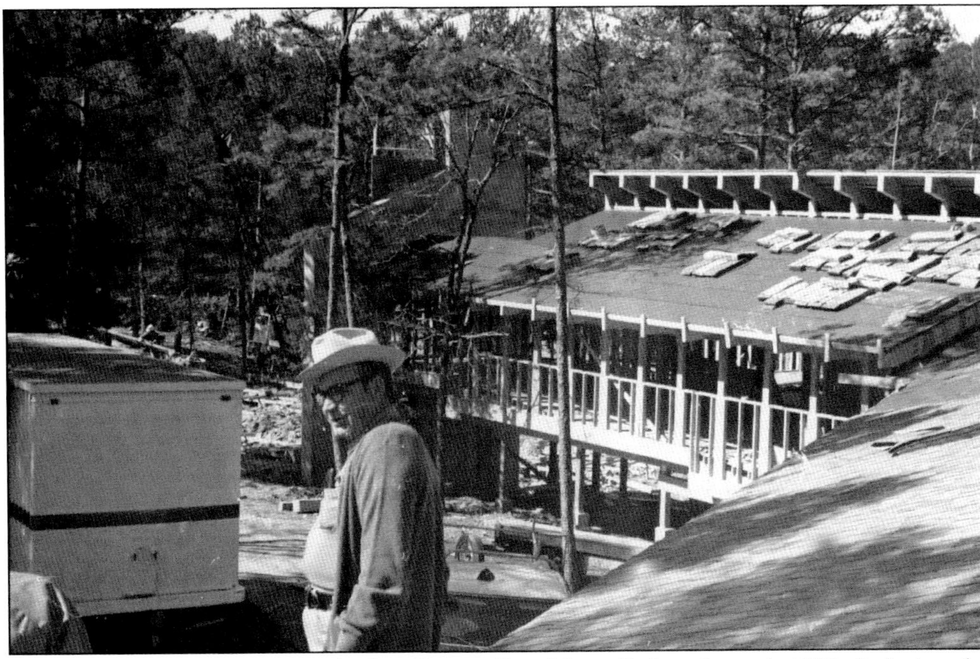

The Forest Heritage Center was built in Beavers Bend State Park in the early 1970s. It depicts the heritage of life in the forest and forestry industry. Here is a picture taken during the construction of the center with Reed Tomlinson, the center's construction committee chair, in the foreground. (Kenneth Sivard Jr. collection.)

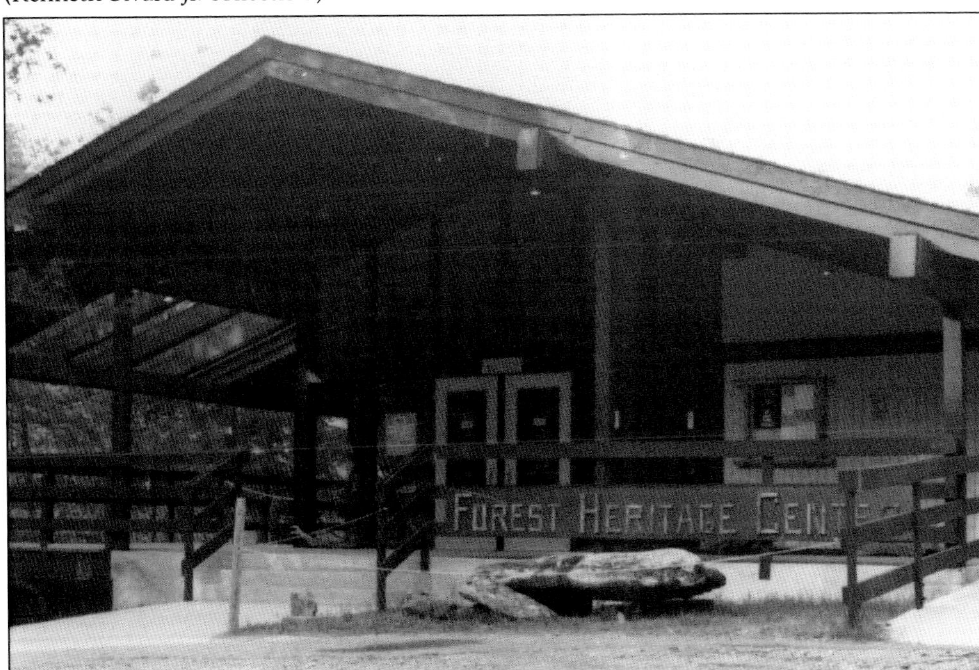

This is the main entrance to the Forest Heritage Center soon after its construction was completed. Today it also hosts a gift shop and serves as an information center for the state park. (Kenneth Sivard Jr. collection.)

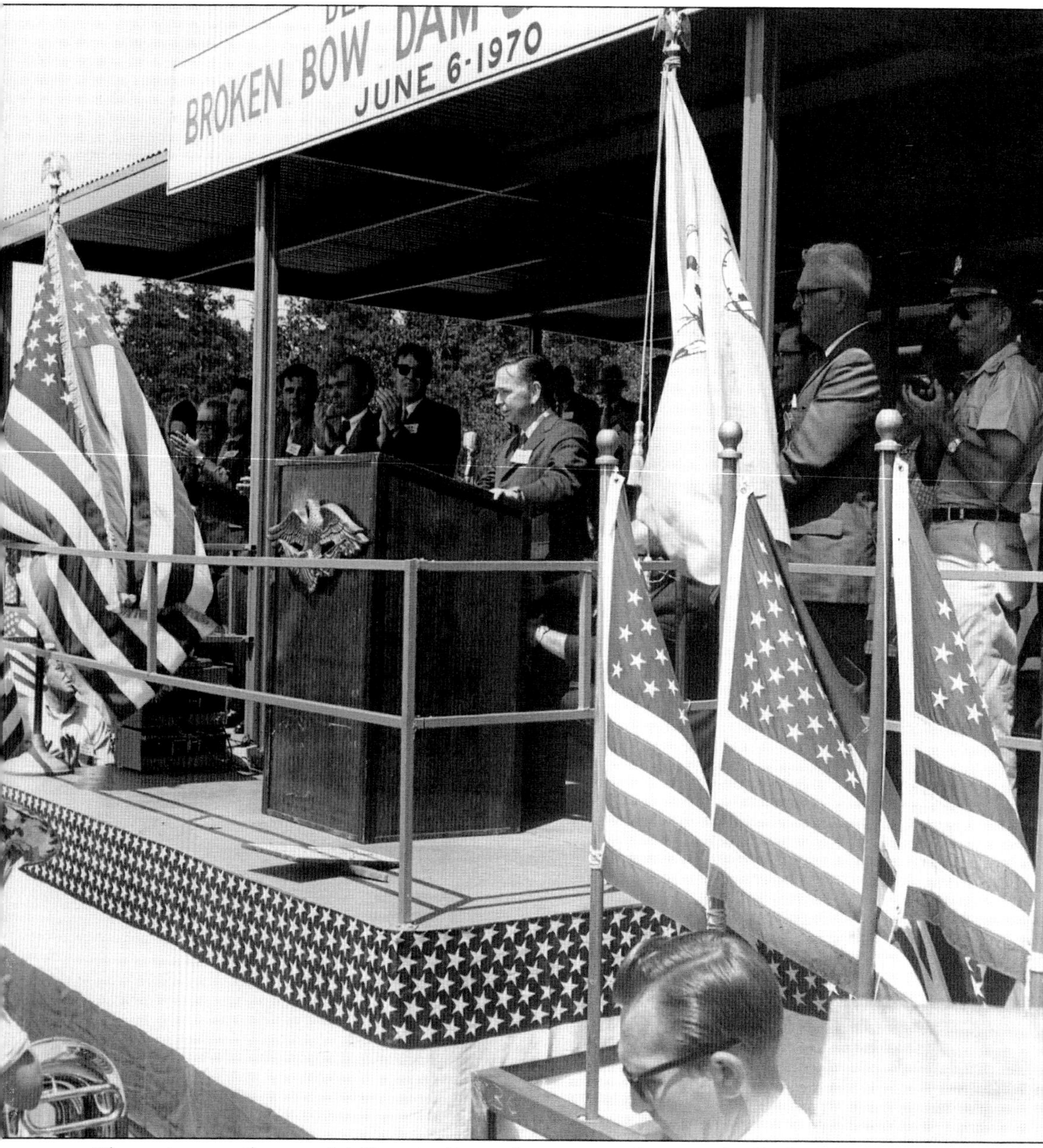

The main contributor to McCurtain County's tourism industry is the Broken Bow Reservoir, or Broken Bow Lake as it is more commonly known. The lake was developed by the Flood Control Act of 1958, and construction began in 1961. It was created by damming the Mountain Fork River, which flooded the Hochatown Valley and covered the original site of Hochatown. Here is a photograph taken at the dam's dedication on June 6, 1970. Congressman Carl Albert was the keynote speaker. (Kenneth Sivard Jr. collection.)

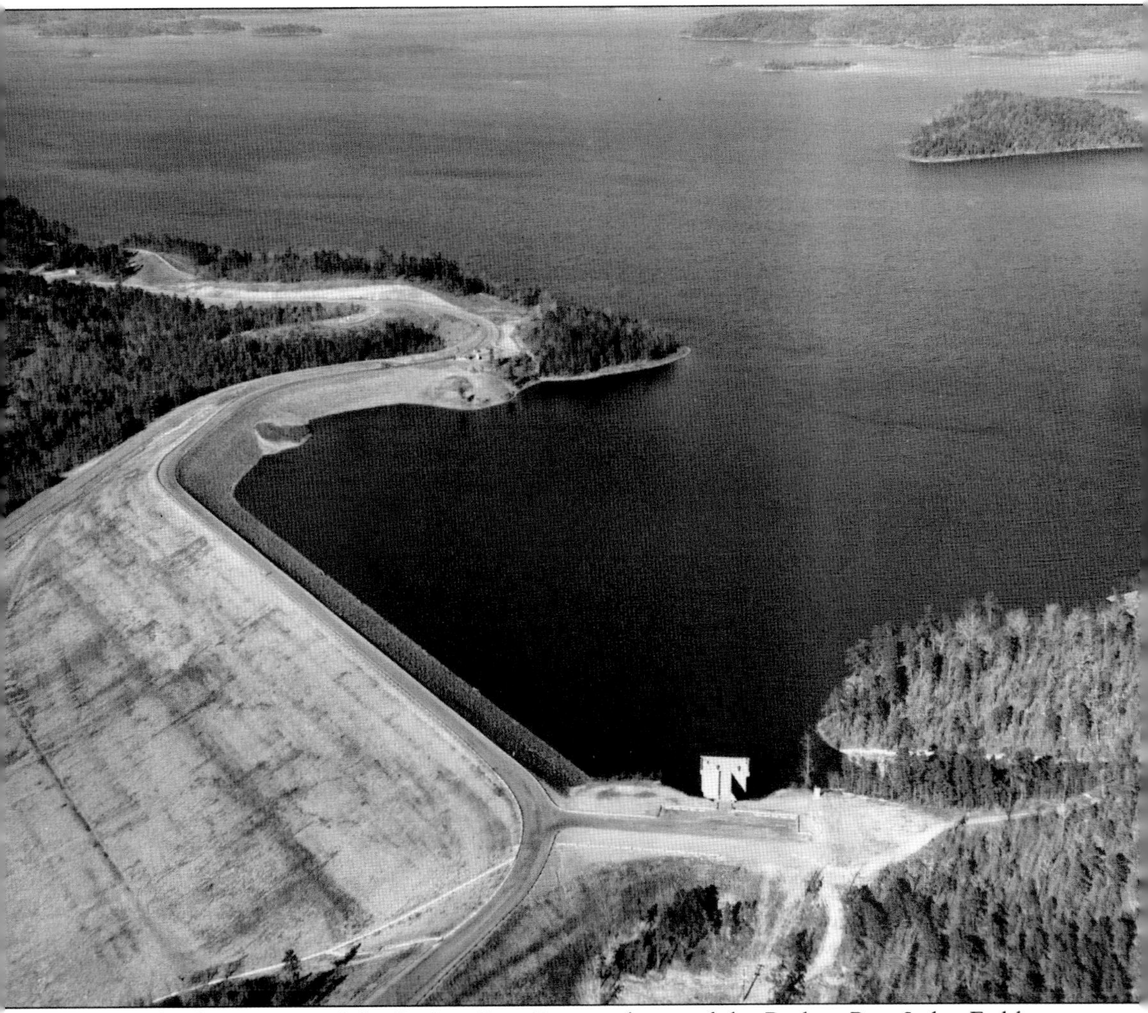

This is a bird's-eye view of the Broken Bow Dam and part of the Broken Bow Lake. Fed by Mountain Fork River, the lake is one of the cleanest bodies of water in this part of the nation; families come from all over to enjoy it every year. (Kenneth Sivard Jr. collection.)